BRITAIN, GREECE AND TI

CW00348263

KONSTANTINA MARAGKOU

Britain, Greece and the Colonels, 1967–74

Between Pragmatism and Human Rights

HURST & COMPANY, LONDON

First published in the United Kingdom in 2019 by
C. Hurst & Co. (Publishers) Ltd.,
41 Great Russell Street, London, WC1B 3PL
© Konstantina Maragkou, 2019
All rights reserved.
Printed in India

The right of Konstantina Maragkou to be identified as the author
of this publication is asserted by her in accordance with the
Copyright, Designs and Patents Act, 1988.

A Cataloguing-in-Publication data record for this book
is available from the British Library.

ISBN: 9781849043656

This book is printed using paper from registered sustainable
and managed sources.

www.hurstpublishers.com

CONTENTS

ACKNOWLEDGEMENTS

The idea of researching the Labour government's relations with the Colonels' regime vis-à-vis their ideological incompatibility surfaced during discussions with Professor Jonathan Haslam, my PhD supervisor at Cambridge University. Further consultations with several other academics, and the advice I received from Professor David Reynolds during my viva, shaped my decision to extend the time frame of my research in favour of studying British policies towards the Greek dictatorship across the Greek Colonel's seven-year military junta, before preparing the book for publication. Consequently, the enlarged project furnished my conclusions with valuable insights, as it allowed me to compare the policies of two governments that were, at least in principle, diametrically opposed. Accordingly, the findings presented in this book make a significant contribution to the scholarship surrounding the tortuous history of Anglo-Greek relations, and serve as a useful theoretical framework in which the transnational dictates of foreign policy-making at the start of the globalisation era can be evaluated. By illuminating competing priorities, such as Cold War realities, alliance dynamics, financial and commercial imperatives, regional instability in the Mediterranean, as well as domestic pressures and the surge in human rights activism, this book seeks to prove that the essence of a national history can only be fully understood by focusing on the relationship between the nation state and factors beyond its domain.

My two postdoctoral fellowships, hosted by the Hellenic Observatory at the LSE and the Macmillan Centre for International and Area Studies at Yale University, were instrumental to the successful completion of this project, an expansion of my PhD thesis. In addition, I am

ACKNOWLEDGEMENTS

hugely indebted to the many institutions and organisations that funded my research for this monograph, and other related projects. The Alexander S. Onassis and A.G. Leventis Foundations financed my PhD research, which attracted funding from the Cambridge European Trust too. The abundance of material consulted at Lyndon B. Johnson Presidential Library, thanks to its generous grant, provided a very useful prism through which I could analyse British policies. Furthermore, several grants offered to me by the superb schemes at Yale University and Princeton University Library helped to further expand the scope of my research throughout my postdoctoral years. Without their generous financial support, my research would never have reached such heights. I would also like to acknowledge the staff at the various libraries and depositories that I have utilised throughout my research, listed on pages 259–261. Their tremendous assistance helped me to navigate through masses of information and their various different archival systems.

The human rights aspect of this monograph has been made possible thanks to the research I have undertaken for my current project, which was funded by a Marie Curie International Incoming Senior Research Fellowship (Project no. 628372). This book has benefited greatly from the resources of institutional and private archives—all listed on pages 261–262—and the utterly crucial interviews conducted with many protagonists at the time. A sincere and special token of appreciation is particularly owed to all of my interviewees mentioned on pages 272 & 273, who have generously lent me their thoughtful insights, enlighting thus my work in a truly unique and holistic way.

Last, but by no means least, the support I received from several colleagues and mentors, including Professors Stathis Kalyvas, Kevin Featherstone, John Iatrides, Evanthis Hatzivassiliou, Mark Mazower, Brendan Simms, Richard Clogg, Matthew Jones, Piers Ludlow and Dr Hubertus Jahn, at various stages of my research has been inspirational. A very special mention is owed to Professor Jay Winter, who catalytically stirred the focus of my research towards the domain of human rights during my years at Yale. A number of friends in addition to my publisher and editors have made significant suggestions that led to this final version, hence my deep gratitude to all of them too. Most importantly, though, had it not been for the encouragement and patience of my family, this book would probably never have come to fruition.

INTRODUCTION

Anglo–Greek relations at the dawn of the Greek Colonels' coup

Many studies of Modern Greek history have traced various aspects of its long, intertwined relationship with Britain,[1] a relationship marked by 'moments of glory, trial and mutual error'.[2] It has been established that the origins of British involvement in Greek affairs predate the founding of the Modern Greek state, with the formation of the Philhellenes—a group of wealthy and prominent Grecophiles, among them Lord Byron and Percy Bysshe Shelley, who supported the Greeks' struggle against Ottoman rule in the 1820s. British intervention became established at the London Conference in 1832 and was entrenched as the newly founded Greek state was placed under the jurisdiction of a triadic protectorate in which Britain assumed a lead role during the nineteenth century.

Active British influence in Greek affairs continued unabated through the early twentieth century with the coming of the Balkan wars and Greece's *Megali Idea* (Great Idea) expansionist campaign. Although Anglo–Greek cooperation was most conspicuous during the First and Second World Wars, the interwar years were equally significant for the strengthening of the bond. Their close interaction was, for instance, evident in the tutelage by British Police and Naval missions of their Greek counterparts. The extent of British participation in Greek affairs was also linked to the degree of British penetration of the Greek economy. It is striking that in 1935 'half of the Greek public debt of 89,000,000 [pounds sterling] equivalent to more than 6 billion today,

1

was held by private British investors'.[3] The literature on informal empire has some bearing, therefore, on the Greek case.

Britain's guarantee to Greece against the Axis powers in 1939 opened a new phase of involvement in Greek affairs. A catastrophic Allied offensive in 1941 was one element; the Caserta agreement of September 1944, which placed all the resistance forces in Greece under the command of Brisith officer, General Ronald Scobie, was another. The years immediately following the end of the Second World War witnessed the apogee of British engagement. This was facilitated by the drafting of the 'percentages agreement' by Churchill and Stalin in October 1944, in which Greece was unequivocally assigned within the British sphere of influence. Two months later, this agreement enabled Britain to control the politics of the Dekemvriana phase of the Greek Civil War in December 1944. British connivance took the form of energetic support for the Greek Nationalists against the perceived Greek Communist threat. By 1947 however, unable to afford the massive injections of foreign financial assistance required for Greece's postwar recovery, Britain had relinquished most of its responsibilities to the United States.

Although British control over Greek affairs had ended formally, Britain's substantial interest in them, not least of 'sentimental and intellectual'[4] nature, persisted. But during the 1950s their previously good bilateral relations were seriously tested due to the escalation of acrimoniousness and violence following the Greek Cypriots' efforts to achieve independence and union with Greece (fiercely resisted by the British rulers) and rapidly deteriorated to their lowest point ever. Additional developments including Greece's detachment from British undertakings during the 1956 Suez Crisis further exacerbated their rift.

The end of the 1950s testified to a progressive thaw in Anglo-Greek dealings. This was facilitated by the signing of the London and Zurich Agreements that resulted in the granting of independence to Cyprus and Greek Prime Minister Konstantinos Karamanlis' visit to London in 1961. The two countries eventually managed to fully overcome the traumas generated by their previous vitriolic disagreements, including the handling of the Cyprus issue and Britain's reluctance to contribute to NATO's funding to Greece; hence, at the dawn of the Colonels' coup on 21 April 1967, they had reached their 'most cordial point since 1945.'[5]

INTRODUCTION

From a strategic perspective, what mattered to Britain initially was Greece's position with regard to safeguarding the route to India that had been part of the wartime history of Anglo–Greek relations. From the end of the Second World War, although Britain gradually withdrew from 'East of Suez', Greece grew in importance given Britain's keen interest in keeping Cyprus, the Mediterranean, and the Middle East out of the Communist orbit. Britain's perceived national interest lay behind the maintenance of continued influence over Greece's internal affairs. In addition, Greece was a quintessential part of the geostrategic Greek–Turkish equation. In financial terms, close Anglo–Greek relations afforded promising prospects. But while there is consensus on the general outlines of this story, there is still scholarly disagreement about the actual nature and exact degree of significance of the 'British role' in Greece in the second half of the twentieth century.

The State of the Art

Most scholars approaching the field of Greece's post-Second World War history have chosen to adopt an American-centric perspective, arguing that since 1947 the United States has been Greece's most powerful ally.[6] This may be true, but it does not justify ignoring or discrediting the influence of Greece's other traditional Western allies, most notably Britain. As Professor John Spraos, Chairman of the London-based Greek Committee against Dictatorship, affirmed in one of his lobbying pleas addressed to the then UK Foreign Secretary Michael Stewart in April 1968, 'Britain's historic ties with Greece place a special responsibility on H.M. government'.[7] To be sure, the Greek authorities were aware that Britain was not any longer the 'main protecting power', but they did not lose sight of the fact that the British were one of their major partners in NATO, the Western European Union and the Council of Europe, whilst Greek membership of the EEC was also a prospect. The latter factor would be of particular importance in the likelihood of a reduced American presence in Europe, which would render Greece more dependent on Europe and hence on Britain too.

In addition, Britain's relevance to the past, present and future of Cyprus was too substantial to be ignored. Greece also held Britain in

3

high respect because it was considered to be 'aware of our [Greece's] problems' and to have political experience with Greece's challenges given their long-standing close relationship. In fact, with regard to its internal affairs, the Greeks had a tendency to look at Britain as 'an example to be followed'.[8] Moreover, Britain maintained a strong influence over developments in the Mediterranean and the Middle East and a role in Greek–American relations in light of its special connection with the US. As this book intends to make clear, the regime of the Greek Colonels consistently attached great importance to the maintenance of cordial relations with Britain: an argument thoroughly corroborated by two of the three coup leaders whom I interviewed.[9]

Given the 'special, historical and emotional relationship'[10] between the two countries it seems odd that until recently the historiography, whether in Greek or in English, had barely touched on the response of British governments to one of Modern Greece's most critical historical phases.[11] The reasons for this scholarly dearth were many, including challenges regarding sources—although these have how dissipated. A pertinent doctoral dissertation that was eventually turned into a book by Alexandros Nafpliotis dealt with British foreign policies towards the Colonels. Although important inasmuch as it represented the first attempt to analyse them during the whole seven year period that the regime stayed in power, this dissertation had a few shortcomings. First, it underestimated the importance of Cyprus as a leitmotif in Anglo–Greek relations during the Colonels' era. To be sure, the author did refer to the island at various points, but the omission of Cyprus from the title of the dissertation is indicative of a certain deficiency. Furthermore, the author did not sufficiently contextualise the fluctuations in Anglo–Greek relations within the Cold War framework, by highlighting the effect of a number of exogenous crises and their bearing on Anglo–Greek relations. The consequent monograph did try to modify these absences, but it did not pay substantial attention to British reactions outside official policy circles and their impact on governmental attitudes. In addition, given the recent nature of the topic, one would have expected the findings to have been complemented by interviews with protagonists—and this is one factor that makes this book stand out as a more comprehensive account.

This book will also show how some arguments in Nafpliotis' subsequent monograph were not entirely accurate, including the claim that differences in Labour's and the Conservatives' policy towards the Colonels were 'too important'; as this book will prove, the emotions and rhetoric, and even initial reactions, of the two parties were substantially different on occasion, but their actual policies were rather similar at least up to Wilson's return to power in 1974. In another instance, Nafpliotis argued that 'London's weak position both financially and internationally was a key determinant of its pragmatic policy'; however, it would be rather counter-intuitive to claim that had the UK enjoyed a stronger status at that time, its policy would have been less pragmatic, especially within the all-encompassing context of the Cold War. This assumption is clearly refuted by the United States' staunch *Realpolitik* despite its undoubtedly hegemonic position, as well as the record of Britain's past policies towards Greece during periods when it commanded greater power.

In line with the recently mushrooming interest in the history of Greece's foreign affairs, this book attempts to address lacunas in the literature through the analysis of a vast corpus of primary material originating from more than twenty different archives, as well as thirty-five interviews with major protagonists during the era under investigation, including high-ranking British officials, senior diplomats, the Colonels themselves, the former King of the Hellenes, influential members of the resistance and prominent journalists. Although several of them spoke off the record, their comments have been crucial in enriching this in-depth analysis.

The book's focus is on the nature and motives of British policy while accounting for its fluctuations in response to various events, not only in Greece but also in Britain as well as on the international stage during the seven years that the military regime remained in power. The main axes around which it will revolve include the two countries' political, diplomatic, military, financial and cultural interactions as well as the irritants that occasionally obstructed their mutually desired good working relationship. It is organised chronologically in order to bring out more clearly the variations and continuities in British foreign policy towards Greece. The chapters do not represent yearly accounts, but are rather arranged in a way that reflects Britain's foreign policy trajectories; in other words, each chapter encapsulates a phase in the relationship.

The examination of Britain's relationship with the Greece of the Colonels is significant not only for the historical record of their interstate relations, but also because through it we can gain a better under-standing of wider British foreign policy trends of the time. From this perspective, we can gauge the different strategic imperatives facing British governments, such as Cold War exigencies, regional instability in the Mediterranean, alliance dynamics and asymmetries, and economic and commercial factors, in tandem with considerable domestic pres-sures. It should be nonetheless clarified that although the present book is a significant case study of British foreign policy, it does not aspire to provide a comprehensive overview of the British foreign policy trends in the period.[12]

At its core, this study aims to assess the extent to which British foreign policy was a matter of ideology or pragmatic analysis, and the degree to which it entailed transnational imperatives, such as human rights considerations. It was in the 1960s that the process we now call 'globalisation' got fully under way; from then on, no nation—and no foreign office—was an island. It was part of a whole—and in the British case, a shrinking part of the whole—in which non-state players within the international field also played their part in the evolution of thinking on foreign affairs. This is the key to understanding the tortu-ous history of Britain and the Greek Colonels, one which has many echoes in our own time.

It also aspires to show how inextricably linked the internal develop-ments of a country on the periphery, in this instance Greece under the Colonels, were with events in the international arena during the Cold War era. In a nutshell, beyond the regional, bilateral and international level, this study fits into the transnational paradigm in that it proves that the essence of a national history can be fully understood only by focusing on the relationship between the nation state, sub-national groups, and forces beyond its control.

The 'rape of Greek democracy'[13]

Prior to embarking on a systematic examination of British policy towards the Greek Colonels' regime, it will be helpful to offer a brief sketch of the events in Greece, which took place on 21 April 1967. The evening before the fateful day of the coup a secret meeting was convened at the house of Lieutenant-Colonel Michael Balopoulos. Fourteen Colonels and

Lieutenant-Colonels participated, namely George and Konstantinos Papadopoulos, Nickolaos Makarezos, Ioannis Ladas, Konstantinos Aslanidis, Michalis Roufogalis, Dimitrios Ioannides, Michalis Balopoulos, Antonios Mexis, Antonios Lekkas, Nickolaos Gadonas, Stefanos Karaberis, Dimitrios Stamatelopolous, Ioannis Anastassopoulos as well as Brigadier Stylianos Pattakos.[14] Their meeting was to prove to be of profound significance for Greece's political future. For it was during this meeting that, despite the slight trepidation expressed by Lieutenant-General George Zoitakis, the final seal of approval was given for the Colonels' long-planned coup to be executed without delay.

The conspirators had come of age during the Greek Civil War and were united by their virulent anti-Communist credo. They were therefore wary of the forthcoming general elections, mainly due to the possibility that Communist sympathiser and anti-NATO politician Andreas Papandreou might gain power as a result of his father's Centre Union party's forecasted landslide victory. They decided to intervene unconstitutionally in order to forestall the Papandreous' anticipated liberalising measures that would destroy, in their view, the institutional framework of right-wing dominance within the state, which had been cemented since the end of the civil war. In addition, they were banded together by their ardent nationalism, distorted adherence to the Christian faith and Ancient Greek civilization, avowed revulsion of parliamentary and democratic procedures, severe intolerance of social non-conformity and indiscipline as well as long-fermented corporate and professional grievances.

Thus, following a period of political turmoil in the 1960s, evident in the weakening of parliamentary institutions, the resignations of Prime Ministers Konstantinos Karamanlis in 1963 and George Papandreou in 1965, and the kaleidoscope of five different Prime Ministers, who governed Greece in the two years prior to the coup, the Greek people woke up on the morning of Friday 21 April 1967 to the sound of military marches and national folk music broadcast on the radio, and with a dictatorship in place, a fait accompli.[15] The events that had shaken Greece a few hours earlier were reported by the Greek Conservative newspaper *Kathimerini* as follows:

> A military coup has broken out—politicians have been arrested: at 2:30 in the morning an armoured division occupied the centre of

Athens. Amidst looks of astonishment from the few Athenians who were out on the streets… armoured vehicles cut off the royal palace, while military forces were occupying OTE (Organismos Tilepikoinonion Ellados—Greek National Telecom), the radio stations, Zappeion and the Ministries.[16]

In the hours following the coup, details about what exactly had happened were still sparse. The coup was spearheaded at 2am with the simultaneous departure of infantry and armoured units from various bases around Athens. Following orders from a triumvirate composed of relatively junior-ranking Army officers—Colonels Papadopoulos and Makarezos and Brigadier Pattakos—'fewer than 500 daring officers'[17] managed to take control of several infrastructural nerve centres, such as the Pentagon, and a number of strategic bases, the airports and ports, the telecommunications headquarters and the offices of political parties and newspapers.

While all communications were being suspended, the country's major political and military personalities were arrested. Among the first to be taken into custody were the caretaker Prime Minister and leader of ERE (Ethniki Rizospastiki Enosis, National Radical Union) Panayiotis Kanellopoulos; George Papandreou, the former Prime Minister and leader of EK (Enosis Kentrou, Centre Union) and his son, Andreas, minister in his father's government; and all members of EDA (Eniaia Democratiki Aristera, United Democratic Left). The detainees were taken to Goudi, with the exception of the caretaker Prime Minister, who was transferred to the Pentagon, where later on that morning he held talks with the Greek King, Constantine II.

The coup met with no resistance. The bulk of the Army, including at least 60,000 soldiers and 5,000 officers, was at that time stationed along the north-eastern border between Greece and Turkey, on account of recent tensions in the two countries—and obviously this was a development that the Colonels knew all too well. The royalist Navy on the other hand was reluctant to make any move since the Colonels were deliberately transmitting through all radio stations that they were acting to enforce a Royal Decree. In order to forestall any countermove from the Navy, the coup leaders had also made sure that the Chief of the Navy General Staff, vice-Admiral Konstantinos Engolfopoulos, was among the first to be arrested, while the second-in-command was abroad at the time.

INTRODUCTION

The critical element in the success of the coup was the implementation of 'Prometheus' (a NATO contingency plan designed to impose internal order and eliminate 'subversive' leftist opposition in the event of war with any of Greece's Communist northern neighbours). Thus the Colonels' assumption of power was smooth and rapid, and by 7pm they were in full charge of the country. After all hopes for opposing the coup had evaporated, the new government was sworn in by the King. Fearful of the possibility of inciting a civil war, the King acquiesced to the request of the mutineers after having convinced them to accept Konstantinos Kollias, the senior Public Prosecutor to the Supreme Court and trusted palace ally, as Prime Minister, and to allocate most ministerial posts to civilians for the sake of the country's international prestige. He also told a Cabinet meeting on 26 April emphatically that he expected the country to 'revert to parliamentary government as soon as possible.'[18] Although the King's actions might have contributed to the country's bloodless transition under the Colonels' regime, as an article in *The Times* remarked prophetically, 'whether this [the King's tacit acquiescence] will in the long run help the cause of monarchy in Greece must be doubtful.'[19]

Although de jure power rested with a civilian, the de facto control of the country lay in the hands of the troika, who had insisted on taking up certain key positions in the new government; Colonels Papadopoulos and Makarezos became Minister for the Prime Minister and Minister for Co-ordination respectively, and Brigadier Pattakos assumed the post of Minister of the Interior and Public Order. In light of these developments, it could be argued that the military regime of April 1967 embodied several characteristics of a typical military dictatorship in that not only was the initiative military, but also the most sensitive and influential State posts were taken up by members of the Armed Forces.

Greece was thus entering the longest period of dictatorship in its modern history. There is no doubt that military interventions constituted rather frequent anomalous episodes in the country's recent history;[20] however, no previous dictatorship had attracted such widespread interest. The news quickly travelled around the globe, causing waves of condemnation as reports about the coup appeared in newspapers worldwide from London to Nairobi, Santiago to Sydney and Moscow to Washington. Before long the media was abuzz with calls for the restoration of democracy and increasingly also the safeguarding of human rights.

People and governments harbouring an interest in Greece declared themselves aghast at the forcible abolition of democracy. As Greece's well-educated middle class and intelligentsia were subjected to imprisonment and inhuman treatment, often even before criticising the regime, many in the West involved themselves in opposition activities. Greece had frequently been portrayed as the cradle of democracy, so there was a degree of irony in that this of all European countries in the Western orbit, was the first to succumb to a dictatorship following the end of the Second World War. According to a Labour backbencher, 'we had learned at school that Greece had taught democracy to the rest of us, and now it was like hearing that the teacher was arrested.'[21] It is no coincidence that most anti-Colonels cartoons and literature had a clear reference to Greece's classical past in an effort to play on liberal foreigners' sensitivities.

In Britain the dramatic news regarding Greece aroused particularly strong public interest, and as it will become progressively apparent the press vigorously pursued the Colonels' throughout the seven years they spent in power. Even a cursory search of *The Times* and *The Guardian* digital archives yields several thousand entries for news on Greece during the Colonels' time. It is also worth emphasising that all milestones during this era—for example the King's counter-coup in December 1967, Greece's forced withdrawal from the Council of Europe in December 1969, and the bloody suppression of students' unrest in November 1973—featured in front-page articles in all major British newspapers.

It was in keeping, therefore, that on 22 April 1967 the print and broadcast media focused on the Colonels' forcible seizure of power. The news was given priority over other top international and domestic stories, such as the Vietnam War and the worsening financial situation at home. The leader on the front page of *The Times* read: 'A military coup took over power in Greece at ten minutes past midnight today. Strong Army units, with tanks and armoured cars, cordoned the palace in Athens, government Ministries and other strategic points'.[22] *The Daily Telegraph*'s front page carried the following headline: 'Martial Law order in Greece: Public meeting ban, curfew shooting, political leaders arrested'.[23] Meanwhile, *The Guardian* reported 'Greeks duped by extremists in right-wing coup'[24] and elsewhere noted 'Greece promised elections—when the time is ripe'.[25]

The British public was astonished. Some gathered spontaneously outside the Greek Embassy in London to protest. Naturally, those who had fought in Greece during the Second World War and the subsequent Greek Civil War were greatly agitated by the news. They were shocked that democracy in Greece, for whose preservation they had fought alongside their Greek allies twenty years before, should have been so abruptly suppressed. There was also a distaste in liberal Britain for dictatorial regimes. Moreover, the long-standing tradition of classical education in British public schools made the products of that system sympathetic to the plight of Greek democracy. According to Sir Michael Stewart, British ambassador in Athens from November 1967, 'there was particular awareness in Britain of the fact that no volume of human thought existed in Europe, in which Greece had not contributed the first chapter.'[26]

Last, but by no means least, as a result of the advent of the era of mass tourism, many British had grown fond of the country and its people thanks to their holidays in Greece.

The British government's challenges at the time of the coup

Although the interest that the Greek news generated among the British public is certainly noteworthy and will come under the microscope of this study occasionally for the influence it exerted on foreign policy-makers, it is natural that the focus should be on the actions of the British government. This book will elaborate that those in charge largely disregarded public opinion when it came to effectuating their policy towards the regime. Indeed, our knowledge of the public's opprobrium further highlights the intransigence of Britain's *Realpolitik*. The Greek military takeover took place at a critical stage in the modern history of Britain, and so before analysing Britain's responses to the news of the so-called 'rape of Greek democracy',[27] we must consider briefly the array of concerns that British officials faced at the time of the coup, both on the domestic front and at the international level.

The sixties was a turbulent decade, witnessing the unfolding of a number of regional crises with potentially explosive global dimensions. These included the increasing unrest in the Middle East and the build-up of the Soviet fleet in the Mediterranean. Most crucial for Britain was the inescapable challenge of having to come to terms with the mundane reality of its loss of status as a world power, as it was embarrassingly at odds with geopolitical facts.[28] When the Colonels came to power, Whitehall, having reluctantly relinquished long-held British claims, was still trying to redefine Britain's role in a post-imperial era and weather the economic maelstrom that was rocking its foundations. The most pressing issues for Wilson's government revolved around 'how to match overseas commitments to resources, how far to retain a presence east of Suez and whether to seek EEC membership.'[29]

Another vexing question preoccupying Britain was the Vietnam War. Although not directly involved, the British government did not remain untouched by it, particularly given constant US pressure to actively commit its forces. Most British officials were unwilling to send forces to Vietnam, for a variety of reasons. For one thing, the escalation of the war coincided with their undertaking to make sharp reductions in Britain's overseas garrisons. Domestic public opinion was also hostile. But they had to ensure that their reluctance would not alienate the American government, on which they relied heavily for security, in terms of intelligence and nuclear cooperation, and financial assistance for the defence of sterling.[30] As Wilson bluntly put it, 'we can't kick our creditors in the balls.'[31]

Britain's intransigence to become entangled in the web of the Vietnam conflict was also associated with the grave challenges it faced in other parts of the world, with either former or current members of its Empire and Commonwealth. Its interest in those parts of the world had continued unabated as it was felt that Britain bore an additional responsibility and also had significant economic interests which it needed to safeguard. Among the most troublesome were the crises in Southern Rhodesia, which had culminated in Rhodesia leaving the Commonwealth in December 1966. In addition, the heated debate about the sale of arms to South Africa, the rebellions in Aden, the Biafran civil war in Nigeria and the imminent troubles in Northern Ireland further ignited Britain's anxieties.

Moreover, British officials faced mounting domestic problems, mostly linked to the country's deteriorating financial situation. These included trade unions' upheaval over income policies. The latest sterling crisis had been recently precipitated by a six-week strike organised by the National Union of Seamen in the summer of 1966. The Prime Minister, commenting in retrospect on the factors that 'forced us [British government] off parity', included 'the economic consequences of the Middle East crisis, and in particular the closure of the Suez Canal' as well as 'the dock strikes in London and Liverpool, and when they ended, financial manoeuvring within the six [member-countries of the EEC].'[32]

In light of Whitehall's reluctant and gradual recognition of Britain's reduced great power status, efforts were made to enhance its position in world affairs by accelerating moves for economic and political union in Europe.[33] Its keen interest in joining the European Economic Community derived from the need to ameliorate its crippling financial situation and to divert the attention of its public away from it. The dismembering of its Empire and the resultant termination of its defence commitments overseas were also a factor: the country was being converted gradually into primarily a European state. As their successive applications were vetoed by the French government, the British became more and more determined. The latest application was submitted on 2 May 1967, only a handful of days after the Colonels' putsch; that too proved unsuccessful, further aggravating the government's dismay.[34]

Chapter outline

In spite of the British government's overwhelming preoccupation with several pressing domestic issues and contentious challenges in the international arena, chapter one will show how the news of Greece's falling prey to a military regime did not go unnoticed. This was unsurprising in view of the significance Britain attached to Greek affairs, not least for sentimental reasons, as we have seen, but also due to considerations of *Realpolitik*. The chapter will document Wilson's government's adoption of a 'business as usual' approach towards the Colonels' newly established regime, despite its ideological incompatibility.

While the first chapter spans the first months of the regime's accession to power, the starting point of the second chapter coincides with the Greek King's abortive counter-coup in December 1967, which had serious, albeit short-lived, repercussions. It covers the period up to the end of 1968, as a number of episodes during that year had a bearing on Anglo–Greek relations. Chapter three examines the British government's sustained efforts to normalise its relations with the Colonels' regime during most of 1969. It extends to the forced withdrawal of Greece from the Council of Europe in December 1969, which inaugurated a new phase of aloofness in Anglo–Greek relations. The fourth chapter is concerned with Wilson's government's attempts to restore normalcy in the period after December 1969 until the 1970 election.

The second part of this book opens with chapter five, whose emphasis lies on the climate of euphoria among ruling circles in Greece following the Conservatives' coming to power. It explains why those expectations were largely misplaced, and shows the more bracing reality presented by the Conservatives' initial reactions to the Colonels' regime. Chapter six covers the period from early 1971 to late 1972, during which Anglo–Greek relations experienced their most uneventful era. It accounts for the efforts made by both governments to establish relations on a friendly footing and the occasional obstacles found in their way. Chapter seven focuses on the British government's responses to the long chain of dramatic events in Greece during 1973, which signaled the erosion of power of the Colonels' regime. It starts with the appointment of a civilian as Prime Minister—Spyridon Markezinis, an Anglophile, who triggered considerable optimism on the part of the British—and continues with his forcible replacement by the hardliner Brigadier Dimitrios Ioannides. Chapter eight examines the policies of Wilson's Labour government upon its return to power in March 1974 and spans the first Turkish invasion on 20 July 1974, which delivered the *coup de grâce* to Ioannides' ailing dictatorship three days later. It is however important to emphasise that this book will not deal with British policies towards the Cyprus crisis, both because it does not form an entirely integral part of the Colonels' era—in fact the latter ended before the second Turkish invasion on 14 August—and because several attempts have been recently made to account for this undoubtedly important theme in its entirety.[35]

The purpose of the concluding chapter is to compare the policies implemented by the three successive British governments towards Greece under the Colonels. This provides the groundwork for a consideration of the policies subsequently pursued by two ideologically differing British governments, epitomising the core argument of this book, which is how a major Western power—a presumed pillar of Western democracy—adopted a permissive attitude, albeit not entirely surprisingly, toward a crude and incompetent military regime: a regime blatantly and consistently antithetical to the principles of Western democracy.

1

FROM 'EXTREME RESERVE' TO 'BUSINESS AS USUAL'

As the *Greek Observer*, an influential monthly anti-regime publication edited and published in London, put it, 'historic ties with the States and with Greece made Britain's position pivotal'[1] during the events of April 1967. In light of the close relations between the two countries, the intensity of British concerns over the imposition of dictatorship in Greece was hardly surprising. As already mentioned, it was nothing other than the continuation of a pattern resulting from a nexus of factors associated with Greece's long-standing importance for British interests. The significance of Greece in the sixties, at the height of the Cold War, was perceived as vital by its NATO allies due to the country's strategic position. Other defining factors that came into play included British worries over the fate of Cyprus, as well as commercial issues.

Indeed, such was Greece's geostrategic value that in the immediate aftermath of the Colonels' coup, a speculative climate emerged regarding the possibility of British and/or American complicity in it. Such allegations will not be treated in detail in this book, as I have already addressed them elsewhere.[2] My conclusion then was that the British kept their hands clean. As a Foreign Office brief succinctly summarised it, 'no British authority was in any way, either directly or indirectly, involved in the Greek coup d'état of April 1967'.[3]

However, while it seems unlikely that there was unethical connivance in the Colonels' coming to power, British foreign policy in prac-

17

tice was not whiter than white, as this chapter will demonstrate. Wilson's Labour government had won the 1966 elections on an ethical foreign policy platform, but once in power a number of pragmatic considerations induced it to adopt a 'flexible' approach which did little to prevent the Colonels' tightening their grip on power.

The British government's first reactions at policy level to the news of the coup, which arrived in London at 3:20am are best summarised in one word: consultations. Immediately the government called its Ambassador in Athens, Sir Ralph Murray, to London for discussions. Meanwhile, a series of meetings took place not only among British officials, but also with their foreign counterparts. The underlying reason behind these lengthy deliberations was the need to acquire a better grasp of the events. For many hours after the coup, most officials were trying to gather information regarding the identity of the perpetrators, an 'unknown group of colonels... of whom we know nothing,'[4] in the words of Sir Patrick Dean, the British Ambassador in Washington. Symptomatic of the confusion was Sir Ralph Murray's misspelling of all the names of the participants in the coup in one of his first telegrams to the Foreign and Commonwealth Office (FCO), as well as his initial assessment that one of the plotters was not actually involved in the coup.[5]

This degree of surprise came despite claims in a document on the origins of the 1967 coup, which suggests that 'there [was] in London information that Papadopoulos himself was considering the possibility of overthrowing the old political system in the early 1960s.'[6] It seems that although relevant alerts about the coup perpetrators were sent before the coup, they either were not treated seriously, or were not communicated by the intelligence services to the civil authorities.

One of the British officials' main priority was to gauge the American and West German responses to the unconstitutional turn of events in Greece and to try to streamline their attitudes according to the West's prevailing orientation. The importance of the American standpoint needs no further elaboration, whereas that of the Federal Republic of Germany must be seen in the light of Britain's intended second application to join the EU just ten days after the Colonels' coup. As was cited at a Cabinet meeting, 'we [the British] were in close touch with the United States and the Federal German government, whose views were in accordance with our own.'[7]

Among the British government's immediate preoccupations was ensuring the safety of the approximately 5,000 British nationals who resided in Greece. In the first few hours following the coup, and while the situation was still in flux, the carrier HMS *Hermes*, which was taking part in exercises near Cyprus, was ordered to be within 20–24 hours distance from Piraeus, Greece's main port. However, it soon became clear that an evacuation would not be required: the safety of all but three British subjects was not in jeopardy. In fact, the arrests of three British nationals, namely the Olympios brothers and Betty Ambatelios, who was the wife of a Greek Communist, were to be dealt with by the British government through diplomatic channels for fear of the outcry they might provoke among the British public.

At the same time, the British government made every effort to keep in close and constant contact with King Constantine, not least because of the traditionally close ties of the British Royal Family with the Greek Crown, and concentrated its energy on restoring his influence. During the fateful hours that followed the communication of the news of the putsch, the British envoy met him at his Palace at Tatoi and strongly urged that he should refuse to accept it as a fait accompli. Another unassailable proof of the British government's dissatisfaction with the turn of events in Greece was its focus on making it public knowledge that the King had acted under duress. This was a line the BBC and the British press were encouraged to take, and was underlined by the government's insistence in Parliament that King Constantine had not been a party to the revolt. As Sir Patrick Dean told Secretary of State Dean Rusk, 'in background briefings to British press and to BBC, Brit Govt sources had discreetly supported [the] King'.[8] In this way the British aspired to protect his image thus contributing to the maintenance of his political leverage vis-à-vis the new government.

The British government's initial vexation was also evident during the frequently heated debates in both Houses. Prime Minister Wilson admitted that his government was 'deeply and intimately concerned' about developments in Greece.[9] Emphasis was placed on the notion that 'recent events have placed a strain on Anglo–Greek relations' and that it was the government's wish that 'advances towards the restoration of democratic procedures and civil liberties will make our relations easier'.[10] In the meantime, the British government decided not to contact Greece's new rulers right away.

In fact, in the immediate aftermath of the coup, they maintained only working-level consular contacts with the new regime and froze all other direct dealings with coup officials and new ministers. For instance, its Embassy Officials deliberately abstained from its custom of joining the Greek authorities for the celebration of the Orthodox Easter, just days after the new regime's coming to power. In addition, it avoided acknowledging the traditional circular note that Pavlos Economou-Gouras, the new Greek Minister for Foreign Affairs, sent to all embassies in Athens upon assuming duties, their thinking being that 'a quick response [would] be interpreted as approval of the new regime.'[11]

This 'distinctively chilly diplomatic situation' crystallised, despite the regime's constant assurances about its genuinely democratic intentions.[12] Everett, the British Embassy official responsible for NEA, described the British stance towards the new regime 'as one of "extreme reserve"' and mentioned that 'British Amb Athens is under instructions… not to approach new govt although Embassy officers have had "informal" contact with officials new government.'[13] Furthermore, it was promptly decided to 'freeze all, if any, exports of arms to Greece for the time being.'[14]

Meanwhile, the British government also expressed concern for the Greek people regularly and consistently. The first statement of sympathy by the government in Parliament came three days after the coup, in the suggestion that 'to see a friend and an ally go through this kind of problem, it is as much of concern to us as it is to them.'[15] A few days later, Richard Crossman, a Cabinet Minister remarked: 'I personally am deeply shocked by and profoundly alarmed at what is happening there, as are all members of the government… It is a shock for us that Greek democracy should be treated in this way.'[16] It should be borne in mind that this was a Labour government so not only did it feel natural distaste for the unlawful imposition of a military regime in Greece, but, equally importantly, it had to publicly manifest it.

Nevertheless, despite its displeasure at the developments in Greece, the British government made no statement outside Parliament, even of the most delicate nature, regarding its official stance towards the Colonels' regime; this was true not only during the first hours after the coup, when the situation was in flux and potentially delicate, but even several days or indeed months later. The only reported governmental statement was the apology offered to the Greek Ambassador for the demonstration and forcible occupation of the Greek Embassy in London a week after the Colonels' putsch. A group of more than 100 Greeks, Cypriots and British had entered the Embassy while the Ambassador was away, and used Embassy radio transmitter and telex.'[17]

The British government confined itself to defending its policies among strictly political circles in a vague and laconic fashion. During confrontations in the House of Commons, not only with members of the opposition but mainly with its own backbenchers, government ministers repeatedly stated that they would wait until the situation became clearer before spelling out a policy. According to one official's argument during a debate in the House of Lords, 'there is time to speak and there is time to be silent. I think it is possible to argue that this is time to be silent, or at least to be discreet, and to let the fruits of our private diplomacy make their appearance.'[18]

Claims regarding the officials' continuous uncertainty about the intentions of the regime were rather specious. Soon after the coup, three members of parliament, namely Francis Noel-Baker, Malcolm Macmillan and Arnold Gregory, were sent to Greece on a fact-finding visit. After spending some time investigating, as far as was possible, a number of allegations against the new rulers of Greece by talking to them, touring the country and recording people's comments, the latter two proceeded to compile a report. In it they expressed their conviction that 'the dictatorship's pretense of normality and claim to its acceptance by the people is a clear fraud directed at foreign opinion and tourists' and that 'overwhelmingly the Greek people feel deeply outraged and betrayed and are utterly opposed to this dictatorship'.[19] The two envoys concluded their report as follows:

> the violent and utterly unjustifiable putsch by the military junta that arrogantly and brutally seized power by the misuse of NATO (including British) arms, supplied for national and allied defence, and not for the assault on the Greek people, their Greek Parliament and democratic life, calls for condemnation of all nation-members of the United Nations Organisation, of NATO and of all the signatories of the Universal Declaration of Human Rights (ratified by Greece). Until and in order that all free Greek Parliamentary and other democratic institutions and rights are fully restored, this fascist-type dictatorship should be ostracized by all civilized nations and every effort should be made to

assist those responsible influences, organizations and persons, inside and outside Greece, active and at the task of securing the release of the political prisoners and restoring the liberties of the Greek people.[20]

The British government had received indications, even from an early stage, about the practices and outlook of the regime in Greece. Consequently, it certainly could not argue that it was allowing time for the regime to reveal its true nature; the forcible way in which it took power as well as some of the methods it employed in the immediate aftermath, proved that, although it was quite idiosyncratic not least in terms of its purported ideology, it had indisputably adopted a dictatorial approach.

As the above litany of rather restrained reaction demonstrates, once the Greek Colonels had assumed control, the British government did next to nothing to influence developments in Greece. The same climate of non-interference, which fits with the conclusion that Britain did not actually connive to bring about the coup, also helps to explain why Britain was less inclined to take action to topple the Colonels' regime. Though direct intervention in Greek affairs was a practice not unfamiliar to British politicians, especially up to the mid-1940s, it was argued that it was not the responsibility of the British government to undertake actions that could influence the evolution of another country's domestic events. This was a belief to which both Foreign Secretary George Brown and Ambassador Sir Ralph Murray seemed to adhere when the possibility of conspiring with conservative Greek politicians to undermine the regime was placed on the table of negotiations.

In addition, according to George Brown, the majority of the Greek public, mainly those living outside Athens and Salonica, apprehensive about a new civil war and disenchanted by the unstable conditions before the coup, seemed willing to give the Colonels a chance.[21] Indeed, most observers agreed that 'though there was little overt support of the colonels, there was, in the early months, a larger than later acknowledged tacit acceptance.'[22] One important factor was that, as Sotiris Rizas accurately observed, anti-Communism enjoyed a substantial mass following 'since memories of the civil war repelled from the left a considerable section of the Greek population'.[23] Writing in *The Times* Philip Howard characterised the Greeks' attitude as follows: 'There is an enormous amount of apathy about everything. People are very tired with politicians, with journalists, with the military ... there have been so many years of psychological acrobatics, of believing in people and losing that belief, of believing again and then being disappointed again.'[24]

A plethora of additional factors contributed to their lackadaisical approach. British officials estimated that there was a danger that factions within the Greek Army, or others, might feel encouraged to initiate resistance, thereby sparking a civil war. This concern was reflected in one of the comments made by George Brown, which reads as follows:

> It is easy to talk about supporting the working classes of Greece in overthrowing the regime. It is easy to talk about expelling Greece from here and there. The fact of the matter is that if that ended in murder and bloodshed, which we were in no position to help or to avert, we would have a hell of responsibility on our heads for those who would then have to suffer and pay the price for it.[25]

In light of the aforementioned considerations, it was not long before British officials started to yield to pressures for sustaining a formal working relationship with the regime and accede to the idea that, as long as it satisfactorily served British national interests from a pragmatic point of view, there was no crying need to disrupt their traditionally close dealings with the country. In fact, the idea of breaking off diplomatic relations with Greece was discussed[26] and overwhelmingly rejected, as in the British Ambassador's words, 'we [the British government] don't want this dictatorship, however much we dislike it, to start its life with an anti-British bias.'[27]

Moreover, the British government considered closing diplomatic channels and admonition to be counter-productive courses of action on the grounds that they would alienate a country whose close cooperation was significant within NATO and would, in return, lead to unwelcome retaliations. They reckoned that such a stance would eliminate any chance they had of exerting influence over the new rulers in favour of democratisation. Besides, as British Foreign Secretary George Brown suggested, the Colonels were unlikely to be overthrown by a policy of condemnation.[28] Robert Keeley, an American diplomat in Athens at the time took a different view—he thought the West could easily influence the regime.[29] One can only wonder whether a systematic anti-junta campaign through diplomatic and economic sanctions and military non-cooperation could have contributed to the demise of the illiberal regime.

In reality the British interests behind the Labour government's decision to resume 'business as usual' with Greece were rather different. They above all included concerns, for both moral and strategic reasons, over the fate of Cyprus, the importance of preserving Greece's cooperation with NATO and averting the spread of Communism in the Mediterranean, as well as safeguarding British commercial interests in Greece, especially given Britain's parlous financial state. The Colonels had in fact made it clear that they were advocates of all these notions Britain held dear; these were neatly summarised on the day of the coup in a statement by spokesman Stylianos Pattakos, to the effect that 'the coup was designed to ensure domestic tranquility, loyalty to the King and allegiance to NATO and the West as a whole, as well as to unify the people.'[30] It could be certainly argued that the early omens received by the British government hinted that the new ruling establishment of Greece was in harmony with the West's interests.

It was Greece's special geostrategic significance to NATO which was the most frequently quoted consideration behind the 'play it cool and burn no bridges' policy.[31] In fact, Greece's position lay in the eye of the vortex, encircled as it was by a number of Communist countries, such as Bulgaria, a staunch Soviet satellite, pro-Chinese Albania and the idiosyncratic Tito's Yugoslavia, as well as Soviet sympathisers Syria and Egypt. British officials were acutely conscious of Greece's pivotal importance for the prosperity of NATO's 'underbelly' and the consequent necessity of being on good terms with it.

The military facilities agreement signed in 1953 'authorised the construction, development, use and operation of military and supporting facilities in Greece necessary for the implementation of, or in furtherance of, approved NATO plans.'[32] The established and expanded facilities following this agreement 'strengthened the NATO forces in the area, provided important communication links, a staging area and supply depots for US and NATO air and naval forces and permitted surveillance and monitoring of the activities of Soviet forces in the Eastern Mediterranean.'[33] They also served the purpose of safeguarding NATO interests not only vis-à-vis the Soviet threat, but also those raised by Middle Eastern and North African countries; for instance, from 'the base at Hellinikon in Athens, surveillance planes had carried out flights over Libya, whereas the base at Iraklion monitored communications from Libya and the Middle East.'[34]

In a nutshell, Greece was contributing both armed forces and an infrastructural base, which were instrumental to the West's common defence of the area; and this sat well with the British Prime Minister's preoccupation with maintaining 'the stability in the Eastern Mediterranean and preventing further encroachment by the Soviet Union into that area.'[35] This necessity was something that the American government, in light of its even greater strategic interests in Greece, made sure did not escape Britain's attention. In an effort to put up a common front with the Americans due to the associated benefits, the British government allowed for the determination of its own interests in accordance with American needs, especially with regard to NATO. John Young noted that 'NATO was one place where Britain demonstrated its continuing importance to the USA, countering the negative effect of the withdrawal from East of Suez and Wilson's refusal to send troops to Vietnam.'[36] In a secret Cabinet Memorandum entitled 'An Anglo-American Balance Sheet', the Secretary of State for Foreign Affairs related that Britain's alliance with the United States was 'the most important single factor in our [British] foreign policy.'[37] The memorandum concluded that 'any systematic attempt ... to pursue independent policies for their own sake, would undermine the basis of the relationship and do great damage to the national interest.'[38]

Moreover, 1967, witnessed many Cold War incidents in areas geographically related to Greece's position. The Six Day War in 1967 between Israel on one side and Egypt, Syria and Jordan on the other, took place less than six weeks after the Colonels' advent to power, and highlighted the Soviets' intention to cultivate good relations with the oil-producing Arab states. By deploying for the first time their surface fleet to challenge the influence of US sea power in a region distant from the Soviet Union itself, the Soviets gave the first tangible indication of their serious interest in the area. At the same time, the Soviet Union offered financial incentives to the Maghreb region and Turkey.

Following Israel's abandonment of its neutral stance, the war also spearheaded 'an American reappraisal of the importance of NATO's southern flank ... in view of NATO's need for over-flight privileges, sea communications, and oil resources.'[39] Given that the various places for rest and rehabilitation for NATO forces were diminishing—the Arab ports were denying access, the Turkish ones were inadequate, Italy had curbed landing rights, Malta was threatening to become a NATO no-go area, and Spain blocked any landing on Gibraltar—sustaining access to the Greek ports had never seemed so essential as it did then. In light of such disquieting developments, Greece figured large in the eyes of NATO as the only reliable ally in the region along with Israel.[40] As John Owens, a State Department Greek Desk veteran, epitomised it, 'the Arab-Israeli conflict dramatized the importance of the Greek land and sea space in the Mediterranean and the need for friendly relations with the Greek government.'[41]

George Thompson, the Chancellor of the Duchy of Lancaster, commented during a meeting with the Greek Minister of Foreign Affairs on 12 September 1967, that 'the United Kingdom attached high importance to relations with Greece both bilaterally and within the Atlantic Alliance.'[42] He added that his government 'considered it essential to maintain an integrated NATO organisation both as a deterrent and as offering the basis for further détente in East/West relations.'[43] A memorandum drafted in 1967 by the Joint Intelligence Committee defined British interest in the Eastern Mediterranean along the following lines:

(a) the maintenance of conditions in which peaceful and orderly development can proceed,
(b) the prevention of Soviet expansion and communist penetration,
(c) the protection of our material interests (predominately our oil interests and supplies),
(d) the preservation of our transit facilities, both civil and military, by sea and air.[44]

Such *Realpolitik* considerations, it has often been claimed, mean that British attitudes towards the Colonels cannot be examined outside the Cold War framework; in other words, had it not been for the Cold War, Britain could have followed a more hostile approach towards them. Such was the view espoused by many of my interviewees. But this argument, though possessing many undeniable merits, ignores the fact that there were other greatly cherished interests at stake, one of them being Cyprus, whose significance was not solely contextualised within NATO.

Cyprus was undoubtedly a very critical and contentious issue for Britain. Despite having granted the island its independence Britain had become along with Greece and Turkey one of the island's guarantors of security. In view of this arrangement, finding a solution to the irredentist disputes of the Greek and Turkish Cypriot communities in Cyprus was considered attainable only through the productive collaboration of all parties involved. This was reflected in a comment made by one member Foreign Office, who argued 'we have always taken the view that progress towards a solution of [the] Cyprus dispute can only be achieved by negotiations between the parties concerned.'[45] This concern was particularly relevant in 1967, as by that time a number of recent crises had led to the belief that both Turkey's and Greece's aspirations with regard to Cyprus were potentially explosive. In fact, only a few days before the Colonels' coup, skirmishes had broken out yet again between the two communities on the island and generalised fighting was only narrowly averted thanks to the intervention of the UN— including British forces.[46]

The Colonels' seizure of power increased British anxieties over Cyprus. It was feared that the Greek Colonels' counterparts in Cyprus might follow suit with a coup against the island's authorities.[47] Another scenario saw the former fomenting, in its anti-Communist ardour, a strike by the Greek Army against the Communists on the island, which would risk igniting inter-community troubles.[48] That the Colonels' coup aggravated the already uncertain and tense situation over Cyprus was made clear in comments by Foreign Secretary George Brown.[49] In light of such dreaded contingencies, he lost no opportunity to specifically warn his Greek counterpart against any use of force by the Grivas-led Greek–Cypriot National Guard.

Britain's desire to maintain peace in Cyprus was not simply due to a sense of responsibility. Though colonial rule in Cyprus had ended in 1960, Britain retained a strong military presence principally in the form of their Sovereign Base Areas and the Retained Bases. These bases, which 'could not be effectively provided elsewhere',[50] had emerged as the only remaining safe British asset for the defence of the Middle Eastern region. A joint memorandum drafted in June 1967 succinctly summarised the significance of Cyprus in the eyes of British officials. Cyprus was important to the UK for three reasons. First, it was a member of the Commonwealth. Second, the Cyprus dispute affected

Britain's relations with Turkey and Greece. And third, Britain's Sovereign Base Areas in the island played a large part in Central Treaty Organisation (CENTO)[51] and other commitments and provided the jumping-off point for the CENTO air route through Turkey and Iran to the Persian Gulf and the Far East.[52]

There is ample evidence to suggest, however, that British officials were not only reluctantly cooperating on the Cyprus issue with the Greek government; on the contrary, before long they appeared quite confident and rather pleased with the Colonels' handling of it. For one thing, the Colonels' regime was fiercely opposed to Communism, thus minimising the possibility of Cyprus becoming the 'Cuba of the Eastern Mediterranean'.[53] This became more apparent towards the end of 1967 when the regime appointed as its Foreign Minister Panayiotis Pipinelis, a well-respected Greek politician, who, as his successor, Xanthopoulos-Palamas related, was 'ideologically attached to the Western monarchical tradition and politically followed the lines of close cooperation with the Anglo-Saxon powers and above all London.'[54] Meanwhile, the replacement of Sir Ralph Murray as British Ambassador in Athens by the more businesslike Sir Michael Stewart infused greater pragmatism into British foreign policy towards Greece.

A further catalyst related to the financial benefits that could spring from maintaining close cooperation with Greece. The British were aware that if they opposed the regime, they would not be able to derive any economic gains. This belief was fortified by the threat issued to the Scandinavian countries warning them that Greece would 'break off all commercial relations with them, unless they revise their hostile behaviour towards the new regime.'[55] Such blackmails were repeatedly exercised in stark retaliation for the Scandinavians' antagonistic, to put it mildly, attitudes towards the Colonels.

A similarly polemical course of action would have certainly appeased the majority of the British public, a large section of which expressed repugnance at the events in Greece and advocated an outspokenly condemnatory stance of the kind for which the Scandinavian states had set a strong precedent. Nonetheless, as the British government would customarily reply:

Our position is not the same as that of the Scandinavian countries. British interests in Greece are far greater than theirs. We have an annual trade balance of 20 million pounds [in excess of 360 millions in today's value] in our favour. There are potential orders worth 100 million pounds [close to 2 billions in today's value] at stake. We also have a position of responsibility towards the Cyprus problem, which we cannot disregard, any more than we can ignore the key-position that Greece occupies on the South-end flank of NATO.[56]

The concerns of the Treasury regarding Britain's relations with Greece were also associated with various considerations stemming from previous Anglo–Greek dealings. These included the settlement of an inter-governmental loan and the administration of the bonded debt, as well as aid obligations within the NATO framework and the OECD Consortium. In view of the above, the Treasury admitted in private that 'in matters of trade, finance and investment our [the Treasury's] wish was for completely normal relations with Greece', and that … 'the criteria by which Greek investment or other projects to be financed by long term credit were judged in London were purely those of economic and financial viability.'[57] As another source put it, 'we [the British] must keep ourselves in a position to take as full advantage as possible of development opportunities in Greece.'[58]

A statement in a Cabinet Treasury report a few weeks after the coup ruled it imperative for Britain to 'maintain working relations with the new regime so that British interests be protected',[59] thereby illustrating the great importance which the British attached to commercial factors. Given Britain's mounting financial problems and its adherence to the 'export or die' principle, it was considered unwise either to risk losing exports or to compromise the possibility of entering into new commercial deals with Greece. In 1967, British exports to Greece amounted to £33.8 million (almost 610 millions in today's value).[60] In addition, following the approach of Greek Embassy officials to the Foreign Office in an effort 'to emphasise their desire that commercial and financial relations should be maintained undisturbed',[61] the British government felt optimistic about promising future prospects.

In connection with the financial factor, there existed another crucial parameter, namely the need to safeguard the conduct of negotiations regarding the possible supply by the UK Atomic Energy Authority of a nuclear power station to Greece, a deal estimated to be worth £20 million (360 millions in today's value). It was for the purpose of discussing this possibility that the Greek ministers of industry and foreign affairs had visited Britain in May 1966. Ever since, British officials had been expressing notable anxiety about winning 'this very valuable order'.[62] There were other potentially substantial deals at stake, including railway rolling stock contracts, a valley irrigation scheme and a number of technology deals that would boost Wilson's 'White Heat' of scientific revolution. In its November 1967 report, the Treasury concluded that 'on the basis of the existing issues pending settlement and the hope that commercial agreements could be enforced, and in conjunction with Britain's poor financial state, the British government had to try to be on good terms with its Greek counterpart.'[63]

Likewise, the debate about whether Britain should refrain from selling arms to Greece on ideological grounds was concluded by recognising that, in view of the need to ameliorate the balance of exports and avoid jeopardising British jobs in the armaments industry, Britain could not impose a ban on the overall sale of arms to Greece. Instead, British officials decided to closely monitor the trade so that they could forbid the sale of those arms which could be used against the civilian population—a fairly spurious distinction. Furthermore, the vacuum created by the US armaments embargo on Greece in response to the Colonels' coming to power created good prospects for increased military sales to Greece. This seemed a lucrative proposition to the British government, which was interested in increasing its share of benefits both in terms of money and creation of jobs for British workers through its participation in the Greek defence procurement programme.

In view of the above considerations and in spite of its serious doubts about the intentions and potential of the Colonels—whom the British Ambassador described as 'political eunuchs'[64]—the British government informed its American colleagues that it intended to resume working relations on 27 April, six days after the coup. The British Prime Minister recognised the established authority of the new rulers, but cautioned against implying approval of the coup's outcome.

This was therefore the line that the British Foreign Secretary impressed upon his Ambassador in Athens when they met in London.[65] A day later, the Cabinet meeting on 4 May 1967 expressed the belief that 'Britain could achieve the most favourable results possible in the circumstances, if we continued to do business with the regime.'[66] While agreeing on the need to deal with the new regime by engaging in normal diplomatic contact, British officials advised against giving any impression of endorsement. In Parliament, the British government presented its decision to resume normal relations with the Greek regime in the following way:

> We have assumed official relations with the new regime. Had we not done so, we would not have been able to make the strong representations … A further reason for the assumption of official relations was to enable us effectively to protect British subjects and interests in Greece which are the government's first concern. But this action in no way implies approval of the regime's policies.[67]

As striving to maintain good working relations with a military dictatorship constituted an ideological discrepancy on the part of the British Labour government, it ended up infuriating the vast majority of Labour backbenchers for whom *Realpolitik* considerations did not carry much weight. It was on those grounds that they repeatedly attacked their own government with taunts of hypocrisy. To be sure, it was this very government that had subscribed to the 'optional' clauses of the European Court of Human Rights in 1966. The Parliamentary Labour Party's statements often reflected the rank and file's disillusionment with governmental policy. Several Labour backbenchers in defiance of their government's official policy, provided assistance to a number of Greek exiles abroad, and contributed to organising and coordinating international resistance against the regime. Labour MPs Samuel Silkin, Leader of British Delegation to the Assembly of the Council of Europe and Chairman of the Society of Labour lawyers, and Joan Lestor from the National Executive Committee of the Labour Party were only a couple of the many high profile politicians who were in close contact with Greek resisters in London and often rallied openly in favour of their pro-democracy pleas. However, despite all the furor, they too proved to be eventually amenable to compromise. No matter how stridently opposed they might have been over a host of foreign policy issues, pertaining not only to Greece, but also to the Vietnam war, defence expenditure, the civil war in Biafra and sales of arms to South Africa, they had no desire to challenge their party leadership and thereby pave the Conservatives' way into office.

It is also worth mentioning that not all members of the Cabinet itself were at ease with the policy the government had implemented. Some members, like Foreign Secretary George Brown, who was allegedly substantially influenced by the Americans, were keener to conduct 'business as usual'. It is particularly noteworthy that the Foreign Secretary was almost exclusively entrusted with reaching decisions regarding British policy towards Greece as the Prime Minister's attention at that time focused predominately on the Vietnam War, joining the EEC, matching Britain's overseas commitments to scant financial resources, and the ongoing Rhodesian issue. On the opposing side, Richard Crossman, Minister for Social Services and Leader of the House of Commons, and Barbara Castle, Minister for Transport, appeared to be among the most disenchanted Cabinet members.

Meanwhile, the British people's perception of Greece as a bastion of democracy, erroneous though it was, meant that there was going to be noticeable denunciation of the British government's dealings with the Colonels' regime, evident in the numerous demonstrations. A number of British citizens were involved in fiercely anti-junta non-governmental and international organisations, including Amnesty International, based in London, as well as the Socialist International, the International Labour Organisation and the International Red Cross. To be sure, the Hellenic ideal projected a certain allure. As Alexander Kazamias related, people regularly referred to 'Hellenism as the highest and most perfect expression of spiritual civilization.'[68] Several resisters were motivated by their political beliefs and some even had close links with chief underground resistance organisations in Greece, such as the leftist Patriotic Front and the centre leaning Democratic Defence. Others became interested in actively participating in the resistance, 'for the anarchic "kick" or to brighten a Chelsea morning';[69] or simply, as one of my interviewees confided because 'it felt like the right thing to do'.[70] Cedric Thornberry, Professor of Constitutional Law at LSE and Human Rights lawyer, like many other instinctive liberals, was disinterested, at least initially, in any kind of 'isms'; instead, as he put it, he appeared 'to have reverted to the nineteenth century liberal values of John Stuart Mill and be practicing them on an international scale.'[71]

London was also home to a plethora of Greek émigrés, who harboured the expectation that a Labour government would be naturally sympathetically predisposed to their protests calling for Greece's democratisation.[72] Those included not only high-profile politicians but also a fair number of internationally known academics, journalists, artists, and Nobel Prize winners, most of whom were quite influential with widely circulating media, including the BBC and *The Times*. As prominent Greek journalist and newspaper owner Helen Vlachos, who sought refuge in the British capital following her flight into exile, attested, 'for a journalist I think, it [London] is the capital of Europe.'[73]

The gathering of such energetic anti-junta momentum was reflected in the creation of a number of resistance organisations, myriad letters of protest sent to newspapers, British MPs, and the Prime Minister's office, and the frequency with which questions regarding British policy towards Greece were raised during Parliamentary debates. The pro-left League for Democracy in Greece, in existence since 1945, and the newly formed Committee against the Dictatorship in Greece were among the main carriers of the opposition flame in the UK through lobbying MPs, channeling information to the press, trade unions and students, and organising rallies and fundraising events, such as concerts and plays. The widespread expression of public revulsion at the military seizure of power in Greece was all the more striking when compared to the, at best tepid, response to the military overthrows in Turkey and Pakistan, another two significant British military allies.[74] So all in all, the government faced a welter of criticism, either generated from or embedded within its own ranks and among the public too. In order to harmonise the paradox of their close, albeit at times frayed, interaction with Greece's illiberal and anachronistic rulers, Britain's leaders offered a number of not always convincing justifications.

The first argument deployed was that the question of formal recognition did not arise in the case of Greece since there had been no change in the Head of State. Indeed, this argument was facilitated by the Greek King's swearing-in of the new government. On those grounds, George Brown suggested to the Cabinet that, 'we [the British government] could avoid any question of recognition of the new regime or approval of it, if we took the line that we were merely continuing relations with a government whose Head of State was unchanged'.[75] The future course of events unquestionably confirmed that this argument was used as a façade, as the British government continued to recognise the regime after the King went into exile, following his own abortive coup in December 1967, and even after the abolition of the Monarchy by the Colonels in 1973.

Moreover, the Foreign Secretary claimed that 'it was our normal practice to have diplomatic relations with governments which were effectively in power whether or not we approved of them'.[76] As Sir Patrick Dean, the British Ambassador in Washington, epitomised it, the 'British believe that coup govt is firmly entrenched for immediate future and nothing would be served by repeated condemnation of coup'.[77] It is actually true that the British Crown had for centuries adhered to the conservative doctrine of the de facto recognition of foreign regimes, democratic or undemocratic; though it is arguably something else for a government to use this as a fundamental condition for choosing which governments to do business with. In addition, on several occasions, as for instance in the cases of North Korea, North Vietnam and Yemen, the British had made exceptions on political grounds to the Communist regimes' firm control of those countries.

It is also noteworthy that in a previous exchange of views between David Bruce, at the American Embassy in London, and Alan Davidson, Head of the Central Department of the Foreign Office, which took place only three days before the British government decided to normalise its working relations with Greece on the basis that the Colonels justified the criteria for recognition, Davidson was recorded as having opined that 'neither condition [had] yet [been] met in Greece'[78]—the Colonels were not in firm control, and the King was not indisputably the Head of State. Of interest was the reaction of the US State Department upon notification of the British government's decision, which was recorded as follows: 'at this end we do not see the need for this haste.'[79]

In a further attempt to justify their chosen policy, the British government's representative reaffirmed his government's belief 'that it is more effective to make our views known in this way than by making public pronouncements and protests which would be likely to drive the regime to extremes and thus frustrate the very purposes which we all have in common'.[80] The Foreign Secretary also insisted that 'the fact that we have diplomatic relations does not in any way imply approval either of the political complexion of the Greek government or of its position'.[81] This argument was embodied in a report drafted by Foreign Office officials which encapsulated British foreign policy towards the Colonels until mid-December:

> … our own policy, following our assumption of an official relationship with the new government on 27 April, is to deal with the new regime, but to avoid taking actions (e.g. visits by British Ministers to Greece) which might be interpreted as signs that we approve of it. We share the misgivings so widely expressed in this and other countries about Greece's reversion to military rule and suspension of many essential elements of democratic life. But an overdose of official condemnation might well have the wrong effect on the government which is still in a formative stage. We do not want to drive it into greater extremism… In answering any criticisms that we are condoning the military rule in Greece by dealing with the new government, [we] should make a familiar point: that dealing with a government is not the same as approving it. We are dealing with the Greek government both because this is necessary for the protection of interests (e.g. British subjects who have been under detention) and because by doing so we have a better prospect of influencing it.[82]

Meanwhile, the Cabinet did try to privately influence the regime with some notable successes. Arguments about the efficacy of secret diplomacy were frequently used by the British officials. This became particularly relevant at the end of November 1967, when the danger of a Turkish–Greek skirmish in Cyprus was averted at the very last moment. More specifically, the three Colonels were secretly invited for dinner at the British Ambassador's residence, but as soon as the triumvirate arrived, the Ambassador notified them of the planned Turkish airstrikes in Cyprus a few hours later, of which the Colonels appeared to have no previous knowledge. Upon hearing the information, they left immediately in order to contact the Cypriot officers, whose actions had precipitated the crisis, in a last ditch attempt to avert confrontation.

The Greek Armed Forces were brought to an advanced state of readiness, and George Thomson, Secretary of State for Commonwealth Affairs described it 'as a very tense situation'.[83] Pilots were briefed and heavy troop movements were advancing near the Greek–Turkish borders, whilst similar preparatory movements were reported on the Turkish side too, thus placing both countries on what admittedly looked like the 'brink of war'.[84] Furthermore, reports were circulating that 'American anxiety over the situation had brought units of the Sixth Fleet to the area of Cyprus'.[85]

Despite the joint efforts of US Special Representative Cyrus Vance, UN Secretary General U Thant and NATO's Secretary General Manlio Brosio to ward off escalation, the British attributed the de-escalation to the British Ambassador's 'personal intervention with the leaders of the military junta on the night of 15 November'.[86] Consequently, British officials argued that it was thanks to their having 'retained an influence in Athens on foreign affairs that the Cyprus crisis at the end of 1967 did not escalate into war in the Eastern Mediterranean'.[87] Interestingly enough, one of the 'beneficiaries' of the crisis seemed to have been Colonel George Papadopoulos himself, and by extension his regime too, as it was reported that he 'actually pulled his country back out of the Cyprus mess, when more hot headed and less intelligent men might well have allowed it to slip into a war with Turkey, which Greece would certainly have lost both in Cyprus and Turkey.'[88]

In the meantime, British officials missed no opportunity in the House of Commons to say that they had indeed received many assurances from the new rulers that they had no intention of imposing a long-term dictatorship. Brigadier Pattakos, the spokesman of the 'Revolutionary Council' and one of the three executors of the coup, characteristically claimed that 'we never stated that we imposed a dictatorship, but just a parenthesis in order to create the appropriate conditions to go to elections'.[89] The government's critics argued of course that no convincing case can be made for the imposition of an Army-backed dictatorship.

Perhaps the most striking example of disapproval of the British government's policy came from the Labour Party itself. During its conference at Scarborough on 4 October, its majority endorsed the proposed Greek resolution with 3,167,000 votes in favour and 2,898,000 against. The resolution's purpose was to express 'indignation at the seizure of power by the Greek military clique, and the British Labour government's recognition of this [the Colonels'] regime'.[90] The motion concluded as follows:

> Conference calls for the expulsion of Greece from NATO, the end of all military aid to Greece and the ending of their association with

European organizations like the European Economic Community and the Council of Europe until the military dictatorship gives way to a viable and proper democracy.[91]

On this occasion, sympathy over the events in Greece was yet again expressed by the Foreign Secretary, who mentioned inter alia that:

in the case of Greece, I feel as deeply as anybody here, and so do all my colleagues, about the destruction of democracy in that very ancient founding land of our democratic faith, and not by one thing, by one word, action or posture, do I want to act other than in a very condemnatory spirit of the present regime and the way it came to power.[92]

However, George Brown asked the conference not to pass the motion, and in its aftermath chose to disregard it, while elaborating on the government's dilemma along the following lines: 'To oppose the resolution would give the wrong impression in Greece; to pass it would put a responsibility on us which we are not at this moment able to accept'.[93] It should be nonetheless noted that the frequency of 'revolt against government policy by the party conference' in the 1960s, over a number of foreign affairs issues, such as Vietnam, the Nigerian Civil War and Rhodesia, made the government treat them often as 'intermittent events whose resolutions could easily be ignored'.[94]

In the wake of the devaluation of November 1967, followed by Britain's decision to terminate its presence east of Suez, Whitehall did not seem to be overly exercised with the morality of its foreign policy, which often came across as lacking 'coherent, long term ... goals'.[95] Instead, recurrent balance of payment crises together with the drain on its financial reserves absorbed most of the government's energy. The consequent mundane reality of the need for retrenchment, reduction of its overseas commitments and rapid retreat from East of Suez as well as from the Persian Gulf and Singapore kept the British Foreign Office's agenda busy; consequently, not much stomach was left for debates about changing British policy towards Greece, even more so as this did not seem to carry any immediate, tangible benefits.

It is noteworthy that British officials wasted no opportunity in those early days to bring to the attention of the Greek government their unease with a number of its practices. In a meeting between Anthony Hohler from the Foreign Office and Panayiotis Verykios Greek

Ambassador in London, the former highlighted to the latter the three issues pertaining to conditions in Greece which the British government found particularly cumbersome when publicly justifying its policy. These were the relatively slow pace of preparation of the new constitution; censorship, especially of the press (a point which was particularly sensitive for British public opinion); and the continuing existence of Courts Martial.[96]

At the same time, most foreign governments seemed to encounter similar quandaries when it came to choosing their policy towards the unconstitutional government in Greece. The initial discomfort that was generally felt by all diplomatic missions in Greece was clearly manifested by the freezing of all contact; every diplomatic mission's representatives declined to attend the customary celebration of Greek Easter a few days after the coup took place. The first and only immediate formal exchange took place when the West German Ambassador in Athens, without consulting his fellow NATO Ambassadors, sent an invitation to the newly appointed Greek Minister for Foreign Affairs for Konrad Adenauer's memorial service, scheduled on 25 April. The new regime took advantage of this development, which it used as proof of foreign recognition of its status. However, Foreign Minister Pavlos Oikonomou-Gouras, who was also accompanied by Brigadier Pattakos, was treated with extreme reserve by all governments during the service.

The government of the Federal Republic of Germany admitted finding itself in an uncomfortable position vis-à-vis the Colonels' regime, as it did not favour economic action, nor was it keen to support political action, but was receiving strong pressure to do so from the Social Democrats.[97] Contrary to internal pressures, it was less reticent than the British at the outset, as it even negotiated with the new Greek government the sale of seventy-five M-47 tanks to Greece in the middle of May. It is nonetheless interesting to note that it grew more reserved as time went by, and five months later the same West German government, unhappy with the deteriorating political conditions in Greece, decided that although it would honour the delivery of weapons agreements already in force, it would not sign any new ones with the Greek government.[98]

The French for their part, slightly more restrained than the West Germans and the British, were admitting that their government 'deplored the coup privately' and that 'publicly, the attitude of the French government is reserved.'[99] In fact, their Ambassador in Athens only called on the King, and was, even as late as the end of May, under instructions not to extend the same gesture to any members of the government. The Ambassador was also told that if convoked by a government minister, he would have to refer the matter to Paris for a decision. These French policy initiatives towards the Greek government echoed the Italian attitude too.

With regard to Turkey, whose attitude was important in the context of the Cyprus dispute and NATO solidarity, its policy was reflected in a comment made by a Turkish official to the effect that 'it would do no good to affront the dignity of the present government of Greece, driving it into bitterness and isolation'.[100] Instead, it was recommended that it should 'be given time to work out its problems'.[101]

At the same time, the Greek government was approached by Soviet bloc countries which had noticed the void that the reserved response of its non-Communist allies created. East Germany, for instance, saw a window of opportunity, which it estimated could result in a 400 per cent increase in its trade with Greece.[102] Its government's evaluation was that, as 'the Common Market could not act favourably on Greece's request for association in the light of the military takeover in Athens ... Greece would therefore be forced to seek bilateral arrangements to dispose of their agricultural surpluses'.[103]

The potential for the increasing rapprochement with the Eastern bloc was a concern vexing the Americans in particular. Daniel Brewster opined 'We [the American government] must walk a narrow line between resisting its embrace and at the same time cooperating with it sufficiently to serve our national interests, which includes gradually moving the government towards constitutional government'.[104] Although they decided, just like the British, to withhold from any public statement on the coup in its immediate aftermath, they were actually faster than the British in restoring their formal contacts with the new regime. They did, nevertheless, refuse to lift their partial embargo of arms on Greece until they received 'concrete evidence that the government in Greece will make every effort to re-establish democratic institutions'.[105]

At an institutional level, the organisation which was least inclined to oppose the Colonels' regime was NATO.[106] De Gaulle's withdrawal of France from NATO's military wing a year before the Colonels' coup had put considerable strains on the alliance as it resulted in the liquidation of its installations in France. The second destabilising factor was the growing sense of disenchantment in some of the Northern European allies, especially in Denmark and Norway due to internal political developments that had emboldened the hand of anti-NATO socialist and far-left political elements.

The British, like the Americans and unlike the Italians and the Scandinavians, who firmly supported an initiative to discuss the suspension of Greece from NATO, dearly wished to avoid the eruption of a debate that might compromise the Alliance's interest in maintaining excellent relations with Greece. In fact, in an effort to maintain stability in NATO's southern flank, the Americans pushed the line that JUSMAGG (Joint US Military Advisory Group in Greece) should pursue its normal contacts with the new Greek regime, and that there should not be any change in the venue of international conferences scheduled for Greece, as a politically punitive measure.

In an orchestrated attempt with the Americans to avoid the inclusion of the Greek issue in the December 1967 ministerial agenda, the British argued that to raise the question of Greece's membership would serve only to disrupt the functioning of the alliance. Besides, as the Greek Ambassador even procclaimed in a rather self-assuring way, '... as far as both countries are loyal to NATO and the western orientation of Greece is one of the basic policies, for which Britain has fought, the revolutions should be considered by the British government as *a gift from God*'.[107] The Anglo-American wing also claimed, in a clear allusion to Portugal, that the North Atlantic Treaty did not specify that membership of NATO should be restricted to democratic governments. Furthermore, they started emphasising the regime's proclaimed intention of drafting a new constitution in an effort to disarm criticism of its undemocratic nature.

In any case, it was felt that the new Greek government deserved the right to be allowed reasonable time to live up to its promises. The other argument used was that if such a punitive action were taken against the government of Greece at an international level, it would serve the purpose of rallying the Greek public behind the coup, thereby fostering introverted nationalism. The Greek people's reaction against the proposed sanctions, it was postulated, would be all the more intense because of the fact that no NATO action was taken against Turkey in 1960 when it experienced similar conditions.

To the relief of Britain and the US, the question of Greece's membership of NATO was not brought up at the NATO ministerial meeting in December, nor indeed at any ministerial meeting thereafter, clearly indicating NATO's tolerance, to put it mildly, of the Colonels' regime. Commenting on the reasons behind this, the Americans concluded the following:

> we believe passage of time, recognition of special relevance of Greece to NATO security at time of Soviet build-up in Eastern Mediterranean, and general desire to project image of united alliance at December meeting have produced a tacit agreement to keep the silence.[108]

NATO's soft approach stands out in sharp contradistinction to the attitudes of a number of other intergovernmental organisations. The Consultative Assembly of the Council of Europe had repeatedly manifested a strong interest and anxiety about the developments in Greece. This was because Greece was a member which had adhered to the European Convention for the Protection of Human Rights and Fundamental Freedoms, therefore it had consented to respecting 'the principles of the rule of Law and the enjoyment by all persons within its jurisdiction of human rights and fundamental freedoms'.[109] Although one can easily advance the argument that the Council of Europe was the organisation par excellence to examine such infringements, it should not be overlooked that NATO's Preamble clearly affirms the determination of the parties 'to safeguard the freedom, common heritage, and civilisation of their peoples founded on the principles of democracy, individual liberty and the rule of law'.[110]

As early as 26 April, the Consultative Assembly adopted an order, which reflected its widespread concern at the coup and the particular consternation of European parliamentarians over the future of democracy in Greece. It passed Resolution 256, which proclaimed that the Assembly 'deplored the overthrow of Constitutional government in Greece, called upon the Greek authorities to restore constitutional government based on parliamentary democracy and to respect the European Convention of Human Rights'.[111] The Consultative Assembly's President, British Labour MP Geoffrey de Freitas, made the following statement at a press conference: 'The Assembly's immediate reaction to the military takeover in Greece is a resounding reminder that Europe cannot, and will not accept any substitute for true parliamentary democracy'.[112]

After the April meeting, there followed another two occasions on which the Political Committee of the Assembly met to discuss the Greek situation. The Standing Committee amended its draft resolution of 12 June with its resolution 346 of 23 June, in order to proclaim its grave perturbation at the present situation in Greece and at the 'many serious reported violations of human rights and fundamental freedoms' and repeated a call for the restoration of 'normal political and parliamentary life.'[113] The wish was therefore expressed that member countries refer the Greek case to the European Commission of Human Rights.[114] It is worth mentioning at this point that when Eric Baker, Amnesty's International Secretary-General and one of its founders, sent a letter to British Foreign Minister George Brown urging him to take action within it, the latter responded in the following way: 'I am not convinced that, in present circumstances, it would be helpful to refer alleged breaches of the Convention by Greece to the European Commission on Human Rights'.[115]

Not every country chose to align with Britain: the Scandinavian countries and Luxembourg openly condemned the new regime. The question of taking the Greek issue to the European Commission of Human Rights was raised for the first time in a seven-column front-page article of the influential Danish newspaper *Politiken* just over a week after the coup.[116] In Luxembourg, all elements of opinion 'varying from the relatively cautious and conditional disapproval of the newspaper *Wort* (Social Democrat), to the violent denunciation of the Communists'[117] criticised the military coup.

It was on 20 September that the governments of Denmark, Norway and Sweden, submitted applications against the Greek Government government under Article 24 of the European Convention of Human Rights alleging various breaches of the Convention.[118] The Dutch government, which expressed immediately after the coup willingness to provide asylum to the 2,500 Greek political detainees, followed suit by making a similar application a week later. By the end of September Belgium, Luxembourg and Iceland had endorsed the Scandinavians' applications. Subsequently, they widened their scope to include allegations of torture, which was explicitly forbidden under Article 3 of the Convention. Having declared their applications admissible on 24 January 1968 as regards both the original and the later allegations, the European Commission appointed a sub-commission to examine the matter.[119]

The British government, on the other hand, did not find itself 'able or willing to involve that machinery [of the European Convention of Human Rights] in the face of a serious threat to human rights and fundamental freedoms in Greece.'[120] This was an allegation made in writing by Lord Shawcross on behalf of Justice, the British sector of the International Commission of Jurists, against the Foreign Office that no doubt echoed the moral condemnations voiced by a large part of the British people. In reply to the numerous calls for action against Greece in the Council of Europe, the British government commented: 'We do not think expulsion of Greece from the Council of Europe would persuade the Greek government to return quickly to constitutional government'.[121] This was the official British stance that was contained in all answers to relevant questions, whether in Parliament or in exchanges with other governments or members of the public. British officials also communicated their stance to the Greek Chargé d'Affaires, reassuring him that they 'had no present intention of taking a lead in condemning Greece,'[122] as they 'did not believe it would be helpful in present circumstances to arraign Greece under the Human Rights Convention.'[123]

However, British Ambassador Michael Stewart warned the Greek representative that an undertaking could not be given that 'there would not be private members from both sides of the House, who would not make stiff speeches, unless there had been some important and visible changes in Greece by that time.'[124] The former urged the latter, to persuade the Greek government to 'take steps to lift restrictions on the press, release the remaining political prisoners and detainees and push on with the programme for the restoration of a parliamentary regime'[125] before the next session of the Assembly in autumn, in order for both their countries to be spared heavy criticism.

Meanwhile, the Parliament of the European Economic Community, with which Greece had signed a Treaty of Association in 1961, keen to embolden its political role in relation to the Directorate General for External Relations of the Commission, manifested a vivid interest. It thus came forth instantaneously following the initiative initially lodged by some of its Italian members, ruling that 'the operation of EEC-Greece Association must in practice be broken off pending return to normal conditions in Greece.'[126] This was deemed unavoidable on the grounds that the EEC–Greece Joint Parliamentary Committee could not be functional in the absence of elected institutions—although no doubt Italian motives might have been rather selfish stemming mainly from their desire to avoid competition with Greek agricultural products.

The Commission's stance on the other hand was rather equivocal, as the Greek crisis only added to an array of troubles. The protracted Empty Chairs Crisis that seriously threatened the Community's very existence had only narrowly been averted and its first president, Walter Hallstein, had recently resigned. At the same time, the Greek crisis coincided with the Community's eagerness to portray itself as a potent international actor in the political sphere too, as was soon to be evidenced by the December 1969 Hague Summit and the subsequent launching of the European Political Cooperation. In addition, the governments of the initial 'Six' and the eventual 'Nine' following the 1973 first enlargement were largely divided in their stance towards the Greek regime, ranging from France's rather friendly stance to Italy's outspoken hostility.

The summer of 1967 was ripe with consultations about how best to respond to Greece's constitutional crisis. The final verdict came five months after the coup and was announced by Jean Rey, the Commission's new President, who emphatically stated that 'the association agreement with Greece was not only an economic agreement, but also an agreement having a political bearing as it would lead to the ultimate adhesion of Greece to the Community.'[127] Soon after, the decision was taken to 'freeze' the Association Agreement, as a way of bringing pressure to bear in favour of the restoration of democracy and respect of human rights. Furthermore, the EEC withheld from Greece $56,000,000 (almost $420 millions in today's value), that constituted the unused balance of the EEC development loan through the European Development Bank.[128] Despite its debatable effect, this was a positive step towards collective policy-making with a view to safeguarding civil and human rights.

Moreover, a number of other international non-governmental organisations showed a very strong interest.[129] The International

Commission of Jurists, for instance, issued a press release on 9 May entitled 'The Rule of Law Abrogated in Greece'—the third since the coup. This report drew attention to the illegal suspension of certain fundamental constitutional safeguards and pointed out that:

> the actions and methods of the Greek military regime clearly offend the provisions of the Convention. Accordingly these events concern not only Greece but all the other High Contracting Parties to the Convention and are highly damaging to the concepts of democracy and legality.[130]

The same press release highlighted that,

> the military officers went even further than the King, the government and Parliament were entitled to go [in the case of grave public danger] in that they purported to suspend Article 18 of the Constitution [that forbids torture, capital punishment for political offence and total confiscation of property] which cannot be suspended even in an emergency.[131]

Indeed, this particular organisation published numerous reports and tabled several resolutions, especially during various milestones of the Colonels' seven years in power.

The Socialist International also passed many resolutions. Its first, endorsed two weeks after the coup, condemned 'the military overthrow of parliamentary democracy in Greece.'[132] A couple of weeks later it sent a delegation consisting of its Chairman, Dr Bruno Pittermann, from the Danish Social Democratic Party and Antonio Cariglia, Chairman of the Foreign Affairs Commission of the Italian Lower House, to Greece in order to hold talks with the new Greek government and press for the release of its political detainees.

The International Committee of the Red Cross had also since May 1967 started visiting a number of detention centres in Greece. However, its lengthy reports containing various incriminating details did not see the daylight given the strictly confidential conditions of this particular organisation's nature of work. They were only made available to the Greek government, under whose jurisdiction it fell to decide whether to publicise them or not. As its legal team affirmed, 'Concerning the reports by the International Committee of the Red Cross delegates on their visits to prisons or prison camps, they are communicated only to the Detaining power; this is a custom from which the I.C.R.C. has never departed'.[133]

The only Red Cross report that the Colonels released was the first one drafted in 1967 as it made no reference to incidents of human rights abuses of political prisoners, thus enabling the Colonels to use it as propaganda. Obviously, the required advance notification had allowed time for the Greek regime to cover its tracks. A formal agreement to widen the scope of its activities was signed with the Greek government in November 1969 as an attempt by the latter to tame public opposition ahead of the Council of Europe's decision about Greece's membership in December; but as it did not yield the anticipated results, it was soon abandoned by the regime.

The World Council of Churches, too, showed serious disquiet against the coercive methods used by the regime despite not cancelling its already scheduled annual meeting in Crete in August 1967 in the face of widespread criticism. The Church of Greece, whose Head was arbitrarily replaced, allegedly due to his old age, by the pro-regime Archbishop Ieronymos, abstained from the World Council's Fourth General Assembly in Uppsala in July of 1968 in protest to Sweden's stance against his country's government. The meeting of the executive committee of the Commission of the Churches on International Affairs reaffirmed that 'the situation in Greece has continued to be a matter of serious concern to the World Council of Churches.'[134]

Drastic action was taken at the International Labour Organisation, which proposed the expulsion of the Greek Workers' delegation. This was felt to be imperative because of the serious deterioration in its relations with the Greek government and the Greek trade unions. In fact, the trade unions, whose members were mostly left-wing executives, were one of the first institutions the military regime purged. By dissolving the grass-roots bodies and maintaining those that were largely subservient to them, the ruling regime sought to neutralise resistance, principally in the form of strikes, thereby throwing into reverse the limited trend towards emancipation that they had started to develop in the 1960s.

In the meantime, Greek shipping faced a possible boycott by a number of European Labour Organisations. In addition, the International Trade Federation recommended retaliatory action against Greece and stated that it was most displeased with the Greek government's labour policy. In response, the Greek government replied that 'paid Communist agents' had succeeded in 'approaching ignorant leaders of the ITF', and warned the responsible leadership not to listen to Communist invitations.[135]

A number of British organisations also adopted a very robust line aginst the British government's dealings with the Colonels. Among the most notable examples was the criticism mounted by the Chairman of the Society of Labour Lawyers, Samuel Silkin. In one of the numerous protest letters he sent to the Foreign Secretary, Silkin expressed 'grave concern at the situation in Greece and at the Greek military regime's flagrant deterioration from the obligation to sustain human rights and fundamental freedoms';[136] he thus urged him to 'take all action… to ensure that the Greek situation is referred to the European Commission of Human Rights under Article 24 of the Convention, as recommended by the Standing Committee of the Assembly of the Council of Europe at its present meeting in Paris.'[137]

The Foreign Secretary's reply to Silkin's request was as follows:

> While I fully share the Legal Committee's concern about the mainte-
> nance of human rights and fundamental freedoms in Greece, I am not
> convinced that in present circumstances it would be helpful to refer
> alleged breaches of the Convention by Greece to the European
> Convention of Human Rights. At present therefore, there is little likeli-
> hood that we would wish to initiate (or participate in) action under
> article 24 of the European Convention. The legal position is too com-
> plex and the process slow. The prolonged dispute, which such a refer-
> ence would entail, might very well retard rather than advance our
> objectives in regard to the Greek regime.[138]

The government emphasised time and again that the most effective way of bringing their influence to bear on the Greek government was by speaking its mind through diplomatic channels; they also reiterated their belief that retaliatory action would not have the desired results. The fol-lowing chapters will discuss the validity and sincerity of the arguments used by the British government to justify its policy in the eyes of its own party members and supporters and of the public in general.

2

FROM 'WRESTLING WITH THE QUESTION OF RECOGNITION' TO 'WORTHY COMPETITORS OF JUDAS ISCARIOT'

The previous chapter accounted for the evolution of British attitudes towards the Colonels from 'chilly' to 'business as usual'. This gradual transformation occurred irrespective of the fundamental displeasure of the majority of British Labour MPs towards both the unconstitutional way in which the regime came to power and its repressive nature. Simply put, the government's stance was based on the need to avoid alienating the new rulers for fear of endangering the geostrategic interests and economic benefits derived from friendly relations with Greece. Thus, the British government for most of 1967 emphasised avoiding public condemnation of the regime in an attempt to prevent retaliatory action against British interests. Its efforts focused on mollifying the fierce opposition its liaison with the Greek military regime provoked both within and outside Parliament. One of the main arguments repeatedly used in order to defend its doing business with the regime was that Greece's Head of State, King Constantine, had remained in his position; hence, no viable reason existed for disrupting their previously normal relations with Greece.

However, the attempted counter-coup by the King in December 1967 further complicated the British government's dealings with the regime in Athens by challenging its previous claims about the regime's legitimacy. It will be the aim of this chapter to account for the impact of the December developments, together with a number of other sporadic episodes throughout 1968, as a result of which Anglo–Greek relations entered a new era characterised by increased tension and notable uneasiness. The most vexing phases spanned mid-December 1967 to mid-January 1968, and from the following June till autumn. By that time, there was such a strain on Anglo–Greek relations that the British government had to reassess its policy, strictly prioritising the need to restore harmony with the Greek regime in spite of the mounting human rights allegations.

The first trigger point came with the King's counter-coup. Following the gradual purges of several royalist elements from the Army, the King was faced yet again with the dilemma of standing up against the Colonels or standing still whilst witnessing his already dwindling influence dissipate. This time, unlike the fateful hours following the Colonels' coup in April, he ruled in favour of drastic action. He believed that the Colonels' inept handling of the November crisis in Cyprus presented the perfect pretext. Thus, at 9am on 13 December, King Constantine's voice was transmitted from the city of Larissa issuing a statement dismissing the key officers of the junta. He also claimed that all Greek forces in central and northern Greece, together with the Air Force and Navy, which were stationed in Crete and had always been loyal to him, were now under his command. With this statement, he sought to make clear that he could no longer legitimise the present unconstitutional regime, which he had felt 'obliged to support at the time of the April coup in order to avoid bloodshed.'[1]

The King justified his proclamation on the grounds that all his previous requests to the ruling regime for a reshuffle, which would have rid the government of the extremist elements that obstructed a return to democratic rule, had met with abject failure. He also claimed that his decision had been catalysed by the 'uncertainty and confusion caused by the proposed draft of the Constitution which set no time limit for a return to democratic government, as well as the danger of war with Turkey.'[2] At the same time as the King was issuing his statement, Lieutenant General General Odysseas Angelis, the Chief of the Army General Staff, received a letter drafted by the King in which the latter notified him firstly that he was personally assuming control of the government of the country, secondly that he was placing the Armed Forces under his command, and thirdly that he required certain changes to be made in the leadership of the Armed Forces.

The King's discontent with Greece's rulers was no secret. In the first few hours after the coup d'état, he had refused to grant the Colonels legal authority by signing the relevant proclamation. Although he did compromise eventually, he never manifested any particular enthusiasm towards them; rather, he concentrated his efforts on trying to convince them to take a series of steps to restore democratic rule. Nevertheless, having concluded that this was not going to be feasible, he missed no opportunity to distance himself from them and their policies and to seek ways to topple them.

For instance, although the official reason for his State visit to the US in September 1967 was 'to explain the aims of the Greek government which came to power in the April 21 1967 coup and to obtain US understanding and support for the government,'[3] the real motive was to 'seek Presidential assurances of US backing in any confrontation he might have with the Greek junta.'[4] In other words, the extent of the King's disillusionment with the regime was such that the overriding objective behind his trip to the US in September was to try to enlist the US President's support for his imminent plans to stage a counter-coup against the Colonels.

President Johnson consented to a meeting with the King, during which he reassured him of the US' recognition of the importance of the Greek Monarchy and his appreciation of the stabilising approach the King had adopted since the April coup. But Johnson was reluctant to accede to the King's request for the Sixth Fleet, which was sailing in the Mediterranean, to be placed at the Royal Family's disposal. The US avoided offering any firm commitments to the King, not on personal grounds—in fact, he seemed to have made a very good impression on the President—but because American officials assessed that a confrontation would most probably plunge the country into chaos, an eventuality which they were extremely anxious to avoid. This position was in line with the CIA's assessment, according to which the country was 'well served with the Colonels, who maintain calm and order in an otherwise unstable area.'[5] Furthermore, it is highly probable that the CIA was aware that the King's abortive coup had been intercepted by the junta and was therefore doomed. In fact, numerous foreign press articles had recorded the likelihood of his abortive coup and the only uncertainty seemed to relate to its precise date. In short, it could be argued that the American administration, despite the fact that it would almost certainly have welcomed a successful counter-coup by the King, was disinclined to contribute to stirring up additional troubles in a country whose stability was greatly valued.

In addition, there is evidence that in parallel with his fruitless over-tures towards the American government, and especially after receiving on 13 November the US government's third refusal to pre-empt their reactions in the event of a counter-coup, the King turned to the British Ambassador. Besides, he deemed Britain as an important ally, especially in view of the two countries' Royal Houses' traditionally close ties. In this context, the King approached the British Embassy pretending to seek advice about his intention to attend the November annual meeting of the Olympic Sailing Committee in London. The Ambassador, pre-suming that the King would use it as an excuse to pay a visit to Queen Elizabeth as well as to Prime Minister Wilson and the Foreign Secretary, highlighted the need to keep his visit private. However, the Foreign Office instructed the Ambassador bluntly that Constantine's visit had to be cancelled on the grounds that it would give rise to large anti-junta and anti-royalist demonstrations, as both the regime and the King were largely unpopular. Although he was deemed to be 'isolated and needed support and encouragement', it was specifically empha-sised that 'her Majesty's government had better not get involved in the King's problems.'[6]

Unable to secure foreign backing for his coup, the King then looked inwards. He rallied the support of his few loyal Greek army officers, namely the First and Third Army in northern and central Greece. On the basis of their promised unconditional support, the King decided to proceed; besides, he had always been resentful about having afforded the Colonels, albeit unknowingly, the opportunity to stage their coup in April on account of his own vacillating authorising of his own. Indeed, his clear intentions to act unconstitutionally to prevent his arch-rival Papandreou's anticipated victory in the May 1967 elections were widely known and reported in foreign governments' documents and various newspapers at the time.

The fate of the King's intended pre-Colonels' coup will never be known; his abortive coup in December, however, was a resounding failure. It displayed both poor planning and coordination, which made it 'as incompetent as the first coup [the one executed by the Colonels in April] was efficient.'[7] Because of the 'primitive level of organisation on the one hand and on the other hand the lack of determination the royalist mutineers showed,'[8] the Colonels, who were made aware of this venture in advance, had no difficulties in crushing it.

The foundering of the King's bid was also attributed to his inexperience and lack of a clear plan of action, both of which were down to his young age as well as the 'atmosphere of suspicion that surrounded the Royal Family.'[9] By 3am the following morning, 14 December, the Colonels had managed to reassert their power throughout Greece. As *The Times* commented on 15 December, the 'ills of Greece have been too much for the King to heal.'[10] Fifteen minutes later, two Falcon aircrafts departed from Kavalla airport, in northern Greece, carrying incognito the King, his family and his closest entourage to an unnamed destination. It was left to others to wonder whether the Greek Royal House would ever again be a 'factor in Greek politics'.[11]

The King's counter-coup not only did not bring about the intended result, but worse, it presented the Colonels with a pretext to acquire unrestricted power, an opportunity they quickly made sure would not be wasted. Colonel Papadopoulos became the self-appointed new Prime Minister of Greece, replacing Supreme Court Judge Konstantinos Kollias, who accompanied the King on his flight into exile; he also assumed control of the Armed Forces. Meanwhile, General Georgios Zoitakis filled the position of the King temporarily by being appointed Regent, thereby completing the total concentration of power in the hands of the military, an event that markedly distanced the country from its declared route towards democracy.

These dramatic changes in the political scene of Greece had serious domestic repercussions, which brought about unavoidable international ramifications too. The foreign missions' attitudes were gravely challenged by the Head of State's departure, which automatically raised the question of recognition. Indeed, the King's counter-coup constituted the first serious incident calling into question the Colonels' previous theory of legitimisation based on the grounds that, upon assuming power, they had not abolished the institution of the Head of the Greek State. In other words, it could be argued that the King's self-exile caused the quasi-constitutional façade of the Colonels' regime to collapse.

The Colonels did of course realise that the appointment of a Regent in the place of the King could complicate diplomatic relations with foreign governments. They therefore persistently reiterated that the Head of the Greek State had remained unchanged. A slight, albeit telling, proof of their efforts was the fact that in the press room at the Greek Embassy in London, pictures of the King and the Queen still hung from the wall. In addition, it was reported by the *Daily Telegraph*, that the 'administrative body of the Greek Orthodox Church [largely under the control of the Colonels and appointed by them on a preferential basis] ... issued, with full governmental approval, instruction to all bishops to continue prayers for the Royal Family.'[12] Self-appointed Prime Minister Papadopoulos clarified in his letter to the American President on 6 January 1968, that 'the regime of this country—democracy together with a hereditary sovereign (constitutional monarchy)—will remain unchanged.'[13]

It was not difficult, however, for diplomatic missions in Athens to perceive that the rhetoric differed from reality, especially in view of actions such as the prohibition of broadcasting the King's New Year message. This realisation caused increased discomfort to foreign governments, which had trouble deciding on the right response to these events. The day following the King's failed counter-coup, *The Times* reported that 'the diplomatic representatives of Britain, the United States, West Germany and France today declined an invitation to call on the new Prime Minister and the new Regent.'[14]

During the first hours and days after the abortive coup, all diplomatic missions in Athens refrained from taking any action, either preemptive or reactive, and awaited instructions regarding their stance towards the regime from their respective governments. The British Ambassador, Sir Michael Stewart, was reported as being under instructions to avoid taking actions signifying or implying diplomatic recognition[15] until further notice.

In the meantime, legal advisers to various governments were working feverishly to try to come to a conclusion regarding the constitutional status of the newly evolved regime and examine the resultant protocol implications. Following lengthy consultations, they ruled that the actions of the junta in appointing a Regent and arranging for the appointment of a new Prime Minister were not in conformity with the constitution of 1952, which still remained in force. In other words, they clearly spelled out that the regime in Greece had assumed an extra-constitutional status. This meant that foreign recognition of the regime would not be automatically renewed. Consequently, the pressing issue that confronted the foreign governments was not whether it was necessary to accord recognition to the new regime—this was clearly the case—but whether it was desirable to do so: a question that occupied the minds of their foreign policy-makers for the following few weeks.

In view of such developments, British government officials found themselves in an awkward position, particularly given their previous good working relations with the Greek regime. The Foreign Office was reported the day after the King's abortive coup to be 'wrestling with the question of recognition now that [the] Head of State [was] gone'.[16] The initial British reflections on the post-coup era revolved around the three following parameters:

a) wait another 24 hours to be sure [the] situation is settled,
b) it [is] in the UK's interest to recognise [the] new government of Greece,
c) the longer Her Majesty's government waits, the more significance the act of recognition will assume.[17]

According to Foreign Office Officials Davidson's and Macrae's assessment, drafted as early as 15 December, 'there [was] no question of Her Majesty's government not doing business with the new regime, merely [the] technical question of how and when to start.'[18] Ironically however, four days later, on 19 December, William Rodgers, the Parliamentary Under-Secretary of the Foreign Office, stated in the Commons that 'the question in Greece remains confused' and claimed that 'it is still too early to take a decision on the recognition of the regime'.[19] Meanwhile, the government seemed to pride itself on refraining from diplomatic contact with the Greek government following the King's flight into exile, as noted for instance in the letter sent to Diana Pym, Honorary Secretary of the League for Democracy in Greece on 11 January 1968.[20]

A series of discussions had already begun with other NATO member governments on the question of their relationships with Greece. The first recorded exchange of views between the US and Britain on the events in Greece occurred the morning after the counter-coup, when British Foreign Secretary George Brown visited Brussels for NATO's 14th ministerial meeting. It was then when the British Foreign Secretary bluntly asked his American counterpart whether his country was a party to the King's undertaking, a question that indirectly proved Britain's non-complicity. Following confirmation of the failure of the King's attempted coup, the Italian Foreign Minister Amintore Fanfani took the lead in proposing drastic action against the Colonels' regime, even to the extent of expelling Greece from the Alliance.

Although the Fanfani initiative was endorsed by some countries, the American Secretary of State, managed to quash it and instead confined the Alliance to an expression of mild sympathy concerning the recent developments. The American Ambassador in Athens, Phillips Talbot, commented that 'any discussion within NATO, along the lines that could develop as a result of Fanfani's initiative, would strike at the junta's *amour propre* and thus reinforce the younger officers, who wished to push Papadopoulos towards a Franco-type regime, away from close association with the NATO.'[21] Besides, as George Denney, Deputy Director of the US Bureau of Intelligence and Research, reasoned, with Salazar's Portugal a founding member of NATO, and with the Turkish coup of 1960 a matter of record, it seemed rather late in the day to try to give significance to rhetoric about the Alliance's ideological foundations.[22] In other words, NATO's overall reluctance, mainly through the machinations of its most powerful member, even to explore the possibility of taking any punitive action against the Colonels' regime unassailably proved the predominance of *Realpolitik*.

Most foreign governments remained indecisive. The West German Foreign Ministry commented on 15 December that it had not yet determined its policy on Greek recognition, as 'the situation is too unclear regarding the constitutional status of the Regent.'[23] The Turkish Foreign Ministry was reported as 'still studying [the] question of recognition [of] the Greek government'.[24] Similarly the Chief of the Quai d'Orsay's Southern Department said that 'France would await the outcome of the negotiations between the King and the junta before deciding what action to take in the light of the events of 13 December.'[25]

The immediate aftermath of the coup therefore witnessed a phase of irresoluteness during which Britain, along with the vast majority of its allies, decided to withhold full diplomatic recognition for some time. In the interim period, the British Embassy maintained only business contacts with the regime, while British government officials were in close contact with the King, who had sought temporary asylum in Italy. The issue of the King was particularly worrisome for the British government not least on account of their traditional affinity, but also due to the 'strong rumours' that he intended to go to London, where he planned to set-up a government-in-exile. This possibility would create, no doubt, a serious complication for Foreign Office officials in their relations with the Greek government. In such an eventuality, the Foreign Office decreed, the British government would be advised that 'members [of] such a "government" would be treated as private citizens, but Her Majesty's government would not wish to de-recognise [the] King himself.'[26] At the same time, John Beith, Assistant Under-Secretary of State at the Foreign Office, buttressed the Colonels in favour of the speedy restoration of King Constantine to his throne on the grounds that this would not only facilitate their dealings with Greece, but would also boost the regime's appeal abroad.[27]

Meanwhile, the British government was subjected to heavy criticism and considerable pressure by various sectors of the public and its own Members of Parliament. Most Labour MPs supported some sort of retaliatory action, including drastic boycotts in investment, financial aid and loans, shipping, and cultural and sporting events. Nevertheless, their persistent calls for condemnatory action were in vain. The anxiety of Labour MPs to see their country's government dissociating itself from the military regime in Greece was not shared by the government and the Foreign Office, whose sole concern was to take care 'in presenting the decision [to resume business] publicly.'[28]

Among those few within the Cabinet who sympathised with the Labour backbenchers' cause was, interestingly enough, the Prime Minister himself. The American Ambassador in London, was reporting that 'somewhat to [the] surprise of pertinent Foreign Office officials, Prime Minister Wilson went beyond his brief in responding to questions about Greece in Commons...' and 'had insisted on replying personally to these questions.'[29] Always embarrassed by his government's policy of doing business with the regime, he spoke in the House of Commons on 14 December of 'the barbarous methods in use in Greece.'[30] His unease about British policy towards the regime had apparently intensified, especially as widespread reports about the systematic use of torture steadily multiplied in media, international and non-governmental organisations, as well as government circles; even more seminally, the organisations' reports started to gradually acquire credibility, as a number of tortured victims found the strength to present signed testimonies of their systematic mistreatment by the regime. Furthermore, he admitted that as a result of the appointment of a 'viceroy' following the King's flight into exile, 'the whole question of recognition does come up for reconsideration.'[31]

Another noteworthy incident was narrated by John Fraser, a Labour MP (the 'most consistent and outspoken Parliamentary critic of the Greek regime');[32] he testified that the Prime Minister was on several occasions reported as having encouraged Labour MPs behind the scenes to 'keep their pressure' on the government for its policy towards Greece.[33]

Despite his personal embarrassment about the Colonels' regime, Prime Minister Wilson, no doubt fearing retaliatory consequences, refrained from causing complications by openly endorsing the serious criticism that a large number of MPs were directing against the regime. This stance was particularly favoured by Foreign Office officials. As he could not obviously distance himself from the Foreign Office's recommended line, he stressed in a House of Commons debate that 'Britain traditionally based recognition not on approval of the regime, but on the question of whether it does have control by whatever means in that country.'[34] He continued his argument by pointing out that recognising a regime was a quite different and separate issue from having diplomatic relations with it.

In the meantime, British Ministers decided on 21 December to 'authorize UK Embassy [in] Athens [to] resume low-level contacts (customs clearances, etc) with the Greek regime,'[35] a decision which was communicated to the Embassy Officials in Athens the following day. The rationale was that the new Greek government was in charge of the country, and since there were important issues and interests in and affected by Greece, the British government had to establish some degree of contact with the regime in order to be able to carry on a working relationship.

While the question was still pending, not so much of whether, but of when and how to deal with the issue of recognising the new regime in a publicly acceptable way, members of the diplomatic corps in Athens abstained from the New Year's official service at the Metropolitan Church, customarily attended by Embassies' representatives. The only foreign representatives present at the service were military officials, mainly the JUSMAGG section chiefs. On the same day, Papadopoulos, the new Prime Minister, made a New Year's resolution promising to 'restore a genuine and modern democracy within reasonable deadlines.'[36]

Meanwhile, the foreign missions in Athens and their respective governments used every opportunity to exchange views on the Greek issue. For instance, a meeting is recorded on 15 January between the representatives of Britain, the Federal Republic of Germany, Italy and Denmark, and the US Deputy Assistant Secretary of State. As the American Ambassador in Athens reported, 'most Ambassadors here [in Athens] are getting itchy to resume business and social contacts' and 'most of those with whom I have talked favour process, suggested by Department, of quiet resumption of business without making a big issue of the recognition question.'[37]

Turkey and the Federal Republic of Germany seemed keen to establish full diplomatic contacts. Turkey was recorded on 28 December as being 'willing to deal with present government of Greece and anxious to get back to business with Greece on Cyprus, over-flights and other questions but unwilling to be the first one to make plunge'.[38] As far as the Federal Republic of Germany was concerned, its legal adviser related in a similar fashion to his British colleague, that 'the question of recognition need not arise so long as Greece remains monarchy and the King is alive and not abdicating' and that as 'backlog of commercial and other day-to-day business becoming urgent ... Ambassador at least, is keen for quick favourable action.'[39]

Although Britain manifested reluctance to publicly accord recognition, and was unwilling to 'get out in front in this one'[40] mainly due to the strong Labour Party opposition, it was considered likely that it would follow the lead of the American government which announced the resumption of its relations with the regime on 19 January. Besides, the Foreign Office was already recorded on 16 January as being disposed to resume normal working relations with the Greek government. However, due to the multitude of other matters on the Cabinet's plate, the Greek issue was not discussed until a further week had elapsed. Among the parallel challenges that the Wilson government faced at the time was the British withdrawal from its military bases in Southeast Asia and the Persian Gulf in January, a decision which was accelerated by the devaluation of Sterling in November and the resulting economic uncertainty. Such initiatives had created considerable strains with their American allies at a time when de Gaulle's recent second veto of the British bid to join the EEC deprived Britain of a counterbalancing alliance; hence, the emphasis on aligning with the US on the issue of Greece.

Not long after, George Brown, in replying to a relevant question raised in the House of Commons on 25 January, publicly confirmed that 'Her Majesty's government are resuming a normal diplomatic relationship with the Greek government through the Greek Foreign Minister, on whom our Ambassador paid a business call today.'[41] With regard to the question of recognition, he stated laconically that 'there has been no need for any formal act of recognition.'[42] This statement fundamentally contradicted the one made on 14 December, when the British Prime Minister pointed out that 'our recognition of the Greek government no longer seems to be valid because the Head of State, to whom our Ambassador is accredited, is no longer in Greece.'[43] In light of the aforementioned evidence, it could be argued that after a long period of procrastination due to the bewilderment stemming from the events of 13 December, national interests prevailed rather expectedly over ideological concerns, proving yet again the predominance of *Realpolitik* in British foreign policy.

Melina Mercouri, a well-known Greek actress living in exile in Paris, who actively campaigned for the restoration of democracy, commented as follows:

> When Wilson spoke against the junta, we had a great hope, but your [British] government deceived us very much. They recognized the junta. How is it possible that a Labour Party in England should recognise gangsters who abolish the Constitution?[44]

Her words seemed to embody precisely the British government's initial policy of superficial hesitancy following the King's departure, which was nonetheless in a matter of weeks readjusted to the principle of 'doing business as usual'.

The British government, like the Americans, had decided not to make any formal statements outside Parliament. In fact, it recommended the avoidance of commenting publicly on that question. It also emphasised that its decision should be justified to Members of Parliament on the grounds that their relations were based on the de facto situation of control.

Needless to say, the opposition of the British public and MPs to their government's renewed cooperation with the Greek regime intensified heavily following the December events. The vast majority of Labour MPs, with few exceptions, most notably that of Francis Noel-Baker, were highly critical of their own government's policy. However, as their lobbying in the House of Commons did not bear fruit, they looked for alternative ways of bringing pressure to bear. With this in mind, they launched a campaign on 24 January to dissuade British tourists from going to Greece, in an attempt to indirectly weaken the regime by depriving it of the much needed injections of foreign currency. On the grounds that 1968 was declared by the UN to be Human Rights Year, they urged prospective holiday makers 'to show their disapproval of the violation of human rights in Greece by not going there.'[45]

This action looked promising, since tourism accounted for 10 per cent of Greece's foreign exchange receipts, amounting to £53 million in 1966 (close to one billion in today's value), to which the 105,000 British visitors contributed a substantial part[46]—in fact, they were the third largest group of foreign visitors in that year.[47] It is worth noting, however, that in 1968, 99,000 British tourists visited Greece, whereas in 1969 their numbers skyrocketed to more than 138,000, accounting together with the Americans, French and West Germans for 67 per cent of the country's tourist traffic.[48] Not only did this campaign not yield the expected long-term fruits, but worse, it had the counter-effect of upsetting the Greek rulers. In an effort to offset the adverse impact of the campaign, the British government sent five MPs to Greece in April—Gordon Bagier and William Garrett (Labour), Antony Buck and David Webster (Conservative) and Russell Johnston

(Liberal Democrat)—with the aim of giving the Greek government the chance to make its case.

During their five-day visit to Greece, they reported that Prime Minister Papadopoulos gave them 'his word of honour as an officer' that he would restore democracy—not that this should have carried particular weight in light of all his previous vain promises. In view of those assurances, as well as the selective evidence to which they were deliberately exposed, they issued a joint statement on 24 April in which they argued the following:

> The information published in the Western Press and the news transmitted by the BBC about the alleged ill-treatment of political prisoners are 'ridiculous' ... The government's intention is to restore as soon as possible normal political conditions ... The general economic situation has improved during the last year thanks to the exceptionally beneficent economic measures the government has taken ... The corruption of Greek political life had been widespread for many years and efforts are being made to overcome and cure it ... and everyday life in Athens now is much more peaceful than it has been in recent years.[49]

Two days later another statement was jointly issued by Bagier and Johnston, emphasising that 'the Greek government is more popular than we had been led to believe.'[50] Bagier nevertheless admitted in March 1969 that he had been bribed to speak favourably of the regime by Maurice Fraser and Associates—the controversial British Public Relations company employed for £100,000 (close to 2 millions in today's value) by the Greek government to facelift the regime's image abroad mainly on the grounds of its performance in the economic field.[51] This revelation stirred up a maelstrom and eventually prompted Prime Minister Wilson to set up a select committee to investigate the MPs' outside interests, finally leading to the establishment of a Register of Members' Interests in 1974—perhaps the only positive side-effect of the Colonels' era.

In the meantime, while foreign governments, one after the other, resumed normal diplomatic contacts with the Greek regime, the Council of Europe voted on 27 January in favour of the provisional suspension of Greece from its membership on the supposition that an acceptable parliamentary democracy would not be restored by the spring of 1969. This step was taken within the wider context of trying to exert pressure on the new regime, which was growing impervious to international coercion. In fact, having attained unassailable power, the Colonels were exercising increasingly authoritarian control over the country. Their recent unconstitutional actions included further purges of the Armed Forces and the Church, the establishment of strict control over the press and broadcasting, leaning on the judiciary, and most crucially the dismantling of the apparatus of the State. Within one year of coming to power, they had managed, as *The Times* reported:

> to drive the King into exile, suppress political agitation and opposition by martial law and massive arrests, subdue corruption through purges at the expense of efficiency, glorify nepotism and lead the economy into stagnation through ignorance and plain incompetence.[52]

Still though, the *Times* Special Correspondent observed that 'one year of military rule would appear to the casual visitor to have changed little in the pattern of Greek life'; he also noted with some puzzlement 'the passiveness with which the Greeks have tolerated their new masters.'[53] Needless to mention, that this latter assessment should not have been generalised, as it could not apply to the sizeable part of the population that opposed the regime, whose actions, by having to remain underground for obvious reasons, could not be directly visible to the casual visitor.

Meanwhile, British officials in London were in no doubt that the countless allegations of torture made against the regime had in them more than a grain of truth, despite Papadopoulos' announcement that he 'would hang in Constitution Square any person guilty of torture.'[54] Two reports compiled by Amnesty International in January and April 1968—the first ever to be published in relation to allegations against a ruling regime's systematic use of torture—revealed 'a strong *prima facie* case of physical and mental torture on a significant scale.'[55] Thus, the British government's most onerous task at that time related to confronting claims regarding the Greek regime's abrogation of human rights, which were surfacing in the spring of 1968. In the light of these revelations, the following statement was made in the House of Commons:

> on the basis of first hand evidence and oral testimony, on the basis of scars on the bodies of those tortured, and on the basis of the testimony

of professional people and relatives, the Delegation can objectively state that torture is a widespread practice against Greek citizens suspected of active opposition to the government'.[56]

However, British officials kept emphasising the importance of waiting until investigative bodies had completed their full evaluation of the extent of the torture suffered by political prisoners, before implementing any condemnatory measures. Their stance nevertheless was vulnerable. It might be argued that in formulating their policy towards Greece, instead of assessing the degree of torture exercised, British officials, should have concerned themselves rather with the question of whether most of the prisoners should ever have been arrested at all; or indeed, after being arrested whether they should have been mistreated at all. In fact, so provocative was the British stance, that the President of the Assembly of the Council of Europe made the following statement on 24 April:

> in the Council of Europe we have certain standards and these must be upheld even if some of the governments—including the British government—want us to look the other way. The Assembly has declared that the Parliamentarians must stand firm in defence of political democracy in Europe, even if our governments run away.[57]

In order to avoid being lambasted as insensitive and untouched by such reports, the British government kept transferring the responsibility for action onto international fora such as the Council of Europe and Amnesty International. This was convenient, because those organisations' procedures for the investigation of alleged breaches of human rights were complex and hence lengthy too. This was also due to the fact that they had to ascertain the credibility of the allegations—a difficult undertaking, as Amnesty had a rather shaky take off and the Council of Europe had never before dealt with a similar case. This protracted process therefore allowed the British some leeway. In the meantime, politicians made sympathetic statements in the House of Commons to the effect that they were seriously disturbed at these allegations of torture, while removing the pressure from their shoulders by acknowledging that 'full cooperation in the proceedings of the European Commission on Human Rights is the right course.'[58]

The line that best summarised their stance was reflected in the following extract from a letter sent by Davidson, from the Greek Desk of the Foreign Office, to Beith at the Parliamentary Office:

> We have said that we share the motives and objectives of the Scandinavian governments in having recourse to the Human Rights machinery. But Ministers have also explained in Parliament that we do not ourselves think that action at the Council of Europe is the best way of obtaining the best results we want in relation to the Greek regime. That is why we did not join in the original applications. (We were also influenced, although we have not said this publicly, by our wish to retain the ability to speak effectively to the Greek government on such subjects as Cyprus). But we wish the Scandinavian initiative well, even if we are not persuaded that it is likely to produce the right results. And for our part we have consistently been exerting our influence on the Greek government in the direction of a speedy return to the constitutional rule and democratic institutions in Greece as well as over human rights.[59]

In another communication between the Foreign Office and Conservative MP Peter Kirk, a staunch opponent of the regime and British representative to the Council of Europe's debate on the situation in Greece, it was concluded that 'the regime in Greece was undoubtedly a dictatorship and since Greece was a member of the Council of Europe, the Assembly had every right to examine the situation there.'[60] Nonetheless, it was also claimed that when similar events had taken place in Turkey eight years previously, the Assembly had waited without resorting to drastic action. Before long they were able to welcome the return to the Assembly of democratically elected representatives from Turkey. Similarly, the British Foreign Office, in an effort to buy some more time, advanced the argument that until the new Constitution that the Greek government had promised to issue in 1968 was examined, it was premature to state that democracy in Greece was a lost cause.

Although the Council of Europe showed determination not to tolerate the undemocratic nature of the Greek regime, NATO had unsurprisingly adopted a completely different attitude. The question of Greece's membership of NATO remained unanswered as most of the member states were not keen to compromise the stability Greece was affording its south-eastern flank. British officials persistently avoided giving any clear answer to numerous requests regarding Greece's expulsion from NATO on the grounds that 'she [Greece] is no longer able to further the principles of the Treaty.'[61] When for instance, John Fraser asked William Rodgers in the House of Commons whether the British government would propose the expulsion of Greece from NATO, the latter replied by denying it and argued that he 'did not really think that action of this kind would lead to the restoration of democratic liberties which we all wish to see.'[62] Indeed, so provocative was the allies' unwillingness even to examine the possibility of Greece's ostracism from the Alliance, that the Norwegian Prime Minister openly expressed regret at the fact that 'we have allies in NATO who are not willing to observe the fundamental rules of human rights.'[63]

The real motives for which British officials did not wish to disrupt their relations with the Greek regime have already been discussed in the previous chapters. However, it should be noted that further developments brought additional considerations into play that made British officials even less willing to antagonise the regime. Most of them were of a commercial nature, including the possibility of selling naval vessels and a nuclear plant to Greece, which could bring large-scale benefits for the British.

One of the most important negotiated commercial deals at that time involved the sale of frigates to Greece. During one of the meetings of the Overseas Defence Policy Committee, the British government debated whether to instruct Vospers to cancel its plans for the conclusion of contracts with Greece concerning the supply of patrol boats for the Greek Navy. It expressed doubt about whether 'it was compatible with our objective of promoting a return to constitutional rule in Greece to sell naval vessels to the present regime.'[64] The government specifically feared that in view of the current allegations about torture in Greek prisons, it would have been a damaging blow for its credibility, if it had become known that it was allowing a British firm to negotiate the supply of arms to the Greek government. In light of such serious concerns, a compromising argument was put forward supporting the idea of advising the firm not to conclude the deal until the European Convention of Human Rights had reached a verdict on the Greek case.

After further lengthy deliberations, however, officials decided to allow the British firm to proceed uninterruptedly with the signing of the contract. The winning arguments behind this unanimous decision, aside from the very substantial financial gains, encompassed a wide range of issues. First of all, it was suggested that since the ships would not be delivered before two and four years, 'there could be no question of strengthening the power of the present regime.'[65] Furthermore, it was claimed that 'patrol boats could not be used to oppress the population or maintain a dictatorial regime in power.'[66]

A point repeatedly raised was that state intervention was only necessary, and thus justified, in 'contracts of this kind when political factors were overriding, for example in the case of South Africa where the supply of arms was forbidden by a United Nations resolution';[67] or indeed in the case of Spain, where there was the lurking danger of an attack against Gibraltar. The Greek case on the contrary bore no analogy to these other two. British officials therefore concluded that it was not necessary to alter their decision to allow the sale of arms for NATO purposes to the regime. Besides, they highlighted that 'if we did not supply them, we might need to increase our own effort in the Eastern Mediterranean' and the danger of the orders falling to the French.[68] Consequently, the Cabinet decided that British aid to Greece should continue unabated, as it was recognised that 'we [the British] had, moreover, to bear in mind the importance of Greece to NATO, particularly in view of recent developments in Eastern Europe, and also the part which she had to play in achieving a settlement in Cyprus.'[69]

Although the justifications that the British government used reflected to some extent genuine considerations, their validity is open to serious challenge. Firstly, the British government was well aware that the Greek government could, as it had already done in the past, use such agreements as a way of trumpeting Britain's recognition of the regime and its success in financial terms. In addition, the claim relating to the impossibility of using such material for the suppression of the population was also shaky. The Colonels had proved themselves capable of exploiting military information and equipment in order to achieve their goals. The most notable example was the modification and manipulation of Prometheus, the NATO-instigated counter-insurgency plan, which they deployed in order to launch their April coup.

Moreover, British government officials recognised that 'it was also important not to risk breaking permanently our [British] links with the Greek navy, injuring NATO relations and provoking trade retaliation by Greece against our exports.'[70] With regard to the latter point, they reiterated that:

> in our present economic circumstances we should consider very seriously whether we could afford to forgo an export order for £18 million (more than 300 millions in today's value) and the possibility of further major export orders, including a nuclear power station, with all their implications for the growth of our industry at home.[71]

In relation to British commercial interests, it became known that British exports to Greece had continued at a satisfactory level. Marconi, a British firm, secured in September 1968 'a contract worth some £700,000 (close to 12 millions in today's value) for the supply of television and broadcasting equipment for the European Games, which were to be held in Greece during 1969.'[72]

The most important negotiated commercial deal concerned the possible purchase by Greece of a British nuclear power station. In fact, the British had been actively trying to sell a nuclear reactor to Greece for the previous eighteen months. The deal represented a stake too high to risk, especially as there was awareness of 'threatened competition from the Germans and the Americans in particular'.[73] Not only did the British not wish to risk missing out on the possible sale of a nuclear plant to Greece, but they also wanted to ensure that the Greek government would commit itself to entertaining a negotiated contract with them alone. In return, they proposed to enter into a contract with the Greek government, which would bind them to purchase Greek tobacco, roughly to the equivalent of the value of the nuclear plant over a period of twelve and a half years.

The British government was aware that undertaking commercial deals with the Greek government would be an unpopular choice both within and outside Parliament. This was reflected in one comment made by Kenneth Clucas, Under-Secretary at the Treasury, who advised the British government that they should start from 'the assumption that this will be a purely commercial deal ... and that there would be no involvement of government either explicitly or implicitly'.[74] Similarly, staunch efforts were made to disassociate any 'connection between Britain's policy towards Greece and the Council of Europe and the negotiations at present taking place in Athens on the sale of a nuclear power station to Greece.'[75]

Advocates of the need to allow commercial exchanges to stand also insisted that it was not only a question of jeopardising one order, but more importantly of putting other orders at risk. They claimed for instance that:

> competition in the Greek market was intensifying and we should not put our order for rolling stock, and perhaps other elements of our substantial exports to Greece, at risk by adopting a harsher attitude than that of other Western countries, including Denmark, who were allowing aid to continue to flow to Greece despite their disapproval of the military regime.[76]

In sum, it could be argued that, although the government was concerned about the serious implications, such as public outcry, of allowing such contracts to be concluded between British firms and the Greek regime, it evaluated that its sizeable economic interests overrode those concerns. A further strong indication of its unwillingness to prioritise ideological considerations was manifested during the Cabinet discussion about the possibility of putting a stop to the offer of aid to Greece within the OECD consortium that was agreed in 1962.[77] One defensive argument stemmed from the fact that 'there have been no proposals to impose economic sanctions against the Greek regime nor any move to exclude it from NATO.'[78]

It is also noteworthy that the British government perceived the Greek regime's foreign policy as achieving some successes, for instance regarding the Greek–Turkish bilateral talks that were first initiated by Papadopoulos in September 1967 with the hope of increasing 'the Colonels' prestige at home and end[ing] the regime's international isolation'.[79] It felt that the Greek government, thanks to the personal contribution of the Greek Foreign Secretary Panayiotis Pipinelis had achieved a good deal of progress in the dispute about Cyprus. It was specifically noted that 'Mr Pipinelis is playing a positive and important role in this', and that 'he has already been largely responsible for putting Greek/Turkish relations back on a good footing.'[80] As a result of his competent dealings satisfaction was expressed that 'the prospects of a settlement of the Cyprus problem, which is of course, very much in our [British] interest to promote, are now better than at any time since 1964.'[81] In addition, the Greek government's efforts to eliminate friction between themselves and Turkey both bilaterally and over Cyprus coincided with its attempts to improve its relations with its Balkan neighbours by proposing a Balkan Pact for friendship and cooperation. Such attempts were very much welcomed by British officials who considered them to be 'a good omen'.[82]

In other words, the damages which the British government would have risked incurring if it had succumbed to both external and domestic pressures against doing business with the Greek regime, were not only of an economic nature, but strategic and political too. And as those interests were considerable, British officials found themselves yet again caught in an unbridgeable quagmire: how to carry on dealing with an ally with whose internal order they disagreed, and avoid upsetting both the British public and the Greek regime? Tangled in this dilemma as they might have been, they still assessed that the stakes were too high, and therefore opted for doing business with the regime, while continually insisting that care was 'needed in presenting the decision publicly.'[83] This was not always easy or indeed successful as the remaining part of this chapter will make clear.

Among those who were particularly disquieted by the hardening practices of the Greek regime during the first half of 1968, was yet again the Prime Minister himself. An interviewee recalled the numerous times Wilson contacted King Constantine in exile, repeatedly expressing his strong antipathy towards the Colonels.[84] The Prime Minister's desire to stay in close touch with the Greek King was also evident in one of their meetings, which took place on 27 May 1968 in London and lasted for two hours, and which was described as 'very informal and encouraging.'[85]

Prime Minister Wilson's displeasure with the Greek government is well documented and beyond doubt. In fact, it was his critical comment about the Greek regime made on 25 June in the House of Commons that seriously threatened a diplomatic rupture between the two countries. More specifically, in reply to a question made regarding his recent meeting with the Greek King, Wilson appeared 'in no doubt at all about the attitude of HMG in connection with the dictatorship in Greece and some of the bestialities which have been perpetrated there.'[86] *The Times* commented on the incident and its consequences in the following way: 'The Greek regime tonight deplored Mr Wilson's statement on Greece in the Commons on Tuesday as an "unwanted and unacceptable intervention" which could do great harm to Anglo–Greek relations.'[87] In addition, it mentioned that according to an anonymous, yet official, release in Athens, 'the Greek government, fully aware of its responsibilities and its duty towards the Greek people as well as to the free world at large, is not prepared to tolerate it [Mr Wilson's alleged intervention].'[88]

Indeed, the military regime's furious reactions were not long in coming. Panayiotis Pipinelis was reported as having been 'angry' at the Prime Minister's comments and 'put off by the fact that they were made at a time when he himself was in London.'[89] Many members of the Greek government were undoubtedly strongly tempted to take reprisals. Foreign Secretary Michael Stewart, a party moderate described as 'a Wilson loyalist and a pro-American,'[90] who had replaced George Brown upon the latter's sudden resignation in March 1968, reported to Wilson that the Greek Ambassador said 'this language would be bitterly resented in Greece and would have repercussions on our relations at a time when Greek government were considering the contract for a nuclear power station.'[91] The Foreign Secretary added that he tried to reassure the Greek Ambassador about the fact that 'we [the British government] had no wish to create trouble between our two countries.'[92] He also made an effort to clarify that 'there was bound to be some strain between us, so long as Greece had an undemocratic and unconstitutional government.'[93]

The Greek regime, mainly due to its accumulation of absolute power, had grown increasingly intolerant of foreign criticism, which had certainly intensified especially following the widespread allegations of torture. It was precisely in an attempt to show determination not to put up with such comments, that retaliatory action ensued. The British Ambassador reported on the 1 July 1968 that:

> this morning Rallides [the local Metropolitan-Cammel and Rolls-Royce agent] was rung up by the minister's chef de cabinet who said, after the Prime Minister's statement in the House of Commons last week which was offensive to the Greek government, and which had included the word 'bestiality' which had offended national pride, the Greek government had no choice but to call off business now under negotiation with Britain. He mentioned specifically rolling-stock, the nuclear reactor ABD, the Athens underground.[94]

Thus, one week after the comment was made, the Foreign Secretary in his memorandum described the emerging situation in Greece as one 'which worries us [British government] deeply.'[95]

By that time, it was unmistakably obvious that Anglo–Greek relations had reached an impasse and a resolution was nowhere in sight. This was a development which was of grave concern to both governments: in the case of Britain considerable commercial interests and in the case of Greece prestige issues were put in jeopardy. Moreover, ironically enough, the British government faced difficulties in the House of Commons as a result of the deterioration in its commercial dealings with the Greek government. Several MPs reacted angrily to the government's putting trade deals at risk by the imprudent use of the word 'bestialities'. Labour's Francis Noel-Baker, one of the most notable advocates of business as usual in the House of Commons and owner of a big estate in one of Greece's largest islands, stated on 8 July 1968 the following:

> Although the present [Greek] government did not come to power by democratic methods, they are not insensitive to public opinion and statements of this kind are hardly calculated to assist British exports and orders under consideration at the present time.[96]

On the opposing side, many other Labour MPs demanded that their government 'is not deterred from calling a spade a spade'[97] by the threat of economic sanctions. Comments like the following, made by John Fraser, Labour backbencher, highlighted the point vividly:

> Would my right Hon. Friend confirm that it never has been, and never will be, the policy of the government to trim and mince their words to appease dictators who are in breach of fundamental rights? Would he also agree that the concern of the Opposition for commercial considerations, above human rights, makes them worthy competitors of Judas Iscariot?[98]

The British stance towards the Greek regime was encapsulated by Anthony Crosland, Labour MP and President of the Board of Trade, who, when confronted with this scrutiny by both sides of the House, stated that 'the British government would continue to make absolutely clear its views about the nature of regimes with which it disagreed', while insisting however that 'political differences should not be allowed to inhibit trade.'[99] In the same instance, he confirmed that Rolls-Royce and Metro-Cammell had assured him that no existing order by the Greek regime was cancelled. In an effort to mend fences, he also mentioned that 'the Prime Minister had told him that the phrase he intended to use was "barbarous methods" and not "bestialities".'[100]

Nonetheless, the American State Department, received a telegram from its Ambassador in Athens, Phillips Talbot, who stated that Simon Dawburn, the Commercial Counsellor of the British Embassy, had in strict confidence admitted to him that there was going to be retaliation for Wilson's remarks in the House of Commons. He specifically mentioned that the Greek importer representing the British firm with which the Greek government was on the point of signing a contract for railway rolling stock and diesel had received a call from Takis Makarezos, brother and Chef du Cabinet of Coordination Minister Nikolaos Makarezos, claiming that Wilson's remarks were an 'affront to Greek national pride';[101] hence, the contract for rolling stock could not be approved. In short, the Greek government had decided to retaliate by hindering the signing of any other contracts for British imports and refusing to buy the intended nuclear power station from Britain.

The news was very unwelcome. Consequently, British officials made it their high priority to normalise relations with the Greek government and restore confidence in Greece's dealings with them. In the light of this consideration, Foreign Secretary Michael Stewart, after discussions with British Ambassador in Athens Sir Michael Stewart, who was called to London for consultations, and communications with Panayiotis Pipinelis, his Greek counterpart, produced a memorandum on 2 July 1968. With this he intended to introduce his colleagues to his 'recently reviewed' policy towards Greece. He explained that a series of factors had been taken into account when formulating his conclusions.

The first factor was the realisation that 'since the time of the coup it has been clear that the present leaders are in full and effective control of the country' and 'there is no real organised opposition to it.'[102] In addition, the memorandum emphasised that in view of the fact that there is no viable political faction and force in Greece which could stand up to the Army, 'if the government of Mr Papadopoulos were to fall, it would probably be replaced by a tougher and more extremist regime, again of a military nature.'[103]

It might have been true that there was no alternative rival power centre in Greece able to challenge the regime successfully. The last one, the Crown, was effectively eliminated with the failure of the King's counter-coup in December 1967. The British officials estimated that this event had contributed to further demoralising the Conservative leadership, which saw in it the loss of its rallying point. The Liberals were also weak. In any case, it was highly doubtful that the two groups would be able to cooperate efficiently in forming a common front against the military regime with the ultimate aim of ousting it.

At the same time, the Greek Resistance Movement, mainly energised by Andreas Papandreou's Pan-Hellenic Liberation Movement (PAK), Mikis Theodorakis' Patriotic Front (PAM) and Democratic Defence had, as *Le Monde* accurately put it, 'too many liberators, too little unity'.[104] Lack of coherence and coordinated direction were known to compromise its large-scale take off. The Greek public too seemed to be generally apathetic about the regime; 'the raya admire the resistance from afar, but do not participate in it,'[105] as it was accurately observed.

Such conclusions did not imply that the Foreign Secretary was prepared to endorse the regime, but rather that he saw no adequate reason for ceasing to cooperate with it, as a means of manifesting disapproval with the subsequent aim of causing its downfall. On the grounds of the above considerations, the Foreign Secretary summarised the British objectives towards Greece as follows:

   i) to promote a return to constitutional rule and democratic liberties and conditions of stability,

   ii) to protect so far as possible the military effectiveness of Greece as a NATO ally,

   iii) to protect British subjects and British interests generally, and in particular to pursue our commercial interests,

   iv) to retain our ability to influence the Greek government in matters of foreign policy, for example Cyprus.[106]

Not all Cabinet Ministers seemed at ease with the Foreign Minister's memorandum, which was attacked for allegedly being 'appallingly right-wing'.[107] Barbara Castle and Richard Crossman were yet again among the most fervent critics during the 12 July Cabinet meeting and protested against the inconsistency between the Foreign Secretary's proposed policy and the tone that Wilson's complaint about the barbarities in Greece had set two weeks before. Their reaction was nonetheless tamed by the Foreign Secretary's assurances, according to which 'there was every sign that the regime would honour its word and switch over to democracy in the course of the summer.'[108]

Despite the aforementioned divisions and differences of opinion about British policy towards the Greek Colonels, not that they were novel, the official policy favoured the encouragement of policies aimed at assuaging the regime's wrath. In order to achieve this, the officials were instructed, when asked about the prospects of Greece's return to democratic rule, to respond by arguing that they had been given many assurances, some of which had already been translated into facts. The most prominent was the promise of a new constitution, on which a referendum was scheduled to be held on 29 September 1968. By showing publicly that they put faith in the regime's proclaimed intentions, they had hoped not only to normalise their relations with the regime, but also to avert public and political opposition to their dealings with it.

As a result, the effort British officials devoted to reviewing their understanding with the Greek government began to bear the expected fruits. On 11 July the Greek Minister of Economic Coordination received representatives of Rolls-Royce and Metropolitan-Cammell and announced that his government was continuing negotiations for the supply of rolling stock for the Greek State Railways 'in the spirit of assuring the best possible relations between Greece and Great Britain.'[109] British officials seemed extremely pleased with this indication of the Greek government's wish to restore its commercial relations with them. They subsequently took every possible precaution in expressing their comments about the regime very mildly, whenever required to do so. On 23 July, for instance, while Wilson referred to the 'impatience with which everyone was watching the attitude of the Greek government to the timetable they had promised', he claimed that 'the Greek government have now, on timetable, produced a constitution.'[110] He concluded his remark by insisting that 'it would be inappropriate for me to comment on it, but it is a step in the right direction.'[111] British officials agreed, though, during private conversations that 'there were no considerable grounds for optimism about future developments in Greece.' Although they did voice slight satisfaction that 'the military had so far kept its undertakings on constitutional procedures and the draft constitution which it had produced was better than might have been expected,'[112] they admitted that the latter repre-sented a setback for democracy, as it tended to institutionalise the interference of the military in Greek politics.

In other words, this sudden manifestation of trust did not mean that British officials were unaware of the dearth of promising prospects. As far as steps towards the democratisation of the regime were concerned, such as the drafting of a new constitution, there was widespread suspi-cion. Furthermore, Michael Stewart was recorded as expressing the view to Stuart Rockwell, the American Deputy Assistant Secretary of State for Foreign Affairs, that 'though the curtailment of the powers of the Monarchy and the strengthening of the executive were necessary, the new Constitution as a whole is "illiberal", and that it is not suited either to the "character or the present-day needs of the Greeks".'[113] In addition, it was clear that a constitution, whose premise in Article 55 was to authorise a Constitutional Tribunal to dissolve 'all parties whose aims or the activities of whose members are openly or covertly opposed to the fundamental principles of the regime, or are designed to overthrow the prevailing social order or expose to danger the integ-rity of the country or internal public security,'[114] restricted in an authoritarian way its subjects' basic liberties.

This was in fact a view that was shared outside government circles too. According to a report prepared for the Council of Europe by Max van der Stoel, Dutch Labour Party MP and one of the most 'tireless defenders of Greek Democracy,'[115] following his fact-finding visit to Greece between 18 and 22 April, there was a 'pessimistic view of the future evolution of the regime.'[116] The nature of the Constitution was attacked by the Consultative Assembly of Council of Europe, which branded its draft as undemocratic and repeated its call for free parliamentary elections in the near future. The fellow member states clearly stated that they were prepared to wait for another six months, after which, if no steps were taken towards democratisation, they agreed to consider suspending Greece's membership at their next session in January.

In the meantime, three former deputies of the Greek Centre Union Party issued a statement on 18 July rejecting the Constitution as 'nullifying the principle of the sovereignty of the people... and...

[being] contrary to the European Convention on Human Rights.'[117] Although it could be argued that such people were bound to produce biased statements, the following view expressed by the Greek judge Petros Zissis, who served on the Constitutional Commission, leaves no room for doubt. According to him 'the draft of the new Constitution is largely inspired by an illiberal and largely anachronistic spirit.'[118] Likewise, the three legal experts of the Council of Europe, namely Professors Christian Dominice, Francesco Capotorti and Lord Lloyd of Hampstead, who were entrusted with studying it at length, concluded unanimously and categorically that it did not 'conform to democratic principles'.[119]

The emerging gloominess was further entrenched following the announcement on 30 September of the results of the referendum on the new Constitution, which was supposedly endorsed by a staggering 92.5 per cent of the vote. There were no doubts outside government circles that it was largely fabricated, 'as except for its own officials' support, enthusiasm for it came only from a few captains of industry.'[120] It is also indicative that the regime prevented other critical aspects, such as an estimated 25 per cent abstention rate, from becoming public knowledge.

However, the Greek government's pledges of a triumphant vote of confidence for the new Constitution were not contradicted by the reports compiled by the delegations of British as well as French parliamentarians, who were sent to Greece as guests of the regime to monitor the voting for the referendum. In a joint statement, Conservative MP John Rodgers and former Conservative MP Peter Agnew described the Greek rulers as 'dedicated and able men, determined to cut through the roots of the old system of intrigue and set Greece on a new path.'[121] They also stated that 'to the best of our ability we have satisfied ourselves that the Greek people, far from groaning under the repression of a police state, are happy and relaxed people.'[122] They concluded their statement by mentioning that 'in spite of what had been written by "hostile writers" about the methods of the regime, there have since the revolution been less arrests than under former regimes... no executions have taken place and no capital sentence has been passed by this new regime.'[123]

Despite all the unassailable counter-arguments concerning the Greek Constitution's contribution to the country's democratisation, the British government was determined not to upset the Greek regime, by avoiding, or at least trying to avoid, any public criticism; the Greek reaction to Wilson's comment in the House of Commons was not easily forgotten. The significance of this decision was reinforced by an international development, which confirmed the importance of being on good terms with Greece—the invasion of Czechoslovakia by Warsaw Pact troops on 20 August 1968. The Soviet Union's forceful attempt to reverse the country's efforts to disassociate itself from Soviet influence sent shock waves to NATO, and served as a very powerful reminder of the omnipresent Communist threat. Utmost emphasis was therefore attached to eliminating the danger of Communism spreading into neighbouring countries, especially as Italy had recently cajoled its NATO allies due to the return of Palmiro Togliatti, one of its most prominent Communist ideologists.

An additional fear for NATO members was that the Soviet Union might take over Yugoslavia once the ageing Tito was off the scene. Greece was deemed a vital regional player in this, as it was felt that 'if Greece was expelled from NATO, then Yugoslavia would collapse';[124] consequently, 'keeping Greece on board and on good terms was part of the defence mechanism against Russia.'[125] So important were NATO considerations at the time that as a result of the contemporaneous events in Central and Eastern Europe, the Americans decided in October 1968 on the partial resumption of deliveries to Greece of Mutual Assistance Programme items, which had been suspended shortly after the Greek coup in April 1967. The approved items for resumption were 'valued at about $20 million ($150,000,000 in today's value) or equal to roughly two-fifths of value of all major items suspended to date'[126]—a decision which was expected to be broadened in the wake of the anticipated Republican victory in the coming Presidential elections.

Regimes as fanatically anti-Communist as that in Greece were perceived as harmoniously serving the Alliance's raison d'être. When the Colonels came to power, they justified their coup principally on the grounds of thwarting a possible Communist takeover. The extent to which Communism posed a real threat to Greece is highly debatable, although many believed it was not 'an abstract threat of an artificial bogy';[127] in any case, there can be no doubt that it was useful for the

Alliance to know of the regime's polemical stance. To be sure, the Colonels' regime had averted the danger, as perceived especially by the US government, of pro-Communist and anti-NATO Andreas Papandreou gaining power as a result of his father's party's predicted victory in the May 1967 elections. Furthermore, ever since they assumed power, the Colonels had shown strong commitment to suppressing Communist elements through imprisonment and censorship; that the detainees were subjected to torture did not seem to bother their allies.

It therefore seemed plausible enough for most NATO allies to be content on strategic grounds with the Greek regime, and hence feel no desire to influence its downfall. In fact, the regime had come to power at a time when an array of international developments put pressure on NATO to endorse it, in order to maintain Greece in its camp. It was argued at that time that 'the Russian invasion of Czechoslovakia and the build-up of the Russian fleet in the Mediterranean have both underlined the importance of damaging NATO.'[128] Therefore, the possibility of inflicting more harm for instance by expelling Greece was a source of dread.

Indeed, the events in Czechoslovakia and the expansion of Soviet naval power, just like the Six-Day War in June 1967, gave a tremendous boost to the regime's grip on power, as they earned the regime NATO's unrestricted backing thereafter. So concerned was NATO with maintaining Greece's close cooperation that, as *The Times* reported on 23 September 1968, 'Northern Greece, one of the most sensitive areas of western defence, is to be visited tomorrow by the NATO Military Committee, the supreme military authority of the alliance.'[129] It is important to highlight that during the seven years that the regime lasted in power, NATO visits and exercises on Greek soil continued unrestricted.

With respect to these exercises, there was no reported occasion of a British government's refusal to take part. This was due to the fact that the British officials were well aware that 'we [the British government] should provide the Greeks with adequate means of external defence: particularly after Czechoslovakia, this was essential to NATO security and to our own.'[130] Moreover, one important factor for British reluctance to do otherwise was that the British government was under pressure not to displease its American counterpart. This was an increasingly crucial priority in determining British foreign policy in the middle and late sixties. The Colonels too had repeatedly noted the American influence on the British stance towards them 'in the context of the two countries' special relations'[131] that effected a wide host of issues ranging from finance to nuclear and intelligence collaboration. On one occasion, for instance, they commented on the impact of the 'American "hawks", who underlined the significance of our country [Greece] for the defence of the free world.'[132]

In other words, the formation of British foreign policy, especially on issues of mutual strategic concern, was determined not only by British interests but also by American ones; and the US, in view of its commitment to NATO, had every interest in not upsetting its balance by risking the loss of Greece's vital membership. As Defence Secretary Clark Clifford bluntly declared in May 1968, 'the obligations imposed on us by the NATO alliance are far more important than the kind of government they have in Greece.'[133]

By early autumn 1968, the regime was perceived as having attained uncontested power and did not appear under any serious threat for the foreseeable future. A number of reports were composed by the British Embassy in Athens attesting to the government in London the central fact that 'the [Greek] government are now in a stronger position than they have been in at any time since the revolution.'[134] One of those reports, drafted on 1 November 1968 by the British Counsellor in Athens, Derek Dodson, presented the following assessment:

> After a year and a half of the suspension of democratic processes, there are no signs of any organized opposition within the country. Economically, the government's policies have not proved the disaster that some critics expected. The reserves are now higher than they have ever been. Business circles in general are content with the treatment they are receiving. The attitude of many Greeks towards the government was favourably affected by the invasion of Czechoslovakia and by the increased fear of a continuing Communist threat—emphasized here by the recent Russian naval activity in the Mediterranean—which this engendered.[135]

After considering such reports, British officials had no reason, apart from wavering public pressure, to start opposing the regime. This view crystallised especially when the attitudes of the other Western countries towards the Greek regime were taken into account and not necessarily because they were indeed convinced about the current regime's potential. In fact, as was noted during a meeting held in order to discuss the British policy towards Greece, 'all the government really amounted to was a low-grade, conspiratorial, military committee, who were reasonably efficient at keeping themselves in power, but whose domestic policy otherwise amounted to nothing.'[136] Even so, President de Gaulle was openly endorsing the regime by brazenly communicating directly with the Regent. France had actually been quite friendly towards the regime, and was, along with the West Germans and the Italians, vigorously pursuing an active trade policy. As far as the West Germans were concerned, they had outplayed the British for an order for fast patrol boats.

The British soon expressed disquiet about the fact that despite their commitment of unremitting efforts in the business as usual direction, they were yet again unfavourably perceived by the Greek rulers. The officials' worries were not unfounded, as a number of indications seemed to testify that Anglo–Greek relations were heading towards deadlock. During a meeting between the British Foreign Secretary and the British Ambassador in Athens, the interlocutors discussed that:

> Greek ministers give the appearance of being unwilling to do business with Britain…, the government is no longer receptive to representations from H.M. Ambassador…, and instructions were recently issued to the majority of Greek army officers who had received invitations to a party of the Defence Attaché of the Embassy to refuse them.[137]

This was due to a sequence of events. First, it was not long since the Prime Minister had provoked the regime's wrath by using the word 'bestialities'. Moreover, the Greek rulers never ceased to complain to the British Embassy in Athens about the 'unwaveringly hostile' attitude of the BBC, and the 'Communist editorials' in The Guardian and The Times, for which they partly blamed the British government. Estia, a Greek pro-regime newspaper, almost daily attacked the staff of the Greek service of the BBC as 'scum of the earth, red speakers in the pay of Moscow, Greek-tongued anti-Greek rogues.'[138] In fact, they regarded the BBC 'as a government agency which must dance to whatever tune the British government may call;'[139] they obviously failed to accept the simple fact, embodied in the following comment by Sir Hugh Greene, its Director General at the time that:

> it [the BBC] is not a commercial company; therefore it is not subject to the legal limitations of Acts of Parliament regulating companies. It is not a government department; therefore it is not answerable for its day-to-day operations, and particularly not for details of its pro-grammes, to a government minister or Parliament.[140]

What was obviously irritating the regime was the fact that the out-spoken BBC, which 'had always been a target for those who could not bear the expression of their opponents' view in a controversy,'[141] as well as the fiercely anti-regime Amnesty International, were based in and thus operating from London. The former transmitted highly caustic statements against them, like the one addressed by the Greek poet and Nobel Laureate George Seferis and the latter was turning its fight against the Colonels' human rights transgressions into its flagship case in a slowly evolving campaign against torture. Even more aggravating was the fact that London seemed 'an island of opposition in an other-wise decreasingly hostile world.'[142]

In addition, a number of rumours about active British involvement in the campaign against the Colonels had been circulating since late 1967 and were steadily increasing in volume. Resisters' supply lines came to depend on foreigners, many of whom were British; British passports were smuggled into Greece in order to get several opponents of the Colonels out of the country. For instance, 'tortured Pericles Korovessis, one of the leading witnesses at the Council of Europe, travelled through the Greek-Turkish borders on a passport of a British lawyer by the name Anthony Thornton'.[143] Meanwhile money was fun-draised by the Greek Relief Fund of the League for Democracy in Greece for the families of the detainees; even bombs were placed by British in Athens and Salonica targeting cars belonging to American agencies, the homes of police torturers and places frequented by tour-ists. Anti-Colonels campaigners did indeed pursue a number of ave-nues. Cedric Thornberry went with Anthony Gifford, a prominent human rights barrister from London, to Athens 'to make a nuisance of ourselves with the lawyers there, ministers and anybody else we could get to talk to us.'[144] In a letter sent from Rustan Thoren of the Reefer and General Shipping Agency in London to the Secretary of Socialist International there was exploration of 'the possibilities of chartering a vessel for broadcasting purposes to operate in international waters off the coast of Greece.'[145]

In light of the above, the Greek government continued to hold Britain accountable for any opposition that it met with in the international arena. For instance, Greek rulers condemned the British for the suspension of the Greek trades unions from the International Transport Workers Federation, a decision reached by the Executive Board of the International Trades Federation at its meeting in London between 4 and 5 November, as well as for the latter's intention to institute an international boycott of Greek shipping. In fact, the Greek Prime Minister was so convinced of Britain's co-responsibility for these decisions that he warned the British Embassy in Athens that unless the boycott was lifted, he would ban all British ships and aircraft from coming to Greece. Papadopoulos became so obsessed with the idea of British complicity in all opposition encountered by the regime, that he even came to believe that the British were somehow involved in the assassination attempt carried out against him by Alexandros Panagoulis in August 1968.

In a desperate attempt to eliminate the suspicion with which the Greek rulers regarded them, British officials briefed the Foreign Secretary to explain to his Greek opposite number that the International Trades Federation was an international trade union organisation over which Britain had no control, and give him assurances that its decisions did not represent British official policy.[146] With regard to the alleged connivance in the assassination attempt, the British government categorically spelled out that it had nothing to do with it and had no foreknowledge of the event.[147]

Nevertheless, tensions continued to mount. The British government had tried hard to gain the Colonels' trust, to the extent that it was accused by its own party of glorifying selfish motives at the expense of ideology and humanism in its dealings with the Greek government. However, its attempts to normalise its relations with the regime during autumn 1968 proved unsuccessful. The Greek rulers continued to misinterpret acts of foreign opposition as being spearheaded by the British government and this mistrust translated in difficulties in their bilateral dealings.

The British government's assessment that 'in the second half of 1968 Anglo–Greek relations deteriorated and by the winter had reached a low ebb'[148] came as no surprise. British officials could not tolerate this for a variety of reasons, some already examined and some others that will be looked at in due course. They therefore decided to concentrate additional efforts on restoring their relations with the Greek rulers, as will be discussed in the next chapter.

3

FROM 'LOW-EBB', BACK TO NORMAL,
AND THEN TO THE 'LOWEST-EBB'

By late autumn 1968 Anglo–Greek relations had reached an impasse. The spiralling uneasiness that characterised them was discussed on 7 November, when the British Foreign Secretary held a meeting with the British Ambassador to discuss various possible ways to overcome it. They then admitted for the first time that these had deteriorated to such an extent that they had entered a new phase. There was increased awareness that British pressure on the regime had not only ceased to be influential, but had now become almost counter-productive. British officials reportedly felt that 'Greek ministers gave the appearance that they were unwilling to do business with Britain' and were 'not receptive to representations from H.M. Ambassador.'[1]

The British government viewed this development with notable discontent, because it was obviously bound to harm its interests. In November, for instance, it noted with regret that no major contracts had been signed since 26 June, the day after the Prime Minister's remarks in the House of Commons. Displeased by the unwelcome deterioration in Anglo–Greek relations, British government officials expressed the desire 'to establish a good working relationship with the Greek government.'[2] It will be the scope of this chapter to account for the efforts made by them in that direction, and the additional factors generated by an array of domestic and international developments, which strengthened their belief in the necessity of having good working relations with the Greek government.

It is evident that in late 1968 British officials showed determination to reverse the worsening trend by taking all necessary action to restore confidence in the Greek regime's dealings with them. In spite of the 'clouds hanging over their relations', as Sir Denis Greenhill Permanent Under-Secretary of State for Foreign Affairs put it during his visit to Athens, 'clouds brought new fertile rain from which new crops sprang' and expressed confidence that 'the same would be true of Anglo–Greek relations.'[3] They therefore decided to keep emphasising the need for 'normalising Anglo–Greek relations and recreating our [British] stock of influence with the Greek government by all means open to us.'[4] They also agreed to exercise 'the greatest care about pressing the Greek government on matters of domestic policy … and avoid exerting public pressure on them altogether.'[5]

British officials immediately adopted this policy, which was to be reviewed after six months. For instance, on 18 November, when the Foreign Secretary was asked whether he was finally willing to propose the expulsion of Greece from the Council of Europe, his response was laconic and negative. On another occasion too, he avoided taking a position on matters within the Greek government's internal jurisdiction by stating that 'the timing of Greece's return to a democratic system is a matter for the Greek government.'[6]

Although the objectives of British foreign policy had remained unchanged since the Secretary of State's Memorandum of 2 July 1968, officials increasingly recognised the imperative of pursuing them with different tactics. Indeed, the great challenge facing the British government had always been to conduct these policy initiatives without appearing to condone the regime. In other words, although the British government was unquestionably committed to reinstating its relations with its Greek counterpart, it did not fail to admit that 'Greece was still a very delicate issue … particularly in the Labour Party.'[7] British officials were aware, as Sir Denis Greenhill had put it while talking to the Greek Foreign Minister on 28 November, that 'one of the difficulties of our [Anglo–Greek] relations was the intense interest that everyone in Britain took in Greek affairs.'[8] Thus they were instructed yet again to keep their contacts with their Greek counter numbers quiet and avoid doing anything publicly provocative 'which would imply approval of the regime's policy.'[9] It was also recommended that they should 'seek to influence the regime by private and direct approaches to Greek ministers rather than by public protests or action against Greece in international organisations.'[10]

Most of 1968 had found the British government in the thick of debates about whether or not to authorise the sale of any arms to Greece. The government stressed yet again that no obstacles should be placed upon contracts concerning military equipment signed between the Greek government and British firms; those included Vospers and Yarrows for the supply of frigates and patrol boats, Westland for the sale of helicopters, and British Aircraft Corporation for Lightning fighter jets.

Ever since the time of the coup, the government had followed a consistent policy of preventing the sale of arms that could be used for internal repression. However, as time went by, officials were prone, for the sake of safeguarding their commercial interests, to relax their policy by drawing a 'clear distinction' between the purpose and the supply of military equipment legitimately required by Greece to fulfill her NATO role.[11] They therefore reiterated that, although the sales of arms whose primary purpose was to suppress the civilian population should continue to be forbidden, the sale of all other arms not intended for the repression of civilians should be authorised unrestrictedly. In the meantime, the US government's military sales to Greece had sharply increased to $33.5 million (almost $230 millions in today's value) in February 1969 compared to a low $8.7 million (close to $63 millions in today's value) in 1968 and a mere $1.1 million (slightly above $8 millions in today's value) in 1966.[12]

There followed another meeting on 19 November to debate British policy towards Greece. It was decided then that the British Ambassador after returning to Athens should seek a suitable opportunity to convey to the Greek Prime Minister a message from the Secretary of State along the following lines:

(a) Her Majesty's government accepts the fact that the timing of Greece's return to a democratic system is a matter for the Greek government.

(b) The sooner the Greek government feel able to apply the suspended articles of the new Constitution, the earlier it would be possible to re-establish the traditional relationship between the Greek and the British peoples. The British people are conscious of the particular part Greece has played in the development of Western democracy.

(c) There certainly are differences between Her Majesty's government and the Greek government, but we are anxious to establish a good working relationship with the Greek government whose importance in the Western Alliance we fully recognise.

(d) We admire and continue fully to support the Greek government's effort to promote a lasting settlement in Cyprus.[13]

The above initiative was compatible with the conclusions that were reached at a subsequent meeting and were summed up as follows:

given that for the time being there is little or nothing we can do to influence the domestic policies of the Greek government, our policy should now be to give pride of place to strictly British interests, bearing in mind that, however illiberal they may be, the Greek government (unlike Spain or Rhodesia) are not doing HMG [Her Majesty's government] any harm. On the contrary, they are fellow members of an Alliance on which we both depend for our security.[14]

The opportunity to convey the Foreign Secretary's goodwill came on 3 January when Sir Michael Stewart, the British Ambassador in Athens, met the Greek Prime Minister to discuss prospects for Anglo–Greek relations. His remarks, which were forwarded to London and a number of other concerned British Embassies, read as follows:

the outlook ... is not very promising but I continue to think it is desirable to be in a position where I can talk to him personally and his question about the relationship between the suspended articles of the Constitution and the character of Anglo–Greek relations is an indication that he cares what we and other powers think.[15]

Despite the relative pessimism emanating from the meeting, British officials emphasised the need not to be completely discouraged, but instead to seize every opportunity to stress their points. The next appropriate occasion was not long in coming, as the Foreign Secretary met with the Greek Prime Minister in the middle of March when both of them were in Belgium for a NATO ministerial meeting.

It is clear that British officials continued to attach the greatest importance to safeguarding their contacts through diplomatic channels. The examples they used, in favour of private approaches, included the closing down of the Yaros concentration camp following private Anglo–

Greek discussions and the Greek government's handling of the episode of the three British seamen who were arrested by the Greek police in Athens on 31 May 1969 for distributing Communist leaflets—following high-level diplomatic deliberations, the Greek government decided to forego their prosecution and sent them back to the UK.

The value of maintaining pressure at a private level was also vividly manifested, as they liked to remind their critics, in the case of Alexandros Panagoulis, who was charged with the attempted assassination of the Greek Prime Minister. Following the announcement by the regime that he would be sentenced to death, Labour MPs suggested that the question should be raised in the House of Commons and that they should also organise a vociferous demonstration. The Secretary of State rejected the suggestion as futile. He justified his decision on the grounds that 'demonstrations and condemnatory speeches ... would be interpreted by the Greek government as interference with Greece's internal affairs',[16] and would only cause them to react resentfully. He underlined his point by asking whether it was more important 'to save Panagoulis' life or to make a big song and dance about the sentence?'[17] Finally, there was unanimous agreement that the question should be dealt with quietly through private channels. In fact, through private representations, British officials did succeed in persuading the Greek rulers to commute Panagoulis' death sentence to life imprisonment.

It is worth noting nonetheless that 'the energetic representations of the British government to its Greek counterpart were mainly mounted on behalf of British subjects, as it was claimed that the Greek government would view British interferences on behalf of Greek citizens as unwelcome interventions in its domestic affairs.[18] Likewise, Andrew Palmer from the Foreign Office soon after confirmed the disparity in his government's standing vis-à-vis British and Greek prisoners.[19]

In the meantime, a number of policy initiatives were being adopted in a further attempt to prove to the Greek government the sincerity of British benevolence. First, the Greek Embassy was informed about the British government's decision to satisfy their recent request to provide them with police training. Aware of the potential outcry that this might cause, British officials carefully accounted for it on the basis that 'given the criticism there has been of Greek police methods, it is to the general good that Greek policemen should learn something of the methods of the British police.'[20]

In addition, British officials agreed to relax their previous decision to avoid any official encounters and meetings with members of the Greek regime. Consultations were therefore due to commence with the Board of Trade about the possibility of inviting the Greek Minister of Industry to visit Britain. The Cabinet approved this suggestion in December 1968 and the minister's visit was fixed for the following May.

However, the most telling indication of British officials' anxiety to normalise their relations with Greece and regain its regime's trust was their keenness to proclaim their opposition to all actions taken against the Greek regime by international organisations. Their repeated refusal to expedite the suspension of Greece from membership of the Council of Europe following the vote in the General Assembly was a typical example of this policy. On every occasion when relevant enquiries were put forward in the House of Commons, officials made it clear that they opposed the ostracism of Greece. 'We shall decide our attitude in consultation with our allies,' was a frequent refrain.[21]

On 25 February 1969, for instance, the Prime Minister himself was asked, during a debate on the Greek issue in the House of Commons, whether Greece should be expelled from the Council of Europe. Mr Wilson said in reply:

> As to the question of fitness of Greece to remain a member of the Consultative Assembly of the Council of Europe, this matter is being investigated impartially by the European Commission of Human Rights at this time and I think it would be wrong for me to prejudge what the European Commission might decide to find.[22]

He additionally argued that ousting Greece could only be counterproductive, since 'it would isolate the Greeks from the main stream of European thinking, and this would reduce, not increase any influence we [the British government] have or hope to have on what happens from now on in Athens.'[23] He concluded his argument by claiming that Greece's suspension from the Council of Europe would do 'more harm than good to the Greek people who ought to be everyone's first concern.'[24]

The ambivalent stance of the British government towards this issue was possible for most of 1969, despite scores of letters received urging the government not 'to vote against the recommendation of the

Council of Europe Assembly that Greece should be suspended from membership of the Council.'[25] This was because the Council of Ministers, which met in early May in London with the initial aim of reaching a final verdict regarding Greece's suitability for membership of the Council of Europe, decided to grant a further extension to the Greek authorities. The member states, some more reluctantly than others, passed a resolution on 6 May, which in effect had set the Greek government a time limit of six months within which to convince European opinion that an evolutionary progress towards democracy had either been completed or was within striking distance. Several protests were staged in London against this oscillation.

The Council arranged a date for its next meeting on 12 December, when it ruled that the report composed by the European Commission of Human Rights would be examined, and on the basis of their findings it would be determined whether Greece should be barred or not. In view of that decision, to whose postponement the British representatives had substantially contributed, the British government found it convenient to avoid taking a clear stance. This was, after all, a policy line that was favoured by the American government as well, although the US was not a member of the Council of Europe. More specifically, American officials were concerned that if Greece were expelled from this organisation, the question of its discharge from NATO would automatically be raised; and that was something that they refused to countenance. Under this additional pressure, British officials did not waste a single chance to publicly draw a clear distinction between their policy towards Greece's membership of the Council of Europe and that of NATO.

During a debate at the House of Commons in May, government officials stated that 'the Council of Europe is a body distinct from NATO' and that 'that is why a decision there would not necessarily be the same thing as a decision in NATO.'[26] In another instance, the Prime Minister put his argument in this following way:

> Our policies in the Council of Europe should be decided in the light of the moral and other issues involved, while questions of military coop-eration should be treated in the NATO context. This distinction reflects the fact that whereas the Council of Europe has a democratic statute, which its members are committed to observe, NATO is the product of a military alliance.[27]

Interestingly enough, although the British government was occasionally under considerable external pressure from fellow NATO member countries to raise the question of Greece's membership, domestic peer pressure about this issue was relatively limited, especially when compared to other controversial issues like the sale of arms to Greece. There is a plethora of comments made by a number of mostly Conservative MPs at various times during 1969 that unmistakably proved the general opposition to the idea of expelling Greece from NATO for fear of weakening the alliance's vital southern flank.

For instance, on 17 February 1969, during a debate at the House of Commons, Conservative MP Douglas Dodds-Parker asked the British government representative 'whether in view of the increased naval activity in the Eastern Mediterranean, he will give an assurance that he will support the continued inclusion of Greece within the Atlantic and European Organisations of which it is a member.'[28] A week later, Conservative MP John Rodgers posed the following question: 'As Greece is the only ally that we have in Eastern Europe and as she is also a member of NATO, would the Prime Minister refrain in future from using such phrases as "bestialities" in reference to that government?'[29]

The same agony over keeping Greece onside was expressed on 1 April by Conservative MP John Biggs-Davison who asked, 'Will the Right Honourable Gentleman deprecate as very dangerous indeed anything tending to weaken the contribution of Greece to NATO?'[30] The reply that he received from the government representative reads:

> We remain firmly opposed to action taken against Greece in NATO, in which Greece occupies a key position of the South Eastern flank. Any attempt to interfere with Greek participation in NATO would be strongly opposed by, among others, the United States, West German and Turkish governments, and would have a politically divisive effect within the alliance in addition to its military implications.[31]

The rationale supporting this stance was founded on the grounds that to do so would constitute a 'threat to European security', therefore it would be 'unwise'. The argument presented in the Memorandum mentioned that:

> Greece is a member of NATO and a bulwark of our south-Eastern flank, which is today threatened not only by the Red Army in Rumania,

Bulgaria and Hungary but by the growing threat of the Soviet fleet. ...
It is essential for the security of every nation represented in this
Assembly that the Greek Navy and the Greek air force should remain
at NATO's disposal. Anything that were to cast doubt on NATO's commitment to Greece, or that jeopardized the confidence and enthusiasm
of the Greek nation for the Atlantic Alliance, could put at risk the best
interest of every one of our countries. To suspend Greece in a fit of
self-righteousness would be to cut off our noses to spite our faces.[32]

In short, the British government was relatively free of internal scrutiny on actions to be taken against Greece within NATO, much more
so than on Greece's membership of the Council of Europe. There
existed no overwhelmingly pressing need to obstruct British participation in NATO exercises. Therefore, a Defence and Overseas Policy
Committee meeting decreed that 'unless there were overriding political objections, we should continue to cooperate with Greek forces in
NATO exercises in which our allies were also taking part' and that 'HM
ships could continue to call at Greek ports while engaged in NATO
exercises.'[33] Moreover, they reiterated that their present policy of
allowing 'the sale to Greece of arms that she could reasonably be
expected to require in order to fulfill her NATO role, and prohibit only
the supply of those arms intended to repress the civilian population'[34]
was as satisfactory as they could achieve. The Foreign Office concluded
its meeting on 19 June by agreeing that:

> miscellaneous military cooperation with Greece of a minor nature,
> such as short unpublicized visits by members of the Greek Armed
> Forces to Britain, could continue, again provided that the Ministry of
> Defence gave the Foreign and Commonwealth Office the maximum
> notice when seeking political clearance.[35]

However, despite the relatively benign climate regarding Greece's
membership of NATO, British officials deemed it prudent that 'purely
bilateral visits ... e.g. by ships not engaged in a NATO exercise—
should be avoided unless there were compelling reasons for
arranging them.'[36]
Whilst most members of the opposition were rather pleased with
the government's pro-NATO stance, a number of its own members
were less content. Labour MP William Hamilton fiercely criticised his
own government on 5 May by saying that, 'on this side we are sick and

tired of the Foreign Office seeking to please, or giving the appearance of pleasing, honourable members opposite rather than the government's own supporters.'[37] During the same debate, another Labour MP openly impugned his government's honour by saying 'we on these benches are united in our adamant belief that it would be unforgivable if Britain showed less backbone than other nations in disembarrassing democratic organisations of regimes such as the one in Athens.'[38] What was also striking was the decision of the National Executive Committee of the British Labour Party to provide the Greek Panhellenic Liberation Movement (PAK) with tangible support, both material and moral.[39]

Furthermore, condemnatory statements regarding the government's tolerance of the Greek regime stretched beyond Parliament to include various sectors of the British public. Public opposition to the Greek regime was expressed in a variety of ways, including sporadic demonstrations outside the Greek Embassy in London—and on one occasion even inside it, when it was forcefully occupied by fifty men in May 1968—and participation in anti-regime rallies co-organised with Greek exiles in London, like the one held on 4 May 1968.

Another example of the British public's active opposition was the signing by five members of the British Athletic team at the European Championship hosted by Athens in September 1969, of a declaration stating that 'I am going to the European Games as an athlete representing Great Britain ... I do not wish my presence in Athens to be used for political purposes to indicate support for the Greek government.'[40] As Cedric Thornberry wrote in *The Guardian*, 'resistance activity has also increased substantially since the meeting of the Council of Europe's Committee of Ministers in London in May.'[41] In spite of the regime's brutal attempts to clamp down on the domestic dissent by initiating a fresh wave of arrests in liberal intellectual quarters, resistance both internally and abroad, whether passive or active, even in violent forms, was steadily on the rise. For instance in mid-August 1969, half a dozen bombs exploded in Athens and Salonica, including one inside the NATO headquarters, just in the course of one week alone.[42]

British officials were nonetheless categorically instructed to turn a blind eye to any pressure to change their attitude. They were advised to defend their stance by arguing along the lines that 'the suggestion that the government have shown, as has been implied, any less resolution in trying to assert democratic principles is totally without foundation.'[43] The officials' determination not to alter their policy rested on their re-evaluation of conditions in Greece at the beginning of 1969. A memorandum prepared for the Secretary of State for Defence and the Secretary of State for Foreign and Commonwealth Affairs concluded that 'in Greece itself, the government have now entrenched their position',[44] and although 'there is no enthusiasm, the government now command the acquiescence of the majority of the people.'[45] The rising tides of resistance did not obviously seem to concern them.

The strong position of the regime was boosted by a revival of confidence, which the British attributed to a variety of factors: the result of the referendum; powerful Greek shipping magnate Onassis' decision to invest heavily in Greece—though they failed to note that this stemmed mainly from the scandalous introduction of Law no. 465 of 1968 guaranteeing the exemption of ship owners' transactions from taxes—and the increase in earnings from tourism in the latter part of the summer.[46] These developments looked quite impressive, especially when combined with other financial successes such as the fact that 'around the end of last year [1968], Bank of Greece reserves reached their highest point since 1964, because of the transfer of gold to the official reserves and because of loans negotiated with Swiss and German Bankers.'[47]

Nevertheless, all British efforts to please, or more accurately not to displease, the Greek regime were in vain. The Greek Prime Minister, George Papadopoulos, continued to assume unjustifiably that as long as manifestations of opposition were taking place in England, then the British government must bear some responsibility for not containing them. This belief was strengthened by actions such as the positioning of an armoured car driven by MPs outside the Greek Tourist Association on London's Regent Street and a bomb planted at the Greek Embassy. British government officials were finding it increasingly hard to convince the regime that they had no involvement in or tolerance of any sabotage. The Colonels' suspicions were exacerbated by a widely shared belief in Greece that 'Greek destinies are shaped in London',[48] with the result that all portents, favourable or unfavourable, tended to be magnified. The fact remained, though, that the Greek people had always been sensitive to what British officials said and thought about them, mainly because of close and powerful shared historical ties—and this is an opinion that was also distilled during the course of my inter-views with two of the three coup leaders.

The Greek authorities were displeased for another reason too. They were well aware that the British government, and the Prime Minister in particular, had kept in close contact with the exiled King, mainly through direct meetings with him during his frequent visits to London or via the British Ambassador in Rome, where King Constantine resided. This, however, did not mean that the King's stock of influence on British policies towards the Colonels was on the rise—in fact, quite the opposite. For instance, in one of those routine communications during his visit to London in June 1969, the King drew to the attention of British authorities a story in the German magazine *Der Spiegel* according to which the Greek government was considering ways of arranging to depose him legally and to establish a Regency in his place.[49] Indeed, knowledgeable analysts had often commented on the various alternatives that the Colonels might have been examining all along regarding how to best deal with the issue of the Regency. Those varied from the interwar model of the Hungarian Regency of Admiral Horthy, who left the throne vacant, to Franco's example according to which Crown Prince Paul and not his father would be allowed to return to the Greek throne. With a view to forestalling any attempt, the King asked the British to warn the Greek government of the dubi-ous wisdom of taking such a step.

The British replied that they 'did not think it wise to comply with the King's request.'[50] They argued their case on the grounds that they 'considered it impolitic to put ideas into the junta's head which may not be there.' Furthermore, they claimed that they 'thought it better to keep the junta in doubt about what response the British might make to a junta attempt to depose the King.'[51] Besides, as they finally inferred, 'the British considered any warning to the Greek government was sure to be rejected as interference in Greek internal affairs.'[52]

While the British wished to keep the King's expectations contained, they affirmed that they would take action if needed. In a meeting on 3 July between the British Ambassador in Athens, Sir Michael Stewart, and his namesake, the Foreign Minister, it was deduced unlikely that

Mr Papadopoulos would depose the King and declare Greece a Republic. They assessed that he would only resort to such action if he considered it essential to allay extremist pressure on him. However, as the British Ambassador recalled, 'if it became plain that Mr Papadopoulos was determined to depose the King, which would probably involve the organisation of some kind of charade such as a rigged plebiscite, the British, United States and German governments could warn Mr Papadopoulos not to proceed';[53] though even such claims were not entirely accurate as the developments in 1973 would prove otherwise.

The State Department had also recorded this event by mentioning in its files that 'should GOG attempt to depose Constantine appear imminent, HMG should consider possibility of warning Papadopoulos of difficulties which such action could cause his regime.'[54] In other words, it did not seem to be a question of supporting the King for his own sake, but instead it was a matter of trying to avoid complications for their governments' dealings with the Colonels that his dethronement would give rise to. The American officials, too, believed that there were advantages in the King remaining on the throne. They specifically argued that 'even though his position and prestige have suffered damaging blows, he continues to have some importance as a symbol of more normal political life and to enjoy a measure of support both within and without Greece.'[55]

British officials had used every possibility to demonstrate forbearance, even if cautious, towards the regime. This was obvious to everyone, to the extent that Panayiotis Kanellopoulos, the former caretaker Greek Prime Minister, during a meeting with a British Embassy official on 28 May 1969 implied that 'a number of ... Greeks whom he described as true friends of Great Britain, found our [British] policy towards Greece at present difficult to understand and distressing.'[56] British Counsellor Derek Dodson sought to justify it by replying that 'British policy towards any one country was founded ... on three considerations: first ideology, secondly a realistic analysis of the state of things, thirdly national interest'.[57]

With regards to ideological factors, the Counsellor reiterated that the British government believed that 'the people of all countries should be free to choose their own form of government.'[58] He furthermore opined that the British government could not realistically see any viable alternative to the present regime, since former Prime Minister Konstantinos Karamanlis was 'silent in Paris', and on the Centre Union side, 'most of the former leaders were dead or very old and no one of the survivors who were still in Greece could decide who should lead the party';[59] as for Andreas Papandreou 'he was abroad and discredited and, in any case, no longer really Greek.'[60]

As far as British national interests were concerned, the stakes were high, especially from a commercial point of view. There was a provisional figure at the end of May of transactions amounting to the value of £22.5 million (in excess of 350 millions in today's value), including contracts such as that of Marconi for the supply of television and broadcasting equipment for the European Games worth £700,000 (over 11 millions in today's value), and that of Telephone Cables Ltd linking Athens to Lechaina worth £500,000 (just over 8 millions in today's value). Those transactions represented a noticeable increase of 43 per cent over the corresponding period in 1968.[61] In addition, there were potential orders worth £100 million (over 1.65 billions in today's value).[62] Apart from the negotiations for the sale of a nuclear power station, and the railway rolling stock contract, there were also various other smaller negotiated deals such as the Serres valley irrigation scheme, worth an estimated £5.5 million (almost 89 millions in today's value).

The untrammeled signing of contracts between British firms and the Greek regime was perhaps the most contentious issue and was fiercely criticised by a number of predominantly Labour MPs and a large sector of the public. Anthony Crosland, the President of the Board of Trade, commented on British trade with the undemocratic regime in Greece during a Parliamentary debate, as follows: 'I am constantly asked to limit trade with different countries because of the views taken in this House on the regimes of those countries. I always reply that if I were to encourage trade with only countries of whose regimes we approve, we should trade with very few countries.'[63] Besides, as he used to argue when an opportunity arose, the British government strove to leave no room for doubt that its promotion of commercial dealings with Greece 'does not in any way alter the very strong feeling, which I and my colleagues have about the nature of the Greek government.'[64]

Such was the degree of Britain's financial decline that most Conservative MPs stood firmly by the government's decision to allow the uninterrupted continuation of trade with the Greek regime. Conservative MP John Biffen, for instance, posed the following question to his fellow parliamentarians: 'Would it not be regrettable if this valuable market were imperiled by those ideological zealots who constantly criticise the domestic policies of the Greek government?'[65] A few months earlier, during a meeting of the Parliamentary Foreign Affairs group, which gathered to discuss British policy towards Greece, the reply to a participant who pushed for a ban on trade with Greece was:

> If however the time came when we took a moral stand and lost exports in consequence, I hope that he [Hugh Gray] would help to explain to the British people how we were failing to solve our balance of payments problem because we felt it necessary to show our abhorrence of the Greek regime.[66]

Despite the fact that the government's policy in general, and not merely in regard to trade with Greece, never enjoyed overall approval, officials showed no willingness to change it. The British insistently refused to take any action that might have been interpreted by the Greek regime as hostile. Furthermore, they committed 'unremitting efforts ... to cultivate correct relations with the powerful Ministry of the Press in order to dissociate the British government from the bias shown by the British press and the BBC'.[67] Moreover, they also disregarded the opposition in the House of Commons, regarding the appointment of a Greek General as the new Greek Ambassador in London by responding that it was 'rather undesirable to criticise foreign governments.'[68]

Finally, after prolonged attempts by the British, for the most part, these initiatives were starting to produce the intended effect. It looked as though Britain was finally restoring a good working relationship with the Greek government. British officials recognised that 'we are now once more in a position to raise informally with Greek ministers matters which they consider of purely domestic policy.'[69] This trend was confirmed on several occasions, such as during the private talk which Michael Stewart held with his Greek opposite number on 16 April 1969, as well as the conversation on 25 June between Mr Papadopoulos and Sir Michael Stewart, during which Papadopoulos actually sought Stewart's advice. As a result of these rapprochements, the Greek rulers were reported as having now 'reversed their earlier decision to put the contract for a nuclear reactor out to tender.'[70] This was particularly gratifying news to British officials. Sir Charles Cunningham, from the United Kingdom Atomic Energy Authority, pointed out in a letter of 22 August 1969, that 'we emphasise that our objective is to sell a reactor and that we should deplore any development which made this impossible.'[71]

Whilst opposition to commercial contracts was loosing its edge, the government's tolerance towards the regime continued unabated. For instance, during the negotiations regarding the next meeting of the Council of Europe, which would decide whether Greece should be deprived of its membership, British representatives were advised to take a clear anti-expulsion stance. In the months leading up to the December 1969 meeting, the British government was under constant pressure to clarify the policy it would follow regarding the question of Greece's suspension. In view of the resolution that the Council had adopted, the British government was well aware that challenging times lay ahead. As the Foreign Secretary notified the Prime Minister, 'we [the British] are likely to face a very difficult meeting in December,'[72] and it was particularly highlighted that 'countless numbers of democratic British people in the trade union, labour and co-operative movement' followed the talks 'with utmost anxiety.'[73] Officials realised that ultimately it would be impossible to avoid voting for the expulsion, 'unless the Greek government had made real moves towards the restoration of democratic rules',[74] a prospect which nevertheless seemed unlikely.

In the meantime, several Labour MPs alerted repeatedly their own government that if it did not support Greece's suspension, 'it will be regarded as shameful and as a blow to every lover of freedom.'[75] They also kept making pledges about taking 'a much more robust attitude to what is known to everyone as a barbarous military dictatorship.'[76] Conservative MPs on the other hand seemed to be more cautious, as they warned that 'the Council [of Europe] should be careful lest the expulsion of Greece and the snub to Portugal turn it unwillingly into a communist instrument.'[77] The British government kept finding excuses to justify its indecisiveness, as it knew all too well that if it were to take the lead in condemning Greece at that time, it would reduce the possibilities for 'our Ambassador in Athens to influence the

Greek government towards democratisation. It might well also result in the Commission on Human Rights finding themselves inhibited from fulfilling their investigatory role which we supported.'[78]

What gravely worried the British government were the threats of retaliation with which the Greek government was expected to coerce Britain in order to avert it from voting in favour of Greece's expulsion. In view of this real fear, the Cabinet meeting on 19 June 1969 concluded with the suggestion that 'we should try to form an assessment of the trade we stood to lose to our competitors in the event of the Greeks taking commercial reprisals against us for having voted for their expulsion.'[79] More specifically, the meeting restated Greece's significance and placed particular emphasis on its 'ever important' role within NATO, as well as in the Cyprus dispute, and for British commercial interests. Two weeks later, the same concerns were expressed yet again.[80] The British government admitted that it did not seem likely that the regime would have adopted by December a genuinely democratic character in view of the lack of action in that direction. Hence, it had to try to clarify to the Greek rulers that under those conditions it would be extremely difficult to avoid voting for the suspension.

The British government made two approaches to the Greek rulers regarding this matter. The first occurred at the end of June and took the form of an informal discussion between the British Ambassador in Greece and Prime Minister Papadopoulos. During that meeting the Ambassador expressed his government's worry about what might happen in December, when the Ministers of the Council of Europe would meet to consider again the question of whether Greece was in violation of the European Human Rights Convention. He therefore urged the Greek Prime Minister to take steps to liberalise his regime, suggesting as examples of such steps the enactment of the press law and establishment of a constitutional court. The second British approach was made on the occasion of the farewell call by Verykios, the Greek Ambassador in London, to Foreign Secretary Stewart. Stewart pointed to the serious problems the Greek case presented to the Council of Europe and expressed the sincere hope that he could report progress in the right direction soon. Otherwise, he warned Verykios, both Britain and Greece would face a very embarassing situation.

Furthermore, British officials decided to make another approach before the next ministerial meeting of the Western European Union in

September. This was to take the form of a démarche to reiterate the following two points. The first was already made several times beforehand, namely that unless the Greek government made some genuine moves toward restoring democratic freedoms before the December meeting of the Council of Europe, the British government would find it difficult to refrain from endorsing the ostracism of Greece. The second point, made for the first time, was that if the Colonels did not take steps to convince European opinion that there was in fact a genuine move in the direction of democracy, then they might wish to consider voluntarily withdrawing from the Council of Europe.[81] After evaluating the ominous conditions, the British repeatedly urged further the Greek government to withdraw in order to be spared the verdict.

Meanwhile, it was decided that reference in public to specific representations to the Greeks should be avoided. It was noted that, 'if ministers were obliged to say something—e.g. in answer to a Parliamentary Question about the W.E.U. representations—they would take the view that W.E.U. discussions were confidential.'[82] In other words, it was recommended that 'we should play this matter long and avoid being drawn into taking a stand.'[83] British officials acknowledged that their posture was 'unheroic', but nevertheless attempted to assuage their guilt with the argument that 'it was correct under the circumstances.'[84]

It was also agreed that, 'until a recommendation calling for Greece's suspension from the Council of Europe is passed, there is no need for H.M.G. to take any action',[85] mainly for fear of trade retaliation. Labour MP David Winnick asked George Thompson, the Chancellor of the Duchy of Lancaster, about the government's intentions at the Council's forthcoming meeting; the latter replied by saying that:

> it would be premature for me to say now how we shall vote when the question of Greek membership of the Council of Europe is discussed at the meeting of the Committee of Ministers on December 12. The Greek government still have an opportunity to convince European opinion that they are prepared to make an early return to democratic practices.[86]

Such answers would buy the officials some time to further discuss the issue with other European states and with Greece; and equally importantly, they would not prematurely condemn the UKAEA's hopes for a successful outcome to the negotiations for the sale of a nuclear reactor to Greece. In view of the seriousness of the situation, the

Parliamentary Labour Party Committee on Foreign Affairs suggested that a decision should not be finalised without a priori consulting the West Germans, whose position also appeared to be critical for the result of the voting. British officials admitted that 'perhaps our present decision to sound out other countries before making our decision was not heroic, but it was sensible and what others were doing.'[87]

In the meantime, international opposition was rapidly building up and the British government was finding it even more difficult to justify its ambivalent policy. 'With no dissenting votes and only a handful of abstentions, the Council of Europe on 2 October made a concerted attack on the Greek regime.'[88] Two and a half weeks later, on 20 October, 'the Plenum of the Parliamentary Assembly of NATO adopted by twenty-six votes to four (with two abstentions) the draft resolution unanimously voted and submitted by the Political Committee, thus expressing for the first time condemnation of the Greek Military regime.'[89]

In view of mounting obloquy, it was becoming increasingly obvious that the recent restoration of trust in Greece's dealings with Britain was bound to founder as the Council of Europe meeting approached. Furthermore, a leak by the *Sunday Times* of the ECHR report on the abrogation of Human Rights in Greece confirmed such a forecast. Its conclusions, following an investigation carried out in Greece over a period of two years, were so intimidating that, as *The Times* put it on 1 December 1969, 'on such report it would be ludicrous to keep the Greek regime as a member of the Council, while Spain and Portugal are excluded.'[90]

British officials found themselves, once more, in a very awkward position vis-à-vis a number of Labour MPs' vociferous criticism, since their previous reasoning (of deferring action on the grounds that they were awaiting the results of a judicial examination by the Commission of the European Convention of Human Rights) no longer stood. They had remained silent for as long as they could, but by that stage it was clear that they had to spell out their stance clearly. Stewart returned to his argument that the best possible course before the next Council of Europe meeting in December would be to 'persuade the Greeks to withdraw voluntarily and thus reduce danger of a row.'[91] This was particularly important under the circumstances, as the British Foreign

Secretary had cautiously implied during his visit to Bonn on 14 November that he found it 'difficult to see, on present evidence, how Greece's membership could continue.'[92] In the meantime, following the unexpected leakage of the report, the Greek rulers warned seven European states, Britain being one of them, as to the application of sanctions against countries voting for the country's expulsion.

The British government in particular was further blackmailed. On 2 December 1969, it was 'officially rebuked in Athens ... for allegedly instigating a campaign of hostility to the Greek regime.'[93] A Press Department release mentioned that 'authoritative circles in Greece have expressed surprise at the unbridled partisan campaign waged by Britain's socialist government against Greece, as well as at the unwanted violence displayed by a section of the British press, presumably under remote-control guidance.'[94]

The Press release, in addition, mentioned that 'the scandalous publication of the Commission's confidential report in British newspapers fully discredits those who either committed or facilitated this indiscretion'; it was also described as tantamount to a 'pre-trial disclosure of evidence.'[95] In other words, although the leak of the ECHR report had originated in Paris,[96] the British government was held accountable in the Greek rulers' eyes because it was actually printed by the *Sunday Times*.

In retaliation, on 7 December the Greek pro-regime newspapers published full-page reports of atrocities allegedly committed in Cyprus in 1957 by the British. As one article put it, 'the view prevails in Athens that certain British circles should hardly be entitled to invoke cases of torture', because 'this means that they tend to forget the fact that a huge file exists in the archives of the Council of Europe itself containing official evidence of the unimaginable methods of torture that the British had been guilty of in Cyprus.'[97]

According to the same report in *The Times*, 'it was the first time since the Cyprus crisis, of more than 10 years ago, that an official Greek statement had used such sharp language in criticising the British government.'[98] Two days later, an article in the pro-regime *Eleftheros Kosmos*, stated the following:

> The British had chosen the Council of Europe to fight against Greece. The British government knows better than anyone else that Greece has no need of Britain. We have excellent relations with other powers,

stronger than Great Britain, both in Europe and outside it, so that our interests need not be affected by the British stand.[99]

By that stage, Anglo–Greek relations had clearly experienced a serious blow. British officials regretted having reached a point where 'if we were to make representations to the Greek government about the conduct of their internal affairs, they would be less inclined to listen to us', as had been the case in the later part of 1968, 'when our stock of credit with the Greek government became exhausted and Anglo–Greek relations reached a low-ebb.'[100] The situation seemed virtually irreversible. As a result, in an attempt to silence at least domestic criticisms, the British government thus hurried to let the Ambassadors of the Scandinavian countries in London know that it stood by their position. In other words, for the first time the British government took openly the line that, on present evidence, Greece was no longer eligible for membership of the Council of Europe.

Contrary to the damning evaluations, Mr Panayiotis Pipinelis, the Greek Foreign Minister and Representative to the Council of Europe sought to convince the Committee, just before the scheduled Council of Europe meeting, that his government's 'timetable' qualified it for continued membership of the Council. Most of the delegations however felt that the programme fell short of guaranteeing a return to compliance with the requirements of the Statute of the Council. In fact, all the Western European Union members, except France, were co-sponsors of the draft resolution. Seeing the weight of opinion endorsing suspension, with the undecided members, namely Britain and the Federal Republic of Germany, having swung the pendulum in favour of the resolution, the Greek government instructed its representative, to deliver a letter declaring the country's decision to voluntarily withdraw its membership from the organisation a day before the meeting.

Following the Greek departure, Resolution 51 of 12 December 1969 was tabled.[101] The Committee of Ministers unanimously adopted it with the exception of the Cypriot Foreign Minister's abstention, hence officialising the Greek exit, which inaugurated a new phase not only in Greek history, but also in Anglo-Greek relations too.

4

'A SERIES OF SHIFTS AND JOLTS, WITH
OCCASIONAL SUNNY INTERVALS'[1]

Following the proceedings of the Council of Europe in December British officials assessed that the action taken against Greece would have virtually no effect on the country's internal affairs. Nonetheless, the British government had decided to endorse the resolution as it realised the need to preserve the standards of democratic behaviour to which the Council was pledged. More specifically, their stance regarding the Greek case within the Council of Europe in December was in accordance with the threefold objectives of the British government towards Greece vis-à-vis the Report on Human Rights. First, they obviously did not wish to damage or weaken the human rights machinery of the Council of Europe. By avoiding discrediting the machinery of the Human Rights Convention, they wished to deprive the Greeks of the opportunity of further denouncing the procedures in the present case, as well as to avoid setting a bad precedent. Finally, they certainly did not desire to expose themselves to 'any charges of letting the Greek government off too lightly', but on the other hand they wanted to 'minimise the risk of further damage to their bilateral relations with the Greek regime.'[2]

Four days after the announcement of Greece's withdrawal from the Council of Europe, British government officials held their first meeting on Greece in order to evaluate its likely impact on their relations with its regime as well as to examine their stance towards it. One of the first views expressed at policy level was that the outcome of the Council of Europe proceedings had turned out to be more satisfactory than they had expected. British officials reckoned that the resultant exchanges had been less acrimonious than if Greece had not resigned and the Committee had proceeded with the draft publication for suspension; hence, their estimate that there was now remarkably less danger of escalation. Greece's voluntary withdrawal was the outcome that they had consistently favoured and had even admitted working for.

It soon became apparent, however, that Greece's retraction had not made the possibility of harmonious relations any more realistic; quite the contrary. Soon after, the British were made aware that Foreign Minister Pipinelis bore 'a particular grudge against us [the British government] for the role he thinks we played in Paris.'[3] In the light of this unanticipated development, the British government emphasised the need not to further 'aggravate these hard feelings.'[4] The British had advocated for Greece's withdrawal from the Council as a kind of safety valve 'for ideological reasons and for reasons of British domestic consumption',[5] and had no intention of pressuring the regime any harder. They also kept clarifying that their attitude did not mean that they 'wished for any damage to be done to Greece's position within NATO.'[6] Whilst admitting that Britain 'did not, of course, show the "understanding" of France of Turkey … [it] carefully distinguished its stance from that of the Scandinavians',[7] who were Greece's staunchest critics.

As the British Foreign Secretary had decreed, 'without being apologetic for the line we took in Paris in December, we should continue to try to keep up a good working relationship with the Colonels.'[8] This chapter will tackle the complex conditions that emerged as a result of the proceedings of the Council of Europe, as well as the renewed efforts of British officials to restore their relations with the Greek government, despite widely felt public expectations that Britain should not 'revert to relations as before.'[9]

British officials agreed with the Greek Ambassador's proposal that the Colonels' regime should be accepted as a 'fact of life',[10] as a result of which their government should 'continue to try to maintain a reasonable working relationship with them.'[11] In the absence of any obvious alternative it was thought that the current regime could last up to five years, and if it fell apart sooner, there was the danger that it would most probably be replaced by 'an even worse regime composed of still more extreme right-wing officers or "Nasserite" captains adopting an anti-NATO stance.'[12] Gamal Abdel Nasser's regime in Egypt, having taken power from President Muhammad Naguib, was considered by the British to be a clear threat to regional security, and the emergence of an equivalent in Greece was highly undesirable—hence 'the considerable decrease in the frequency and tone of the attacks against the Greek regime',[13] as it was noted.

Maintaining good relations with the Greek regime was also a pragmatic step to ensure some £2–3 million (32.3–48.5 millions in today's value) a year in orders from Greek state agencies and a further £6–9 million (97–145.5 millions in today's value) of private business were not jeopardised, according to Michael Stewart's estimates.[14] In fact, between 1968 and 1969 British exports to Greece increased from £40 million (681 millions in today's value) to £58 million (937 millions in today's value).[15] Moreover, British firms were seeking several large contracts at that time, including an irrigation scheme near Corinth for which Mowlems had made an offer, and eleven sub-stations wanted by the Public Power Corporation. In addition, although there had in fact been no significant sales of British arms to Greece since the coup, and the previously expressed Greek interest in British frigates and aircraft had receded, the Greeks had made enquiries about purchasing sophisticated electronic equipment, as well as Chieftain tanks.

Equally importantly, there were concerns yet again about the United Kingdom Atomic Energy Association's prospects of obtaining the nuclear reactor contract being at 'very great' risk.[16] In order to maximise the plausibility of selling the reactor, Edwin McAlpine, of the UKAEA, suggested to Prime Minister Wilson sending a private letter to Mr Papadopoulos, ahead of the scheduled arrival of the UKAEA team led by Sir Charles Cunningham and Mr Chaleb on 4 February for the final round of their negotiations with the Greek government. The aim of such a letter was to show interest and express enthusiasm as a way of improving the chances of success.

The UKAEA considered the undertaking of such conciliatory action essential. Foreign Minister Pipinelis had hinted indirectly, albeit deliberately, that Greek government contracts would be concluded only with countries amicably disposed towards it. In his telegram, Edwin McAlpine stressed the point that this was Britain's first real opportunity of selling a nuclear system, a feat which could open up future markets. In view of such benefits, and despite the fundamental ideological objections, the possibility of sending a message was discussed. However, British officials instead instructed the Ambassador, on his return to Athens, to convey orally and informally to Pipinelis 'the warm personal regards of both the Secretary of State and the Chancellor of the Duchy of Lancaster.'[17]

Furthermore, the extent to which the British government was determined to restore its frayed rapport with the Greek government is also evident in its decision to detach itself from its normally close relations with the Greek King—another very sensitive issue which had in the past caused ruffled feathers. That the British decided to distance themselves from the King showed them to be 'anxious not to get drawn into the quagmire of GOG-King relationships.'[18] To be sure, they realised that it would be difficult to avoid offering the King the courtesies which he had received on previous occasions, especially as he visited London quite frequently. It was nonetheless recognised that for HM government 'to be seen conspicuously to pay attention to King Constantine in present circumstances did no good to Anglo–Greek relations.'[19]

Meanwhile, the US Secretary of State clearly stated that he was perfectly prepared to resist pressure for action against Greece in NATO. This was particularly important as the Americans had shown considerable concern that the proceedings on Greece in the Council of Europe might 'overspill' into NATO, with consequences that clearly frightened both allies. In an attempt to clarify the British government's stance on this issue George Thompson commented:

> We have never considered that Greek membership of the Council of Europe was relevant to Greece's role in NATO. The Council of Europe is essentially a forum which deals with matters of parliamentary institutions, human rights and the rule of law. I will seek to explain the distinction which I think can legitimately be drawn. We feel that the Council of Europe is the right forum in which such questions can properly be pursued. NATO is a defence alliance.[20]

This argument was neither straightforward nor entirely accurate; indeed, it seemed paradoxical that NATO should number among its members regimes like that in Greece, which had not come to power through democratic procedures and against which there were proven allegations of lack of respect for the rule of law and its citizens' individual liberties. Even among government officials it was admitted that 'the existence of an undemocratic regime in any member of the North Atlantic Alliance serves to weaken the Alliance as a whole.'[21]

The British Prime Minister was of the latter opinion. However, he was constantly cautioned by Foreign Office officials against estranging Greece from the Alliance. One such occasion occurred as the Prime Minister was due to visit the US at the end of January 1970. He was then advised that, should he wish to 'raise the question of Greece with President Nixon, he should not press the Americans to take action against Greece in NATO.'[22] Prime Minister Wilson stuck to the Foreign Office's line and agreed with President Nixon that it would be wrong to put Greece's position in NATO in jeopardy.

It was evident that the British government remained largely convinced about the necessity of not endangering NATO's stability. On 16 December 1969, government officials in Parliament clearly said that Greece must be kept in the alliance. They expressed their view by arguing that 'actions against Greece in NATO would not necessarily help the Greek people, but would undermine the security of the south-east flank of NATO, thus putting at risk democratic ideals and parliamentary institutions on a scale far greater than Greece.'[23] British officials appeared content that despite the criticism that had constantly been leveled at their policy towards Greece, 'our [British] military cooperation with the regime ... has never, to the best of the Department's knowledge, attracted any adverse comment in this country'[24]—and although this is a rather inflated claim, it certainly bore elements of truth.

Keeping Greece within the Alliance was considered even more necessary as another perturbing factor had come into play. Towards the end of 1969, a number of intelligence reports sent from Athens drew attention to the fact that the authorities in Moscow were predisposed to having 'relations as cordial as the [Greek] regime will allow.'[25] This was of course problematic in light of the increasingly thorny problems the Colonels faced in their relations with Western organisations, which the Soviets hoped would result in alienating Greece from the West. In fact, a number of trade agreements were signed in 1970 with the Soviet

Union, Bulgaria, Romania and Albania[26] and an opening into Africa was established by exchanges of official visits with Ethiopia, Libya, Congo-Kinshasa and the Central African Republic.[27]

The reports were particularly alarming as they testified to the Soviets' proclivity to support the regime, if Greece were to leave NATO and close the bases of its Alliance partners. Though due allowance should be made for exaggeration, developments such as 'the recent signing of a new trade agreement and the laying of the cornerstone for a power plant to be built by the USSR',[28] which contributed to the strengthening of Soviet–Greek economic relations, added credibility to the expressed fears. That such an agreement was concluded publicly two days before the December meeting of the Committee of Ministers of the Council of Europe was in fact partly recognised as an attempt 'to shake the ministers' nerves.'[29]

Although a rapprochement between such diametrically opposed regimes appeared unlikely to most of NATO members, there was a nagging consternation that Greece could well go the way Nasser had gone a few years before. A more accurate assessment was that of the *Times* correspondent who noted that 'there is of course no ideological resemblance with President Nasser's regime at present, not any parallels on the modus operandi'. Instead, he wrote, the Colonels' regime aimed 'to avert the danger of a communist takeover, now and forever, and in the process to tackle some of the nation's problems left unresolved by incapable parliamentary governments.'[30]

Even so, the reports were viewed with notable caution and uneasiness by the West, which correspondingly showed all the more willingness to reverse their disaffection. The pressure of the Soviet fleet in the Mediterranean continued as Colonel Gaddafi in Libya, who forcibly came to power in September 1969, was making clear his disdain for the American base at the Wheelus Field and a British outpost at El Adem. The omnipresent menace of the spread of Communism, especially in view of European Communism's increasing appeal, threatened not only Greece, but Italy and Turkey too—the other two countries that constituted the Alliance's southern flank.

Given this increased uncertainty in strategic terms, most NATO partners realised not only that Greece should not be ostracised from the Alliance, but, on the contrary, its relatively weakened military ought to be strengthened. For instance, the British Ambassador, in a report drafted at the end of December, recommended that the allies should not overlook the country's shortage of equipment and spare parts resulting from the suspension of the United States' military assistance. In the same report, he emphasised the fact that the country's difficulty in maintaining any effective fighting units would become even more pronounced if its NATO allies continued to deny Greece arms indefinitely. The US, the major post-war supplier of arms to Greece, had restricted the supply of heavy items since the coup in 1967; and although they released some aircraft and two minesweepers in 1968, they were still withholding essential items, such as tanks. At the same time, it was feared that the fundamental need of the Greek Armed Forces for new equipment in order to fulfill their NATO role satisfactorily could raise awkward problems for the British government, should Greece turn to it in search of arms supplies.

The report's final point focused on the conviction that 'Greece's present leaders are not in a position to threaten to withdraw from the Alliance or adopt a Gaullist position as a means of bringing pressure to bear on the United States for a full resumption of military service.'[31] This belief was based largely on the grounds that the Greek government itself had discounted reports that, following its withdrawal from the Council of Europe, it would reduce its cooperation with NATO or, even worse, withdraw from it. In view of all the aforementioned considerations, British officials met again on 6 January 1970 to re-evaluate their stance towards Greece. The following aims constituted the backbone of their agreed lines of policy:

a) to promote the return to Greece of constitutional rule and democratic liberties in conditions of stability;
b) to preserve as far as possible the military effectiveness of Greece as a NATO ally;
c) to protect British subjects and British interests generally, and in particular to pursue our commercial interests; and
d) to retain our ability to influence the Greek government in matters of foreign policy, e.g. Cyprus.[32]

As far as the first objective is concerned there is a fair degree of doubt about whether it was realistic. Not because the British government did not honestly wish for a rapid return to democracy, but because they seemed fairly convinced, especially after the Colonels had stayed in power long enough for their perceptions to be emboldened, that this would not happen in the foreseeable future. As they admitted during the same meeting, when they outlined the parameters of their policy, 'real progress towards a return to democracy cannot be expected soon.'[33]

In the meantime, during the Western European Union ministerial meeting in Brussels on 9 January there was general agreement that although the grounds for Greece's return to democracy were not particularly solid, the British government and other fellow governments should nonetheless continue to pursue their goal of promoting it. This cannot be interpreted as anything else than wishful thinking, as they were aware that their ability to substantially influence the Greek regime was strictly limited. In fact, in another communication between government officials, Michael Stewart admitted that 'among members of NATO only the Americans, through their military aid programme, are in a position to exert any real leverage on the Colonels.'[34]

In addition, they noted that although the regime had a timetable for the full implementation of the Constitution by the end of 1970, 'many of its provisions are so hedged around with qualifications as to provide no guarantee of democratic conditions.'[35] For instance, the regime's new press law, although praised as a liberal breakthrough by the regime, was indisputably restrictive by British standards. Besides, as aforementioned, the regime had kept announcing deadlines for implementing steps to initiate its process of democratisation, which it consistently failed to meet. In effect, the Council of Europe's resolution of 12 December alone suffices to prove beyond doubt the lack of progress towards the restoration of constitutional rule and democratic liberties.

Most importantly, the pursuit of democracy for Greece would unavoidably conflict with Britain's other three foreign policy priorities: safeguarding British interests in Cyprus, cooperation of Greece with NATO, and Anglo–Greek commercial dealings. Fulfilling the other three objectives was not possible unless the British government was prepared to sacrifice the first. The Greek regime had left its allies in no doubt about its unwillingness to deal with those countries critical of its governing methods. The British government, entangled in this insoluble dilemma, opted for reluctant cooperation so as not to jeopardise their last three objectives, while making private representations in pursuit of the first.

The British government was aware that such a trade-off was no automatic guarantee of harmony in its relations with the Greek regime—great challenges lay ahead. Among the most potentially troublesome was the next meeting of the Council of Europe's Committee of Ministers' Deputies scheduled to take place from 2 to 6 March in order to discuss the report of the European Commission of Human Rights on the Greek case. This report, which had emerged, as already discussed, following the application brought in 1967 against the Greek government by the governments of Denmark, Norway, Sweden and the Netherlands, was transmitted to the Committee of Ministers in November 1969. It presented findings which were overwhelmingly critical of the Greek regime, and made clear that 'the Greek government have subjected people to torture.'[36]

The Greek government, in anticipation of the report's adverse findings, had advised its delegation, in parallel with their submission of the country's withdrawal from the Council of Europe, to denounce the Human Rights Convention. However, as the legal advisers of the British government ruled, the proceedings of the report could not be affected by either of these actions. The denunciation did not affect proceedings relating to acts performed before then, and, in any case, it would not become effective until six months from the date when it took place.

Consequently, although Greece was not allowed to participate in the meetings of the Committee, the case regarding allegations of torture brought against its government would still be considered in the forthcoming meeting of ministers. British officials were aware that these documented allegations of torture were bound to cause even more friction in the regime's relations with Britain.

Still poisoning the relationship was the part the British government was thought to have played in Greece's withdrawal from the Council of Europe. There was no doubt that the Greek government continued to feel humiliated. The Greek rulers strongly resented the Council's turning against them and held Britain largely responsible. The Greek government's state of mind was made known during a conversation, on 11 February 1970, which took place between the Greek Ambassador and Thomas Brimelow, Deputy Under-Secretary of State at the Foreign

Office; the former pointed to the latter that 'governments which had initiated action against Greece in the Council of Europe would be considered by the Greek government as hostile.'[37]

Meanwhile, the Greek Foreign Minister opposed the publication of the report. He argued that 'early publication would produce a strong reaction in Greece ... and would revive the tensions and dangers which had arisen after the Council of Europe decision of December.'[38] In other words, he warned that the effect on Greece's relations with Western countries could be serious. Besides, as the Greek Ambassador pointed out, the withdrawal of Greece from the Council of Europe did not bring about the changes that the supporters of Greece's expulsion had anticipated. On the contrary, as he argued, it contributed to increased internal solidarity and support for the government, due to the fact that the Council of Europe's action against Greece was widely interpreted as an attempt to interfere in Greece's domestic affairs.[39]

In light of the forthcoming meeting of the Council of Europe in March, Mr Pipinelis raised this subject with the British Ambassador on 23 February, and inquired about the stance that the British government intended to take. Sir Michael Stewart avoided giving any clear answer by replying that he 'very much doubted whether British ministers had yet decided what they would wish to do.'[41] A new emphasis was placed, on considering whether there was any action the British government could usefully take to allay Greek suspicions about its policies towards Greece. At the same time, they reached the following conclusion: 'We must recognise that the Greeks are at the moment in a sensitive frame of mind; while we cannot allow this to affect our policies unduly, we would be wise to exercise more than usual care in our presentation of these policies.'[42]

In the meantime, the British government clearly expressed to John Robey, British representative in Strasbourg, the wish 'to keep the political temperature down' and avoid appearing to the Greeks 'to be conspicuously in the lead.'[43] Furthermore, Robey was advised in favour of discreetly seeking the agreement of all parties to the dispute on the adoption of a clear-cut resolution on the report. It was expected that the meeting would endorse the findings in the report of violations of the Human Rights Convention in Greece, while prescribing a reasonable period in which the Greek government should take the measures necessary to remedy these violations.

Another meeting scheduled for March at NATO's headquarters in Brussels gave the British additional headaches. This evolved around the lingering dispute between the Greeks and the Norwegians in the Defence Review Committee of NATO over the handling of a sub-group report on the needs of Greece's Armed Forces to fulfill their NATO role. The Greek government emphatically noted that it would judge the British government's value to them on the basis of its attitudes vis-à-vis this dispute. More specifically, the British had come to believe that the Greek regime would assess 'how far it is in their interest to favour us [the British government] or even treat us neutrally in respect of the nuclear contract, by the extent to which we are prepared to support them in this instance against the Norwegians and if necessary the Danes.'[44] Soon after, another telegram sent to the Foreign Office by the British Ambassador in Athens alerted the British government to the fact that 'over the last weeks a growing body of evidence here [Greece] that HMG is regarded as both the most determined and the most formidable opponent of this regime.'[45]

In view of this, British representatives urged the Norwegians and the Danes not to make difficulties in NATO over the handling of the report.[46] In fact, so preoccupied were the British government that the British Ambassador in Athens requested permission to 'inform the Greek government without delay ... that HMG think the Norwegian government's objection to the sub-group's report is unreasonable' and that 'we support the Greek government's position.'[47] The Ambassador also drew attention to the fact that this evidence did not spring only from government sources, but also from important former political figures. It therefore seemed imperative that, as he put it, if the British government wished to restore its ability to exercise some influence with the regime in Greece, it should not be seen as taking the lead against it in international proceedings for the second time in three months.

Although the British government believed that they had taken as favourable a line as circumstances permitted towards Greece in both of those organisations, there was trepidation that the Greeks would be minded to make scapegoats of the British yet again if developments took a negative turn for them. In view of those fears, the Foreign Office's Reginald Secondé stressed that it was:

therefore a good moment to remind the Greeks at a high level of the seriousness of our proclaimed intention of maintaining a good working relationship with them, and, by stressing the efforts we are making on their behalf in Brussels and in Strasbourg, to seek to correct some of the wild talk about us now circulating in Athens.[48]

Another parameter in the worsening of Anglo–Greek relations was the strong language often used publicly when referring to the Greek government. More specifically, some parliamentary questions about Greece were couched in unnecessarily offensive terms, according to the Colonels, without any comment or intervention made by the Speaker of the House. For instance, the characterisation 'political mafia' used by MP John Fraser in one of his questions in Parliament on 2 February[49] had prompted a complaint by the Greek Ambassador to the Chancellor of the Duchy of Lancaster. Moreover, the Greek ruling authorities felt outrage that the British government was doing little or nothing to curb the activities of Greek émigrés, politicians and students in London and beyond. They obviously failed to comprehend the limitations that a non-dictatorial government has regarding its citizens' activities. Even so the British government did engage the services of both the MI5 and the MI6 in investigations regarding its citizens' activities, and questioned certain individuals.[50]

Various highly publicised protests had recently added to the Colonels' exasperation, including the Garden House Riots in Cambridge in February 1970, which disrupted a banquet that was to be the culmination of a week sponsored by the Colonels to promote tourism; the staging of a number of fundraising concerts and campaigns for Greek prisoners were among many other examples. Another irksome and rather embarrassing incident for the British government unfolded during Nixon's first visit to London in late February 1969. A number of anti-regime campaigners saw this as the perfect opportunity to voice their criticism against Britain's principal ally's unsavoury dealings with the regime that had intensified further due to its lifting of the arms embargo. A well-attended demonstration marched across London to coincide with the President's visit. Some of these activities derived genuinely from the special concern felt in Britain about Greece, while others were believed to be skilful PR work by Greek émigrés. A number of prominent British citizens, including Oxford Professor Sir

Maurice Bowra actress, Dame Peggy Ashcroft and author Olivia Manning, showed unwavering support.

Furthermore, the Greek regime repeatedly expressed serious discontent about the fact that several strident anti-junta papers were edited and produced in England, including the *Greek Observer*, the *Greek Report* and the *Hellenic Review*, all publishing uncensored news and information as well as articles by distinguished analysts of contemporary Greek affairs. In addition, the British press was accused of making 'a big fuss about tortures but seldom presented the other side of the coin e.g. its treatment of the Agreement with the ICRC.'[51] Occasionally, even British officials became exasperated, for instance by admitting that 'the BBC are no more balanced—in particular, the BBC's smug little film on the "Pimpernels" was a disgrace.'[52] There were some problems on the military side too. These included the cancelled naval visit the previous year, the attendance of a Greek army officer at the Old Sarum Course, and the long delay in giving the Greeks any reply about the order of medium tanks.

In view of the aforementioned nuisances, the British Ambassador wrote to the Foreign and Commonwealth Office in mid-March in order to express his recommended approach to his government's handling of the Greek issue. This followed his communication with General Angelis, Chief of the Greek Armed Forces, who warned the British Ambassador that 'if the European Countries were to continue to treat Greece in this way, there were always other possibilities.'[53] The Greek General specifically cited the Bloody Sunday turmoil in Istanbul and Smyrna following the American Sixth Fleet visit in February 1969, hinting thus at the possibility of imitating such anti-NATO riots, so that 'Greece would perhaps teach some of Greece's allies in NATO that she could not be pushed around indefinitely.'[54] Consequently, the British Ambassador advised the following:

> I venture to suggest we ought to do what we can to help Mr Pipinelis in regard to Human Rights Commission's report. I think you will agree that we need Pipinelis and Papadopoulos' help in regard to Cyprus, and the fresh resentment in the junta, which the publication of the Human Rights report would arouse... could be dangerous.[55]

In the same telegram, the British Ambassador repeated his opinion that it was extremely unlikely that the Greek government would wish to change its present defensive alignment, or would tolerate the 'so-called spontaneous anti-NATO demonstrations.'[56]

Meanwhile, the Deputies' meeting at the Council of Europe took place in Strasbourg, as scheduled, in order to discuss the report of the European Commission of Human Rights. A draft resolution was tabled by the fourteen attending delegations that provided, amongst other things, for the immediate publication of the report. However, following the request made by the Cypriot delegation, the final discussion of the report was postponed until the meeting of the Committee of Ministers on 15 April, when a decision was due to be taken.

The British government was clearly against the suspension of publication until the meeting of the Committee of Ministers. They maintained that the whole issue would have been disposed of with relatively little publicity and embarrassment if the deputies had adopted the draft resolution in March. At the same time, realising how much contempt the Greek regime might feel as a result of the continuation of the processes relating to the by now infamous report, it advised the British delegation that their policy should be to avoid any initiative to amend the resolution. In general, their instructions cautioned against taking the lead and avoiding as much surface exposure as possible.

Following the temporary suspension of the announcement of the report, the Greek authorities tried to exercise as much pressure as they could bring to bear on Britain in an attempt to influence its voting in the forthcoming meeting of the Committee of Ministers. Ioannis Sorokos, the Greek Ambassador in London described the draft resolution as 'a text for revenge' during his conversation with the Chancellor of the Duchy of Lancaster on 8 April. The Ambassador warned the Chancellor that the Greek regime's relations with the Western allies would be seriously prejudiced if the Committee of Ministers were to decide to adopt the draft resolution agreed by the majority of the ministers' deputies in Strasbourg in March. He argued that the principal reason for his stance was the economic, social and political progress that the regime had made. In addition, he maintained that it was essential for the country to be allowed some time to repair its relations with the member states of the Council of Europe. He also insisted that it would be easier for the Greek government to implement their constitutional timetable in the absence of publicity and controversy about the report. He summarised his point by indicating that 'if the Committee of Ministers adopted the present draft, the Greek government would quote defend itself and retaliate unquote.'[57]

In reply to this, Mr Thompson had no alternative but to honestly report to the Greek Ambassador that the overwhelming mood of the majority of member countries was to endorse the draft; hence, it would be exceptionally difficult for the British government to oppose it. A number of recent reports of political trials in Greece, including those of Professors Karageorgas and Mangakis and thirty-two other people by an extraordinary court martial in Athens in March and April had outraged British public opinion and made opposition even more pronounced. He continued by arguing that 'if the regime in Athens had enabled the Council of Europe governments to feel confident that satisfactory reme-dial measures would be taken by the Greek regime in good time, or if Greeks had couched their reply to the Secretariat's invitation to be rep-resented at the March meeting in more moderate terms',[58] a different draft could well have emerged. In the light of all this, he observed that the draft was difficult to alter, but he reassured Sorokos that the British representation would do nothing to inflame the proceedings.

In the meantime, the Scandinavian governments had launched a new application on 10 April alleging that the Greek government had vio-lated Articles 3 and 6 of the European Convention of Human Rights dealing with torture and fair trials respectively. In response to this initiative, the British government decided that its line should be 'strictly non-committal'[59] on the grounds that a further round on Greece in the Council of Europe in the near future was highly unlikely to have any real advantage. On the contrary, it was argued that it could be counter-productive as it would unnecessarily overload the Human Rights' machinery and result in its slowing down. The British govern-ment maintained that member countries had already made clear their feelings about the Greek government's internal policies, hence their attention should be focused on guarding against any further deteriora-tion in relations with Greece. The Western Organisations Department concluded that:

> We sympathise with the constructive moves designed to bring about a speedy return to democracy and human rights in Greece. This remains the first objective of our own policy and we hope that by retaining

some bilateral influence in Athens we can continue to work to this end. But such influence as we have in Athens would be seriously jeopardized by our joining in this application.[60]

As we have seen, British officials' decision not to join the Scandinavian countries in their application was not their only action directed towards the achievement of amelioration of Anglo–Greek relations. In fact, British officials had made unremitting efforts to resolve the issues that rocked the Greek regime's trust in them. They had advised Mr Pipinelis to pre-empt Greece's expulsion from the Council of Europe by submitting its resignation, they had shown resolute resistance to any intention of raising the Greek issue within NATO, and were particularly helpful in dealing with the difficulties that had arisen in the NATO subgroup. The extent of British officials' determination to improve their government's rapport with the Greek regime was such that their policies in the early part of 1970 were particularly unpopular among the British public.

Wilson's government lost on both fronts. It failed to assuage the electorate's contempt—at least one factor in its defeat in the June 1970 general election—and the Colonels remained thoroughly displeased. The British Ambassador, in his report regarding the overview of British relations with the Greek regime in 1970, wrote:

> Our own relations with Greece, overcharged with emotion as these tend to be on both sides, fluctuated throughout the year. During the early part of the year my staff and I were conscious of the deep resentment and sense of injury caused by the Council of Europe episode, of which the United Kingdom bore the brunt. Mr Papadopoulos avoided seeing me until November and I had a difficult passage with General Angelis, Head of the Armed Forces, in March. Further trouble arose over the unfortunate scenario at a military course at Old Sarum which a Greek officer was attending, and for a time it looked as though our relations with the military here had foundered permanently. The outcome of the general election at home, however, was greeted with relief and enthusiasm by the regime who assumed at once that a new page could now be turned in our relations.[61]

The extent of the deterioration of Anglo–Greek relations during the Labour government's last months in power becomes obvious when taking into consideration the number of post-election Greek press reports supporting the view that the Greek government was counting on the change of government in Britain to bring about a substantial improvement in Anglo–Greek relations.[62] The British Ambassador observed:

> there has been a marked change in the Greek official attitude and policy towards us since the British General Election; even the more cautious and experienced members of the government entertain high hopes of a new attitude and policy towards Greece. The Greek military in particular, who were the more embittered, have shown the strongest swing.[63]

Britain's change of government in June 1970 was welcomed wholeheartedly by the Greek rulers, who seemed to harbour expectations of greater sympathy from a Conservative administration. A Conservative government, they reasoned, would be more business oriented and 'therefore susceptible to a little gentle blackmail on this basis.'[64]

5

FROM 'UNWARRANTED EXPECTATIONS
OF GREATER SYMPATHY' TO 'SATISFACTORY'
RELATIONS

In contrast to the mistrust generated by the Labour government's policies that gradually became embedded in the Greek Colonels' minds, the Conservatives' coming to power was met with a considerable enthusiasm, notwithstanding several inhibiting factors; those included the Conservatives' belief in 'liberalism', their sensitivity towards the Greek King and their past 'bitter' experience of public outcry against their sale of arms to South Africa.[1] A number of Greek press reports published in the immediate aftermath of the elections supported the view that the Greek government was counting on the change of government in Britain for a substantial improvement in Anglo–Greek relations.[2]

The Colonels based their expectations on previous good contacts with a number of Conservative MPs, including Edward Heath, the new Prime Minister, that they had established when Labour was in power. Another factor was new Foreign Secretary Sir Alec Douglas-Home's well-known conservative credentials. This ardour on the part of the Greek rulers was reflected in the visit of the Greek Foreign Minister to the British Ambassador on the very day Heath's government was sworn in. The Greek Foreign Minister, after expressing his wish for better relations, emphasised his hope that 'both sides continue to show good sense and appropriate control over their nerves whenever contentious matters came up.'[3]

The new Conservative government's pre-electoral emphasis on supporting the NATO framework as the basic pillar of Britain's defence had fuelled the Greek rulers' optimism for greater military cooperation. Furthermore, the Colonels gathered that they would particularly benefit from a likely 'rapid contraction of British influence in the Mediterranean, east of Suez and elsewhere.'[4] Besides, it was expected that a right-wing government would be naturally more inclined to do business with a right-wing dictatorship.

In view of the lack of any serious left-wing scrutiny within the government's ranks it was believed that British dealings with the Colonels were likely to be more accommodating. The Conservative government would not be sensitive to the internal pressures Labour felt—and this 'auspicious point' was also highlighted by the British officials themselves.[5] In fact, just one day after the elections, during a visit paid by the Greek Ambassador in London to Snodgrass and Palmer at the Foreign Office, the latter attested to the new government's limited amenability to either internal or external constraints. In contrast to Labour's susceptibility to 'terrible interparty pressures', the Conservatives were deemed to be less vulnerable to endogenous divisions on the issue; and in any case its party discipline was presented as 'stricter' compared to Labour's whip.[6]

To be sure, a few notable sources of opposition did exist, mostly originating from MP Christopher Montague Woodhouse. A former British secret agent, who parachuted in German-occupied Greece during the Second World War, he was one of the staunchest antagonists of the Colonels in Britain. An acclaimed author of many authoritative studies on Greek history and politics and one of the best informed contemporary British authorities on Greece, he was a rare but firmly critical voice on the Conservative benches, and was prepared to speak out against the idiocies of the Colonels' military dictatorship.

British policies were much more likely to be exposed to right-wing calls for endorsing the Greek right-wing regime as a way of countering the danger of Communism within NATO's underbelly; especially as the British presence east of Suez was the Conservative's greatest sensitivity vis-à-vis Soviet penetration of the Mediterranean',[7] hence their increased interest in their bases in Cyprus and Malta. And such calls, as already noted in previous chapters, did occur quite often during Parliamentary debates when the Conservatives were in opposition.

It did not take long for the Conservative government to become aware of the Colonels' 'unwarranted expectations of greater sympathy for their domestic policy from a conservative government.'[8] In response, the new British officials stressed the need to 'continue to dampen any exaggerated hopes the Greeks may entertain.'[9] They insisted that the optimal course would be to tactfully discourage those hopes by warning them about the new government's attachment to the principles of democratic government, but without deflating their proclaimed commitment to improving their dealings.

At the same time with their strong emphasis on joining the EEC, the Conservatives deemed it imprudent to be seen condoning a military dictatorship in Europe. Thus, at the first official meeting between the British Ambassador in Athens, Michael Stewart, and the Greek Foreign Minister, Panayiotis Pipinelis, the former expressed the view that their bilateral relations had to be considered within the context of Whitehall's deliberations to enter the EEC. Sir Michael Stewart pointed out that his government should avoid alienating EEC country-members, such as the Netherlands and the Federal Republic of Germany—both critics of the Greek regime—as they were of 'utmost importance to Britain in connection with the forthcoming Common Market negotiations.'[10] The British Ambassador therefore tried to temper the Colonels' exorbitant hopes by pleading for their patience with the pretext that this was 'still [a] very new' government.

Indeed, to the dismay of the Greek rulers, the new Conservative government's policies toward the Greek regime did not change dramatically—at least not initially. According to a confidential report about British policy towards Greece 'the objectives of our policy towards Greece should remain those set out in the then Secretary of State's dispatch of 20 June 1968'.[11] The only noticeable shift came not on the basic principles but in a 'change of style'[12] 'with the aim of improving the present working relationship.'[13] This was evident through the consideration of suggestions such as sending a friendly message to the Greek government, arranging a Greek ministerial visit to Britain, abstaining from condemning the resolution on Greece at the International Labour Organisation Conference, and making military cooperation less grudging by streamlining some procedures for transferring armaments.[14]

British policy towards the Greek Colonels was not the highest priority on the new government's agenda, as other turbulent issues, such as the troubles in Northern Ireland, necessitated much prompter action and closer attention. Nevertheless, the new government did not miss the opportunity to reassert the importance it attached to Greece especially vis-à-vis NATO. Sir Michael Stewart reassured the Greek Foreign Minister that any official Greek requests for the availability of British arms for Greece would be granted careful consideration.[15]

This statement was particularly targeted at mending fences with the by then rather embittered Greek Armed Forces. In order to prove the validity of their reassurances, the British officials decided to grant approval to Greek requests for forty-four torpedoes and engines for patrol boats. They also agreed to process a few others, including anti-tank guns,[16] in sharp contrast to Labour's overall more cautious stance. Although the new government emphasised the need to avoid advertising it, as 'the South African arms issue was still a major political issue in the UK',[17] it continued to insist on the exigency to 'actively promote such sales'[18]—and this was obvious to the Greek rulers too.[19]

Thus, with regard to the issue of enhancing military cooperation, a certain shift in British policy was detectable. In other words, the new British government adopted 'flexibility on questions of military cooperation and arms supply'[20] in order to improve the record of Anglo–Greek trade mainly in the form of armaments. To this end, in juxtaposition to Labour's previous restriction on arms that could be used to repress the internal population, a decision was reached favouring conciliatory responses to all requests for arms. The government realised that given the niche created by the Greek government's serious need of new equipment, it had to become more pro-active, just as the West Germans and French had done, in order to derive comparable financial benefits. It should be borne in mind that the financial situation the Conservatives inherited from their predecessors was critical, with serious inflation contributing greatly to a sense of a spiralling crisis.

Meanwhile, military cooperation was due to be facilitated via the exchange of visits and participation in courses. Expediency became the order of the day, as can be seen in a note from the Foreign Secretary, who after being informed of the sale of the latest French tanks to Greece, claimed that 'we are handicapping ourselves too much and we should go out for business with them particularly in the air and naval fields.'[21] Consequently, British officials wanted to dispel the impression that the Greek government might have of them 'still being cold-shouldered.'[22]

A serious blow to Whitehall's positive predisposition towards the Colonels was dealt as a result of the death of Foreign Minister Pipinelis in July, which was widely accepted to be a 'major loss for the regime.'[23] Experienced diplomat par excellence, he was one of the very few members of the Greek government whom the British held in high esteem and whose credibility was substantially augmented thanks to his commitment to negotiating a viable modus vivendi with the Turks. The British Ambassador was moved to comment that 'we in Britain and particularly in this Embassy have lost a friend.'[24] On another occasion, he noted that 'the death of Mr Pipinelis makes it probable that Greek reactions to difficulties in NATO will be dictated more by wounded national pride than by detached assessment of the national interest.'[25]

Pipinelis' death deprived the Colonels of a balanced voice in the running of foreign affairs. The situation was further complicated by his succession by Prime Minister Papadopoulos, who added the Ministry of Foreign Affairs to a portfolio that already included the Ministry of Defence. Fearful of the deepening of the rumoured rift with his regime's hardliners and the public's growing dissatisfaction, mainly due to his overt accumulation of power, Papadopoulos attempted to pacify his opponents by asking another veteran diplomat to assist him in the conduct of foreign affairs. Christos Xanthopoulos-Palamas, former Ambassador in Washington and Papadopoulos' newly appointed deputy in Foreign Affairs, was weighed up as having notable acumen by the British Foreign Office. Although aware of his lack of the 'exceptional strength of character... the skill ... and the international stature of Mr Pipinelis',[26] the Foreign Office was also conscious of the paucity of viable alternatives. The note drafted on Xanthopoulos-Palamas drew particular attention to his anti-Americanism and Gaullist sympathies, which hinted at an increase in the influence of the French Embassy at the possible expense of British interests, most likely in the commercial sector[27]—a prospect that was rather disturbing.

The British Embassy in Athens feared that these changes at the helm of the Greek Ministry of Foreign Affairs would render 'normal business with the Ministry more difficult to transact than in the past.'[28] Furthermore, British officials were wary that the impact of such developments would transcend the purely bilateral Anglo–Greek relations and spread to other issues pertaining to their interests. More specifically, they argued that the absence of Pipinelis' astute diplomatic manoeuvres, together with the increased influence of the hardliners, would most likely give rise to renewed calls for reconsideration of Greece's membership of NATO.

Concurrent regional events of strategic bearing highlighted the vital importance of the Colonels as one of the very few remaining pro-Western bastions in the eastern Mediterranean. The Colonels naturally capitalised on Middle Eastern tensions by reaffirming Greece's staunch allegiance to NATO. Consequently, Foreign Minister Sir Alec Douglas-Home paid tribute to Greece's increased leverage vis-à-vis growing Middle Eastern strains and signs of Soviet preponderance.[29] The British Ambassador in Athens specifically recommended that the British government should 'ensure that the natural concern for Greek constitutional liberties is not allowed to spill over into the councils of the Alliance.'[30]

Another disquieting factor that further demonstrated the importance of safeguarding Greece's cooperation emerged from the regime's opening up to the Balkan countries in the early 1970s. The regime's rapprochement with its Balkan neighbours included a number of initiatives in political, commercial and consular terms that resulted in the establishing of formal diplomatic relations with Albania for the first time after more than thirty years[31]—and the improvement of relations with Yugoslavia, Bulgaria and Romania. It was unclear whether these initiatives were undertaken in a genuine effort to profit in strategic and financial terms from improved relations or as a way of blackmailing the West—a tactic not entirely alien even to previous democratically elected governments. However, they succeeded in foregrounding the need not to underestimate Greece's significance within NATO.

Having come to the tacit realisation that there was no incompatibility between Papadopoulos and British interests, the Conservatives decided that they should strive to 'avoid action which would help to strengthen their [hardliners] position at his [Papadopoulos'] expense.'[32] Throughout 1970 attention was focused on the regime's internal rivalries and Papadopoulos' precarious balancing act between the moderates and extremists. The fear always existed that he could be overthrown by internal dissidents, who could be either much more radical and oppressive or exhibit Nasserite tendencies, both options being obviously unwelcome. Such concerns became further ingrained in view of the British Ambassador's assessment that Papadopoulos' 'freedom of manoeuvre and action is considerably less than it was a year or six months ago.'[33] As he bluntly concluded, 'Papadopoulos as moderate should be supported in every appropriate way.'[34]

The British government evaluated Greece's friendliness, of course, in connection with not only NATO, but also its vital interests in Cyprus. Overall, Britain had appeared appreciative of Greece's efforts to 'keep the temperature down and ensure a continuation of the intercommunal dialogue.'[35] They were quickly endorsed by the Turkish authorities, and had yielded improved relations all those years, with the brief intermission of the already examined incident in November 1967. Thus, the Foreign Office recognised that 'the generally sensible policy which the Papadopoulos regime has followed with regard to Cyprus has been very much in our interests.'[36] In addition, British officials who had remained fearful of the Cyprus imbroglio opined that Papadopoulos stood a better chance of preventing the situation from disintegrating than 'any of the immediate alternatives to him as Prime Minister of Greece.'[37] They also emphasised that Papadopoulos was their only hope against 'the further estrangement of Greece from western Europe, which is good for neither Greece nor Europe.'[38]

It was within the context of Greece's enhanced value for British and NATO interests that they scheduled a meeting for the end of September in order to discuss the various developments. Another source of alarm for the Foreign Office was the perceived imperviousness of Greek Chief Military Officers due to their embedded suspicions of the British government. In fact, Reginald Secondé from the Southern European Department confirmed that already in June the incoming government was 'giving thought to how we might now deal with the various sources of friction' with the Greek regime.[39] The issues that were to be addressed included Greece's position within NATO, the sale of British arms to the Greek authorities, British contact with the King, and the British authorities' strong interest in the exchange of official visits.

With regard to the latter, a number of options were put on the negotiation table. The first breakthrough was achieved with the stop-over of Christos Xanthopoulos-Palamas in London on his way to New York, which created a precedent for the eventual positive climate of high-level consultation. The Greek Deputy Foreign Secretary's meeting with Sir Alec Douglas-Home took place on 20 September and ended with the former welcoming 'an extension of British commercial interests in Greece' as it was the government's wish to redirect such opportunities to its 'true friends'.[40] Two days after the meeting, Xanthopoulos-Palamas reflected on his time with the British Foreign Secretary as having been 'constructive and most helpful'[41] and repre-senting a noticeable amelioration in Anglo–Greek relations, which were thought to be 'at a good point'.[42] Three days later, Xanthopoulos-Palamas offered assurances to Sir Thomas Brimelow on behalf of the Greek Prime Minister that 'it would be possible to give British firms a better share of business in Greece.'[43]

The issue of paying a naval visit to Greece was also seriously debated. Although this option was temporarily ruled out, another high-ranking Official Air Chief Marshall Derek Hodgkinson, was sent to Greece at the end of the year following General Angelis' invitation. The British government took this initiative in an effort to provide 'concrete evi-dence of the importance which HMG ... attached to cooperation with the Greek Armed Forces, particularly the air and navy in the Mediterranean'[44]—especially following the news of the opening of a Soviet base close to Alexandria.[45] So positive was the effect of the visit that the argument in favour of additional national visits gained credence on the grounds that they would have a very beneficial effect on the perception of British goodwill by the Athens authorities.

The Conservatives' determination to show more resolve in bridge-building was evidenced by their desire to eliminate various lingering sources of friction with the Greek Colonels, for which the latter held the British responsible. These included trying to contain the intense anti-junta activities of the many Greeks exiled in London, as well as the lengthy and hostile articles in the British press, which had turned London into one of the centre stages of international opposition to the regime. Further thorny issues to be dealt with included the offensive terms often used in formulating questions relating to Greece during Parliamentary debates.

The government therefore decided to take 'any action sanctioned by the law to control or stop any illegal activities of the exiles';[46] indeed even the police and MI5 got involved in several investigations in the UK with a view to clamping down particularly on the activities of resistance organisations, whose aim was to support the domestic anti-Colonels campaign by supplying weapons and explosives, and external resistance by creating and spreading negative propaganda. One of the policy directives issued included the banning of any official contact with Andreas Papandreou, especially during his various London visits, as well as dealings with openly anti-regime members of the British public, such as Richard Clogg, a lecturer at King's College London, who took part in many resistance activities and wrote several scholarly books on Greece. Meanwhile, Martin Packard, a British naval intelligence officer, former peacekeeper with the British Army in Cyprus and active member of the resistance recalls being berated at the British Embassy in Athens for 'conduct prejudicial to good relations between London and Athens' and specifically instructed to 'cut himself off' if he wished to remain in Greece.[47]

British contact with King Constantine was particularly problematic for the Greek leadership and pleas were delivered for open association with him to be restricted. The Foreign Office even advised the Prince of Wales to refrain from attending the baptism of the King's third child in January 1970 despite the two Royal Houses' close familial relations[48]—another striking example of British pragmatism prevailing over symbolism and sentimentalism. The British regretted that the prospects for his return to Greece were bleak, but equally, had no wish to offend the Greek rulers by appearing to condone high profile political figures who had opposed their regime. Meanwhile, a low profile meeting between Edward Heath and the King was described as 'unproductive' as the Prime Minister did not appear forthcoming[49] and another with the new British Ambassador in Athens in July was carefully handled and given minimal publicity. Such attitudes were largely consistent with the previous government's decision to exercise caution and restraint in its dealings with the King, who was offered only discreet consultations and a chance to have an occasional chat with the British officials. It comes as no surprise, therefore, that the Greek Ambassador pointed out in his end-of-year report that British interest in the Greek royal issue had subsided to 'a relatively contained extent'[50] by the end of 1971. There were nevertheless isolated instances when irksome moments did arise in his name, as for instance when Lord Limerick, Parliamentary Under-Secretary for Trade and Industry proposed a toast to the Greek monarch at an official dinner in Athens given in his honour by the Greek government.

Interestingly enough though, British officials did hold unofficial meetings with a number of Greek politicians whom they esteemed highly, such as ex-Foreign Minister Evangelos Averoff in June 1971. Despite the possible complications that such actions could precipitate, they reckoned that it could be 'valuable to keep a line open to Mr Averoff.'[51] This sounding out of future alternatives unavoidably contrasted with their tactfully maintained distance from the King.

Such a policy of minimising pre-existing sources of friction with the Greek government was further accentuated following the 'not-so-encouraging' fact-finding visit to Greece by Reginald Secondé, Head of the Foreign and Commonwealth's Southern European Department. According to his report, 'it remains true to say that the present regime or something like it is likely to be with us for the foreseeable future.'[52] In another document, Papadopoulos was described as 'an adroit political manager',[53] who succeeded in surviving despite the strong pressure he was under from the regime's extremists. Such assessments seemed all the grimmer in view of the rather tepid state of Anglo–Greek relations during the first six months after the Conservatives came to power. Michael Stewart appraised that during the course of 1970 their relations had 'fluctuated disturbingly'.[54]

Consequently, it was felt that a more assiduous effort had to be made to warm up Anglo–Greek relations, especially in 1971. Although British officials considered it wiser to refrain from making public statements in favour of the Colonels' regime, they decided that they would nevertheless support the Greek government in the event of an anti-regime initiative taken by Denmark within NATO. In fact, Greece's cooperation with NATO was deemed so important that the British government was prepared to go so far as 'to compare and contrast importance and contribution in NATO of Greece and Denmark.'[54]

Despite the fact that the NATO meeting in December 1970 was largely uneventful, except for a few easily contained objections raised by the Scandinavians, Athens continued to express scepticism concerning the sincerity of London's commitment to reviving the Greek bond. Greek officials specifically singled out the lack of clear British initiatives at the political level. The British response sought to reassure them that the passage of time was a key determinant in the establishment of a better understanding and a pre-requisite for the strengthening of political cooperation too. British officials kept emphasising the robust domestic pressures stemming from the fact that 'regrettably the eyes of the whole world' were focused on the prospect of democratic elections in Greece.[56]

Nevertheless, though far from crease-free, Anglo–Greek relations became better than at any point during the Labour government's term in office. The one significant change was the Conservatives' decision to row back on their predecessors' number one target, namely Greece's return to democracy. The latter was therefore significantly downgraded and its desirability confined to a passing reference, as outlined in this Foreign Office memorandum:

> The Greeks should not be allowed to forget that Anglo–Greek relations would benefit from the restoration of democracy. But, in reminding them of this, we have to take account of their sensitivity and the possibility that the pursuit of this objective might prejudice those at b [preservation of the military effectiveness of Greece as a NATO ally], c [the protection of British subjects and interests generally and in particular Britain's commercial interests] and d [the preservation of the ability to influence the Colonels in matters of foreign policy, and especially in Cyprus].[57]

A year after the Conservatives had come to power, their dealings with the Greek authorities seemed to be void of any particularly contentious issues and were described as 'satisfactory'.[58] At the same time, a general wish was expressed that 'these relations should be good and constructive and that they should be strengthened, especially within NATO.'[59] Robin Hooper, the newly appointed British Ambassador to Greece, wrote to the British Foreign Secretary, Sir Alec Douglas-Home, in June 1971 that:

> We thus have a considerable interest in the preservation of order and stability in Greece and maintaining—in a time-honored and perhaps by now somewhat part-worn phrase—a good working relation with her

government. This is not to say that we should go out of our way to condone the more unpleasant features of the regime, or that we should identify ourselves with it on an extent which would destroy our prospects of good relations with an eventual more democratic successor. But at least let us be sufficiently civil to Greece's present rulers to prevent them drawing the obvious contrast between the way we treat them and the favours which we shall increasingly be obliged to seek from them; and let us go easy on preaching them sermons whose recommendations we know will not be accepted.[60]

This tactic was to be followed for the remainder of the year despite Papadopoulos' declaration that there would be no change in the political/constitutional order in Greece in 1971. It was common knowledge, though, that Papadopoulos had at the backstage initiated contact with a number of former politicians with a view to eventually transitioning to democratic rule. The optimism that such rumours gave rise to was reflected in comments made by Pavlos Vardinoyiannis, former junior minister in the Papandreou government to the *Times* correspondent Mario Modiano, in which the former stated his absolute conviction that 'Mr Papadopoulos wants to lead the country to parliamentary democracy—the real thing, not anarchy.'[61]

Betraying a similar euphoria, the newly instated British Ambassador was recorded as being 'impressed' by the Athens regime.[62] In a report drafted on the occasion of the fourth anniversary of the Colonels' coming to power, he opined that although 'Greece is a police state ... the government has a general popular acceptance,' mainly because people were living better.[63] In much the same tone, he stated that the country continued to be 'prosperous and orderly'.[64] He obviously failed to acknowledge, or even worse observe, that the regime had managed to consolidate some levels of support throughout the country by pursuing, disciplining and intimidating, to put it mildly, its people and administration. Interestingly enough, however, the Ambassador would admit a year later that 'the regime has ridden [the] crest of [a] wave of economic expansion and growth inspired by former Prime Minister Karamanlis.'[65]

It was therefore concluded that a policy of 'scolding' would be of no benefit. Instead the approach the Conservative government had adopted was gauged as 'about right'.[66] The Greek government's reciprocation was reflected at a meeting between the British Ambassador and the Greek Prime Minister, when the latter admitted that there was 'no lack of goodwill'.[67] Similarly, Papadopoulos in his personal message to the British Foreign Secretary in March 1971 confirmed that they too attached 'great importance to the continuous improvement of these [Anglo-Greek] relations in all domains.'[68] The British for their part stressed that the visits to London of Xanthopoulos-Palamas in September and Angelis in October unquestionably proved their government's positive intentions. As a result they pointed out that although the Greeks were 'obsessively suspicious ... they have now had ample demonstration of our wish to maintain a good working relationship with them.'[69] The Athens Embassy seemed to particularly welcome the fact that such initiatives had a positive bearing on Anglo–Greek relations at the Armed Forces level, which as a result experienced 'a distinct warming'.[70]

Nonetheless minor complications continued to emerge. One instance of tension was experienced in March. As the regime's fourth anniversary approached, the British press launched an assault on the Colonels, with *The Times* even branding the regime a 'tyranny'.[71] At the same time, the 150th anniversary of the inception of the Greek struggle of independence on 25 March 1971 gave rise to several demonstrations in London, including outside the Greek Embassy and in front of Lord Byron's monument on Park Lane. A further complication took place in August with the arrest of Lady Amalia Fleming, a Greek citizen and widow of Sir Alexander Fleming, the world-renowned British scientist who had invented penicillin; she was charged with conspiring to free Alexandros Panagoulis, who had attempted to assassinate Papadopoulos. Even on this occasion, however, tensions did not escalate to the same degree as in the past, and the British noted that overall Lady Fleming had been fairly treated. This was rather unsurprising as the regime, obviously aware of her high status in view of her late husband's international recognition, made sure that she was not mistreated; not only that, but it also seized the opportunity to promote her as a showcase of their decent handling of their prisoners—much in the same way as they had done with other high profile prisoners in the past, like Mikis Theodorakis and Andreas Papandreou.

Before long the establishment of the European–Atlantic Action Committee on Greece added irritants. It was founded in the summer of 1971 under the chairmanship of Sir Hugh Greene, the recently retired Director-General of the BBC, with the purpose of making representations against the 'blot on the political map of Europe' that the military dictatorship in Greece represented and with the conviction that 'international action can play a very important part in restoring democracy in Greece.'[72] It was the offspring of the European Atlantic Group that was set up in 1954 to provide a regular forum to discuss developments within the European and Atlantic Communities and maintain contacts with members of both Houses of Parliament, Diplomats and Civil Servants in London.

It promulgated a declaration calling for 'effective action within the EEC and NATO for the restoration of democracy in Greece'[73] and received a substantial boost in September with the adoption by the NATO Assembly of a resolution urging governments and members of the Alliance to press for the restoration of democracy in Greece. However, the official mechanism of NATO remained untouched by such calls and no further action ensued. As the British repeatedly claimed, both out of conviction and as a means of placating Greek reactions, 'pressure in NATO is unlikely to accelerate the restoration of democracy and could even delay it.'[74] In another effort to avoid enraging the Colonels, the latter were offered assurances that 'although the declarations [of the EAACG] had been signed by a number of Conservative MPs (including the highly esteemed Monty Woodhouse), this did not of course mean that the organisation enjoyed government support.'[75]

Furthermore, the rumoured replacement of Ioannis Sorokos, the Greek Ambassador in London, who had 'performed his duties excellently for 2½ years'[76] by Nikolaos Broumas, a General lacking in previous diplomatic experience, aroused a fair degree of scepticism. At the same time, Xanthopoulos-Palamas' resignation on 20 December caused further disquiet, as it was generally accepted that it would be difficult for the current government to find an equally able successor. Such concerns were for the moment dispelled as he was persuaded by the Colonels to postpone his resignation for another year, when he was finally replaced with Phaidon Anninos-Kavalieratos.

Despite these instances of tension, relations remained largely stable in 1971. Upon receiving the new British Ambassador, Sir Robin Hooper, in March 1971, the Greek Prime Minister spoke of 'satisfactory' relations between their two countries.[77] One aspect of this good working relationship was reflected on the increase of Britain's exports to Greece, which were 'running at an annual rate of £58 million (£805 million at today's value) compared with £54 in 1970, an increase of almost 8%'; at the same time, 'exports of ships had risen exceptionally from 2.8 million (£42.5 million at today's value) in 1970 to 14.3 million (£198.5 million at today's value) in 1971, an increase of 400%, not unsatisfactory despite the 36% decrease of exports from Greece to Britain.'[78]

This was not, needless to say, the fruit of any major advances towards democratisation. In fact, the British regretted that in the political sphere the situation had changed very little in the course of 1971. In August, Papadopoulos undertook a reshuffle with the aim of putting civilian ministers at the helm of most departments even at the expense of two members of the initial triumvirate, namely Brigadier Pattakos and Colonel Makarezos, who were significantly downgraded. Papadopoulos employed such tactics, including the relaxation of martial law in April, as proof of his genuine wish to return the country to democratisation 'when the conditions permitted'—a catch phrase he liked to use frequently to delay this process indefinitely. Britain assessed that in essence little had changed, especially as those new officers in charge, although quite competent, were primarily the 'Prime Minister's men'.

A series of other relevant developments within the Cold War context were occurring apace. With regard to Greek–Turkish relations, the 1971 Turkish coup brought to power a military government, which was familiar with the political and social militarisation taking place in Greece and regarded the Colonels as a significant opportunity to reach a consensus on matters of mutual concern. As a result, with the American government's encouragement a period of vigorous negotiations began between Greece and Turkey in an effort to establish a constructive dialogue and find a common resolution to their disputes. This was undoubtedly facilitated by the fact that the two NATO members were brought together by strong feelings of anti-socialism within the wider framework of Cold War politics.

The apogee of the Greek regime's diplomacy was reached with the visit to Athens in December of General İsmet İnönü, leader of the Turkish Republican People's Party. Britain was undoubtedly gratified by the fact that Greece had made the amelioration of their relations with Turkey its top foreign policy objective. At the same time, and despite the various Balkan rapprochements, the regime continued to confirm its allegiance to NATO. As a result, the British Defence Attaché in Athens noted at the end of 1971 that Greece was 'wedded firmly in NATO'.[79] The visits to Greece of various allied commanders in 1971 culminating in the December visit of Dr Joseph Luns, the Secretary-General himself, affirmed such assessments. Further signs of intense NATO activity included the large-scale NATO exercises and major NATO conferences hosted by Greece.

This loyalty, especially evidenced by Greece's accommodating stance during the Black September crisis in Jordan that erupted in 1970, was partly attributed to Nixon's decision to lift the arms embargo and resume heavy arms shipments. Papadopoulos' approval of the operation 'Fig Hill' for the provision of Jordanian relief via Athens during the 1970–71 crisis, just like the Six-Day war in 1967, clearly proved the need to safeguard Greek cooperation. At the same time, American Ambassador in Athens Henry Tasca recorded that 'in November 1970 alone, units of the sixth fleet made more than 250 calls to Greek ports',[80] further underlining the critical importance of the Greek role in the defence of NATO interests in the Mediterranean. Moreover, Malta's new Prime Minister, Dom Mintoff's decision to close down the US military base and impose restrictions on duty-free fuel further highlighted Greece's logistical contribution. The Greek government seeing in this development yet another window of opportunity consented to making staging and refueling facilities available in Crete.[81] As was remarked during a meeting of the Greek Ambassador with Anthony Royle and Charles Wiggin from the Foreign Office, Greece's significance for NATO is linked to a) the alliance's South-East flank, b) Cyprus—although the British bases on the island were not connected with NATO, they largely serve the alliance's scope, c) the Eastern Mediterranean, which has become a serious place of contention in view of the Arab–Israeli rivalries and the developments in Malta.[82]

Britain's commitment to avoiding any talks on the suspension of Greece from NATO became manifest yet again before the next NATO ministerial meeting at the end of December. The British Foreign and Commonwealth Secretary went so far as to meet with his Danish colleague in order to discourage him from initiating any talks on Greece's poor progress towards democracy. In the meantime, he spared no opportunity to bring such initiatives to the attention of the Greek government. As a consequence of the efforts of both governments, the British Ambassador could admit to being on easy terms with most government and senior military officers. In fact in the end-of-year report he particularly noted that 'Anglo–Greek relations on the military side have been warm and a pleasant contrast to the immediately preceding years.'[83]

At the same time, the Greek side characterised the British stance as 'pragmatic', as they realised that the West had to remain united vis-à-vis 'the Communist East, whether it was employing Cold War tactics (e.g. increase of Soviet naval presence) or pursuing *détente* (e.g. through proposals for mutual force reduction).'[84] The notable, albeit rather short-lived decrease in tensions was also, according to the Greek Foreign Ministry, attributable to the strengthening of Greece's international standing.[85] Greek officials admitted, however, that the Conservatives' initiatives did not come easy, and further commented on the variety of factors that might have influenced British anti-Hellenism, including past memories of EOKA (the National Organisation of Cypriot Fighters), their pro-Turkish feelings and their paradoxical complex of both inferiority and superiority towards the Greeks.[86] In addition, the Greek Ambassador in London in his end-of-year report of Anglo–Greek relations likened the British government's concerns over human rights abuses in Greece to a 'covering robe, which they put on or take off according to their various objectives' as it had been 'amply proved repeatedly in Northern Ireland.'[87] Although the Conservative government introduced no groundbreaking novelties in its policy towards the Colonels, their efforts testified more to just their proclaimed 'change of emphasis and style.'[88]

Sir Robin Hooper remained adamant that his government could show even greater commitment to reaching an understanding with the Colonels. No doubt putting Hooper at the helm of the British Embassy in Athens contributed as much as wider international developments to increased cooperation with the Greek government. Hooper's insistence on trying 'to seek more opportunities within the limits of existing policy to demonstrate our interest in Greece,'[89] constituted an unmistakable departure from his predecessor's cautious policy. In fact, Hooper was, during his meeting with the Greek King, said to be 'rather impressed'[90] by the government in Athens. This conviction was reinforced by a statement in which he compared the Greek Prime Minister with Charles de Gaulle[91]—and, despite de Gaulle's famously fraught relations with London during the Second World War and negotiations surrounding British entrance into the Common Market, it was clear that the comparison was not made 'with the intention of insulting the French President.'[92] At times, when the British government was seriously engaged with a number of inflammatory issues, such as the troubles in Northern Ireland, Foreign Office officials like Hooper certainly enjoyed greater leeway in influencing British foreign perceptions and policy.

Hooper's more pro-active stance is well brought out in the following paragraph, which concluded his annual review for 1971:

> There are obvious limitations on HMG's freedom of action. But it seems to me that even without those limitations, we are being a bit unimaginative and doing less than we could or should to keep our relationships with the Greek government in repair. Unless we make a determined effort not only to do this but to put ourselves positively on the map, we shall lose out politically—and slip back economically and culturally—under pressure from rivals with less inhibitions.[93]

Despite Hooper's realisation that it was quite difficult to communicate with Papadopoulos, whom he described as 'a strange little man', the latter's regime appeared to be firmly entrenched and the alternatives were less alluring. There existed in his view, then, the realistic need to draw on their valuable intangible assets in Greece. Such suggestions found a number of Foreign Office officials rather perplexed as they considered that a modus vivendi had already existed between the two governments.[94] As the following chapter will highlight, even Hooper soon became more reticent in expressing the urgent need to engage further with the Colonels, due to a number of developments that led to yet another cooling phase.

6

'A POLICY OF "DOING GOOD BY STEALTH"'[1]

The previous chapter discussed the effect the change of government in Britain had on its relations with the Colonels up to the end of 1971. This generally good working relationship, void of 'negative points',[2] was put to the test in 1972 as a result of the Colonels' increasing demands, as well as the emergence of a number of additional vexing issues, such as the two countries' dealings with the EEC. This chapter will account for the various complications which Anglo–Greek relations experienced during 1972 and the first half of 1973, and will contextualise them within the other concurrent British foreign policy concerns.

The most pressing preoccupation of the British Foreign Office at that time was the crisis in Northern Ireland, which reached a new climax with the Bloody Sunday massacre in January 1972. The violent hostility that erupted between the British government and the IRA was unprecedented and rapidly escalating, consuming most of the government's energy. Whatever capacity remained was directed at securing the prospects of Britain's entry into the EEC. In fact, Britain's long desired admittance to the EEC, although a naturally welcome event, proved to be a watershed for Anglo–Greek relations.

In light of these mounting challenges, British foreign officials sought to avoid opening up further areas of friction; consequently, they clearly wished their dealings with Greece to continue on the same solid footing that their previous eighteen months in power had witnessed. This desire did not mean that British officials were unwary of the stiffening reflexes of the Greek regime and the collapse of the Greek–Turkish inter-communal talks that also took a toll on its image. Though the regime's concessions were expected to be followed by the relaxation of restrictions on constitutional liberties, such hopes were shattered in 1972.

An initial indication of the reversal of the trend was Papadopoulos' unconstitutional assumption of the Regency in March, when he replaced his appointee General Zoitakis. This was undertaken due to the latter's alleged siding with 'disgruntled former revolutionaries, who disapproved of Mr Papadopoulos' methods and his tendency to concentrate all power in his hands.'[3] This resulted in further accumulation of unrestricted personal authority. The intransigence, which characterised his rule yet again, was exemplified by a number of incidents, beginning with the arrests of students protesting against the increasingly sclerotic regime and culminating in internationally-renowned economics professor Ioannis Pesmatzoglou's banishment to a remote village in May. The Pesmatzoglou case gave rise to public outcry in Britain, and caused widespread protest across the political spectrum. Anthony Royle from the British Foreign Office therefore underlined to the Greek Ambassador that in light of such developments and the resultant pressures, it would be very difficult indeed for the British government to avoid re-examining its policy.[4] British scepticism was further exacerbated following the re-incorporation of the hardliners Ioannis Ladas and Konstantinos Aslanidis in the regime's inner circle as a result of the governmental reshuffle in August, a year after they were removed, on the basis that 'he [Papadopoulos] felt that they no longer posed much of a threat to him.'[5] No doubt any close observer could not but wonder whether it was the exact opposite belief that prompted Papadopoulos to reintegrate them so as to contain the threat they posed.

One additional indication of the regime's growing intolerance was reflected in its handling of the Mangakis affair in April. George Mangakis, a German-educated Greek university professor, whilst being tried for attempting to topple the Greek military regime managed to escape to the Federal Republic of Germany thanks to arrangements made possible by its Embassy in Athens. Such interventions—at US, French or British instigation—had previously resulted in the release of other internationally known personalities including MP Andreas

Papandreou, composer Mikis Theodorakis, and Lady Amalia Fleming, as well as tortured prisoners, whose testimonies at international organisations were instrumental in proving beyond doubt the regime's authoritarian character and systematic use of torture.

However, the regime's indignation on this specific occasion served as an additional signal of its uncompromising approach to acts of foreign interference. Prime Minister Papadopoulos, accusing 'some foreigners and their lackeys' of carrying out 'an unprecedented act of gangsterism,' abruptly declared the West German Ambassador Peter Limbourg persona non grata.[6] This was of couse not the first time the regime had barred the entrance of foreign officials into the country: for instance Max van der Stoel, the Council of Europe's Rapporteur on Greece, accused by the Colonels of being a Communist stooge, had also been declared persona non grata. But there was a big difference between the attitude of the Council of Europe and that of the Federal Republic of Germany towards the Colonels, which meant that this latest incident was perceived abroad as a 'vigorous reminder of how hysterically the regime can react to what they regard as attempts to interfere in their domestic affairs.'[7] It also prompted the British government to adopt a less engaged stance towards the Colonels, described as a 'cautious middle-of-the-road policy'.[8]

Despite the anxiety that these initiatives generated, the British Ambassador interpreted them as confirmation of Papadopoulos' unassailable position. He clearly failed to note that the over-accumulation of power in Papadopoulos' hands and his occasional and deliberate acts of bravado were rather spasmodic responses to his slowly eroding support base. In spite of potential threats emanating from discontented military officers, the British still reckoned that, thanks to 'his talent for political management' Papadopoulos would be able to contain them by taming his internal rivals, just as he had for the previous five years.' It was therefore reiterated that 'we [the British government] must expect the regime, or something like it, to be with us for the foreseeable future.'[9]

In light of such estimates, Hooper kept emphasising that, while watching carefully and exercising caution, dealings with the Greek government should proceed as normal as Britain needed 'Greece in NATO and over Cyprus and we must safeguard our national and economic interests.'[10] Thus, at the beginning of 1972, the British Ambassador spoke of 'a more favourable' British foreign policy towards the Greek government. Specific reference was made rather often to 'the warm and pleasant state of relations' with the Greek Armed Forces, a development attributed to the Conservatives' determination to cultivate the good working relationship that their predecessors had failed to achieve.[11] At the same time, British officials during a routine meeting with their Greek counterparts were 'expressing satisfaction at the improvement in Anglo–Greek relations during the last two years, and highlighted that the current British government had no intention of mingling with [Greece's] internal affairs.'[12] This realpolitik approach towards Anglo–Greek relations was also noted by the Greek authorities, who confirmed that it had continued unabated during 1972.[13]

Quite unsurprisingly, therefore, Britain's inability to translate its good relations into tangible benefits for the British economy, mainly in the form of arms sales, caused a substantial degree of dismay. Notwithstanding the Conservatives' unremitting efforts to increase them, the record was still 'poor'[14] and the prospects remained 'uncertain'.[15] When accounting for this, the British Defence Attaché in Athens invoked various explanations including the Greeks' proclivity for American armaments, their 'Byzantine' style of negotiation, their foreign exchange strains and the current difficulties in repaying 'the recent French and German loans for tanks, fast patrol boats and submarines.'[16] Given this relative stagnation, the British Ambassador in Athens continued to reiterate the need to be more pro-active, including acceding to the Colonels' wishes for British official visits to be organised. As Hooper specifically pointed out, 'naturally one would like to see it [more forthcoming British policy] result in the purchase of British military equipment'[17] and he recommended that suitable opportunities should be sought.[18]

The visits of American Vice-President Spiro Agnew and French officials in October 1971 and January 1972 respectively seemed to strengthen Hooper's conviction about the need for Britain to actively show its goodwill. He opined that such visits juxtaposed Britain's reluctance to appear as eager, which would in turn leave the French 'one up',[19] especially when it came to the contested field of trade prospects. As a means of keeping the 'momentum going', Hooper encouraged the arrangement of a visit by Lord Carrington, Secretary of Defence, as he judged this to be a move that 'would go down extremely well.'[20] This stance was grounded not only in his assessment that 'with the Greeks … one has to run quite hard to stay in the same place, let alone advance',[21] but also in the official statistics, which clearly revealed a sharp decline in Britain's share of the Greek market. This was tantamount to 8 per cent, placing it in fifth position behind the Federal Republic of Germany, Italy, France and the US.[22]

Another vexing issue for British officials at the time was the breakdown of Greek–Turkish negotiations following the deadlock of intercommunal talks in September 1971. Despite all parties' agreement to resume talks in January 1972, this prospect was torpedoed by the crisis which arose in February over Archbishop Makarios' importation of a large consignment of Czech arms. The impasse was surmounted when Makarios succumbed to Greek pressure to entrust the arms to UNFICYP control, and talks resumed in the following June. Ambassador Hooper, during one of his routine meetings with Papadopoulos, expressed specific concern over the failure of the Greek Prime Minister's initiative on Cyprus, an evaluation which, despite being rejected by Papadopoulos, certainly represented the stalemate that the once promising discussions had reached. The deteriorating atmosphere was further reflected in the Embassy's annual review for 1972, according to which in the context of Greek–Turkish relations, 'Cyprus and Grivas remain a time bomb with a fuse of unknown length.'[23]

So concerned was Hooper that he even confided his fears to his American counterpart during their meeting in early February. His apprehension was further aggravated by his estimate that 'Papadopoulos was not as confident as he appeared.'[24] In addition, during his meeting with Xanthopoulos-Palamas, he tried to persuade the latter to make a statement to the effect that Greece continued to abide by the London and Zurich Agreements and that it welcomed the resumption of intercommunal talks. This tense atmosphere in Greek–Turkish relations was clearly at the forefront of Britain's policy towards Greece for the fear of igniting a serious crisis over Cyprus, leading to a 'serious political or military loss of face for Mr Papadopoulos' government',[25] and even its demise. Needless to say that from such estimates we may infer that Britain was placated with his regime as long of course as it continued to serve British interests.

Hooper's colleagues in the Southern European Department, more susceptible to domestic pressures, cautioned him about the risk of appearing too accommodating, as this would provoke public criticism at home. Britain, they reckoned, should be content with the maintenance of its 'modestly successful policy' towards the Colonels.[26] In other words, they seemed by comparison more concerned about the balance they needed to strike in their dealings with the Greeks, which they described as 'delicate'.[27] They believed that it was a challenge for Britain to stay 'on an even keel' both in its relations with the regime as well as with the internal critics.[28] They also admitted to being 'stuffy' in relation to the Ambassador's pressures for more pro-active actions, and promised to become more amenable. This promise was aired following the relatively limited 'public fuss' concerning the Greek regime in 1972.

In the light of such diverse approaches, British policy towards Greece was re-examined in London. Hooper categorically stated that 'the retention at the top of the list of our policy objectives of the "promotion of the return to Greece of constitutional rule and democratic liberties in conditions of stability" had become inappropriate.' Although a number of participants expressed qualms, they appeared convinced that 'outside pressure was not going to achieve this.' Hooper thus summed up the feelings of his colleagues by arguing that their decision, although realistic, was arrived at reluctantly.[29] The meeting concluded that:

> It would be more realistic to confine our objectives to the three approved by the Secretary of State in July 1970, i.e.:
>
> i) To preserve as far as possible the military effectiveness of Greece as a NATO ally;
> ii) To protect British subjects and British interests generally, and in particular to pursue our commercial interests;
> iii) To retain our ability to influence the Greek government in matters of foreign policy, for example, Cyprus.[30]

Although with considerably less fanfare than the Labour government, the Conservatives' policy towards Greece's democratisation amounted to mere lip service. This line was further cemented by the expectation that the Papadopoulos regime, 'which is important to us politically, strategically and economically' was 'likely to be around for some time to come';[31] according to a report in September 1972, the regime was 'digging in for a long 15-year haul.'[32]

Fully aware of the potential public outcry, participants in the meeting particularly emphasised that 'our objectives, and any change in them, are not made public'.[33] At the same time, they agreed that the sale of arms to Greece should be pursued more vigorously; especially as they noted with relief that parliamentary pressures on this matter, following the recent conclusion of the controversy over arms to South Africa and Spain, had eased considerably. The Inter-Departmental Working Party Report on Policy Restraints on Trade evaluated that 'the only remaining restriction of arms sales to Greece is the need to exercise a certain degree of caution to take into account the possible parliamentary repercussions.'[34] With regard to the discussions about the ministerial visit, however, the Foreign Office was sceptical, as the benefits of such a visit were thought to be outweighed by the adverse publicity it would most likely attract.[35]

This reaffirmation of the British government's determination to do serious business with their Greek counterparts was particularly encouraged by Hooper, who continued to press for a British ministerial visit. He pointed out the Colonels' awareness of the British Secretary of State's visit to Francoist Spain and the adverse effect of British intransigence in denying the Colonels' regime a similar gesture of goodwill. While endorsing the conclusions of the meeting on Greece, he insisted that 'the objectives in para 4 (a), (b) and (c) of the 11 February record will be much easier to achieve if we do so [keep our contacts in repair].'[36]

Before the first British official visit to Greece took place, the Greek government sent Dimitris Tsakonas, the new Under-Secretary for Foreign Affairs to London, on an unofficial visit in May. Aside from the usual compliments, which were followed up by mutual assurances about the 'friendly'[37] relations among the two governments, the new element in their relations that stood out from this meeting was Greece's efforts to secure British support for the thaw of the freeze imposed by the EEC on its Treaty of Association immediately after the Colonels' coup. As Brigadier Baxter British Defence Attaché in Athens related in his end-of-year report, the Colonels 'look to Britain to pull her chestnuts out of the fire in Brussels.'[38]

A number of comments made by British officials reveal that the British government was not in principle opposed to the idea of mustering support for the Greek political claims within the EEC, as it was widely recognised that this would result in their gaining 'a share of the civilian public contracts.'[39] Instead, their apprehension arose from the unfeasibility in practical terms of such an undertaking in view of Britain's newly granted admission to the EEC. They were painfully aware of the weak bargaining power of their country, which had already been denied entry twice, in 1963 and 1967. An additional aggravating factor was associated with the fact that Norway and Denmark, fierce critics of the Greek regime, were scheduled to join the EEC concurrently. They thus deemed it wise to dampen the Greek regime's high hopes by expressing the conviction that their government's wish to contribute to Greece's accession would be 'particularly facilitated, if need be, by the speedy restoration of democracy.'[40]

It was no secret that the Greek regime was facing fresh tides of criticism. This was the result of Papadopoulos' taking the extreme measure of arresting tens of students following demonstrations at Athens University in an effort to placate hardliners. So concerned were the British officials that Hooper, in view of 'a worse press abroad than usual'[41] expressed slight doubts about the prospects of an official British ministerial visit to Athens.[42] He advocated a wait-and-see approach.[43] At the same time, he confided to his American colleague in Athens that while 'he [was] fully prepared as Ambassador to be expendable to meet UK national interests', he was 'not willing to be [a] sacrificial lamb for political opposition to present regime to further their ends.'[44]

Ironically enough, by the time Hooper's slight shift occurred, his colleagues in the Foreign and Commonwealth Office seemed convinced of the need to demonstrate perseverance. Their stance—pragmatic, to put it mildly—was embodied in the following statement by Andrew Palmer, who was of the opinion that 'the pendulum of repression will continue to swing; Greece's allies will continue to take their turn in the dog-house.'[45] Indeed, the Foreign Office repeated this view on a number of occasions, albeit less cynically. On another occasion, Brooke Turner commented that 'in light of the interests we have in Greece, I do not consider that the pursuit of these should be affected by the undoubted evidence of a recent hardening on the regime's internal policies.'[46] What seemed to worry the British officials most was the intensifying student unrest, which was seen as a 'set-back in recent months to the slow process of liberalisation.'[47]

It is telling for instance that in spite of the Colonels' veering to extremes, British officials eventually ruled in favour of arranging a ministerial visit in order to palliate Papadopoulos' marked dissatisfaction about their government's unforthcoming stance towards official visits.[48] However, as caution was required in handling this potentially inflammatory matter, they asked Defence Secretary Lord Carrington to combine his customary summer holiday in Greece with a last-minute low-profile visit to the Greek government. They put forward this suggestion in order to 'keep pace with others such as the French and the Americans' and 'to assuage Greek susceptibilities ... while minimising the risk of hostile criticism here [Britain].'[49]

The proposed visit took place between 6 and 7 September and included meetings with Papadopoulos, Pattakos and Xanthopoulos-Palamas. Lord Carrington was specifically instructed to make openings to Pattakos to the effect that his government 'would be very willing to supply whatever arms Greece required for NATO purposes.'[50] As Sir Thomas Brimelow also highlighted during his meeting with the Greek Ambassador in London, Heath's Conservative government manifested 'increased interest in matters of defence in comparison with its predecessor Labour government.'[51]

However, to the slight disappointment of the British it failed to provide the anticipated breakthrough in relations.[52] The Colonels did not deem his visit of ministerial calibre, as they opined that 'he [Lord Carrington] was simply making a brief break of convenience in his holiday.'[53] His encounter with Papadopoulos failed to extract anything more tangible than the Greek Prime Minister's vague assurances about his intention to bring about the restoration of democracy in Greece, as well as the by then worn-out confirmation that he had noticed 'a satisfactory recovery in Anglo–Greek relations in the economic and defence fields, though this had yet to be extended to the political level.'[54] The latter point assumed further significance in the context of the Colonels' view that 'trade relations could only prosper in an atmosphere of friendly political relations.[55]

With regard to the Cyprus issue, Lord Carrington, after expressing to Xanthopoulos-Palamas his government's support for the inter-communal talks, reaffirmed Britain's wish to refrain from getting involved by stand-ing 'in the crossfire between the parties'; he also insisted about the need to reach a settlement acceptable to all parties involved. He nonetheless specified that should a situation emerge that might jeopardise the consid-erable British interests in the area, then 'a more active policy would be necessary.'[56] Ironically, the course of events in July 1974 in retrospect made such statements of intentions look rather spurious.

Despite realising that the visit was rather 'unremarkable',[57] the Foreign Office still deemed it useful as the first initiative taken in the direction sketched out during the recent meeting on Greece.[58] Paradoxically, the visit was treated by the press both in England and Greece as denoting no major development. In stark contrast, a number of questions raised in the British Parliament reflected the low levels of leniency among political circles. Both in Parliament and publicly via a BBC interview, Lord Carrington defended his visit to Greece on the following grounds, which constituted one of the basic pillars of British foreign policy. He specifically argued that:

> It never seemed to be necessary that you should approve of the politics or the manner of a regime in order that you should have ordinary rela-tions... So this does not seem to me to be really a very exceptional circumstance. I also—and my country—happen to think that Greece is a very important part of NATO—and what happens in the South East of Europe and the survival of Greece and of Turkey is a matter of enor-mous substance to NATO, and therefore as Greece is a member of the NATO Alliance and so we are, we must be friends.[59]

In the light of such pragmatic considerations, the Foreign Office ruled in favour of arranging a visit by another minister to Greece, this time in an official capacity. However, instead of yielding to the regime's pressures to send the Foreign Secretary, they thought it preferable that their first official visitor to Athens should not be more political than a 'technical minister';[60] hence their decision to send Lord Limerick, Parliamentary Under-Secretary at the Department of Trade and Industry. In this way, they aspired to promote their interests in Greece whilst minimising public outcry. Besides, both Heath's government and its predecessor always strove to draw a distinction between 'trade and politics', which 'should not be confused.'[61]

Lord Limerick arrived in Athens on the last day of October, two weeks after the conclusion of the week-long visit to London of the

Commander of the Greek Navy, Vice-Admiral Konstantinos Margaritis. Central to the aim of his visit was the promotion of commercial prospects in Greece; emphasis was placed on confining his discussions to commercial, economic and trade matters and refraining from commenting on politics.[62] He was specifically instructed that if his interlocutors touched upon British assistance for the reactivation of Greece's Association Agreement with the EEC, he should express sympathy, but appear non-committal by clarifying that until it had formally become a member of the Community, Britain's leverage was constrained.[63]

During his meeting with Nikolaos Makarezos, Deputy Prime Minister and the regime's chief economic policy-maker, Lord Limerick vigorously explained how committed Britain was to regaining 'her rightful place in the league table of suppliers of the needs of Greece.'[64] To this open call, Makarezos replied by promising that 'favourable consideration' would be applied to 'British bids for public sector contracts, provided they [we]re competitive';[65] he reciprocated on the last day of his visit by expressing his conviction that with regard to Anglo–Greek trade, there were more opportunities than obstacles.[66]

Although it can therefore be argued that the first ministerial visit concluded on a promising note, it should not be overlooked that, according to Hooper, it was a harbinger of future complications in Anglo–Greek relations arising from Greece's pressure on Britain vis-à-vis its relations with the EEC.[67] This became particularly manifest during Lord Limerick's discussion with the Greek Under-Secretary for Foreign Affairs, when the latter openly sought Britain's support on entry.'[68] In fact, Hooper's following assessment fully illustrates the chasm between the expectations each government cultivated with regard to its relation with the other:

> ... the visit has shown very clearly that there is a difference of approach between ourselves—whose objectives are primarily commercial and concerned mainly with bilateral trade—and the Greeks, whose objective, ... has been predominately to secure our support, after we enter the EEC, in achieving their aims there.[69]

Five days later when reporting on the recent British official visit, the British Ambassador repeated his opinion that 'the Greeks no doubt wished to suggest that our [British] chances of getting a greater share in public sector contracts here depend[ed] upon the degree of political support we can give them in the EEC.'[70] Such expectations did not bode well for the future of Anglo–Greek relations, especially as he rightly observed that within the context of the EEC his government would have 'more important fish to fry.'[71]

In the meantime, in November 1972 Hooper was sharing with the American diplomatic mission in Athens the view that Papadopoulos' position was 'weaker' and that his regime was 'getting shakier'.[72] Both the British and American Ambassadors agreed that the regime's inefficiency was on the rise and the level of government corruption was skyrocketing, while signs of severe strain were beginning to be apparent. Obviously, Hooper's dynamic impression of Papadopoulos seemed to have been substantially tainted as he described him as a weak administrator.

At the same time, and withstanding all previous efforts, Hooper voiced British concerns over the less than impressive British record in winning public sector contracts despite 'a time of rapid economic development in Greece, when British knowledge and technology might have been expected to be in demand.'[73] Although falling short of British expectations, they were described as continuing to hold up, including the recently signed contract for gas turbine generators for a power station in Crete with John Brown Engineering.[74] The prospective difficulty for any increases in Anglo–Greek commercial exchanges was also linked to the Greek rulers' fear about a possible return of Labour to Whitehall resulting in the cancellation of any arms sales.[75] Such concerns were grounded on alarming reports that Labour's left wing 'had succeeded in building a formidable organisation at the grass roots level and would be in a powerful position to fight the next election.'[76] However, faith in the sustainability of good Anglo–Greek relations was instilled on the assumption that 'it would be impossible for a hypothetical future left-wing British Labour government to unscramble even if it wished to do so.'[77]

The British, although clearly disappointed, were not dissuaded from vigorously promoting further contracts. Another British official, this time the Ministry of Defence Sales Manager, was sent to Greece to encourage the sale of missiles and frigates by giving assurances that any potential arms sales contracts would be brought to completion regardless of which party governed Britain. In a clear effort not to fend them off, the Greek officials put their reticence down to the need to weigh up all offers before reaching any decisions.

This was the last British official visit to take place in 1972, and in fact in what remained of the Colonels' time in power. Despite the rather remarkable amounts of energy that the Conservatives devoted to the improvement of their dealings with the Greek government and the relaxation of several inhibitions, their relations, albeit more cordial, failed to bring about the highly anticipated fruits of increased commercial exchanges. The usual complaints pertaining to the British public's largely hostile attitude and the various vociferous campaigns against the Greek regime continued to take their toll. Events such as the publication of less than flattering articles, periodicals and even books about the Colonels' regime in England in 1972, including 'Inside the Colonels' Greece'[78] and 'Greece under military rule',[79] certainly did not help matters. Other impediments arising in 1972 involved the Colonels' fear of a Labour come-back as well as Anglo–Greek relations vis-à-vis the EEC. With regard to the latter, Hooper related:

> The question of British support for Greek objectives in the EEC will be one which will be in the forefront of Greek preoccupations in the coming year; and how we are to confront and if possible, turn to our advantage the pressures to which we shall certainly be subjected will be one of the major problems—if not the major problem—of Anglo–Greek relations in 1973.

Notwithstanding the knotty issues, knottier in 1973 than in 1972, Hooper's end-of-year report stressed the need to continue living with the regime for as long as it lasted. One of the achievements in the domain of Anglo–Greek relations was thought to be that the British:

> have made some further headway in taking the emotional overtones and double standards out of our relations with the regime, and putting these more closely on a footing with the relationships we maintain with other regimes, whose internal policies we deplore, but with which for better or worse we have to live.[80]

Hooper's main argument rested yet again on Greece's relative, even if enforced, domestic stability, which he called the Colonels' 'principal—and sometimes underrated—contribution to this sorely tried country.'[81] He expressed satisfaction at the fact that 'economically Greece continues to prosper', while 'externally the regime had done quite well'; with regard to the latter aspect, however, he appeared sceptical about Xanthopoulos-Palamas' resignation from the position of the alternate Foreign Minister in September. His successor Phaidon Anninos-Kavalieratos, although described as 'amiable', was considered to be less solid and independent-minded; overall 'not [a] particularly impressive successor.'[82] Such estimates gained further significance, as Hooper opined that current alternatives to the Colonels' regime would not necessarily be 'the sort of orderly, liberal, western-orientated set up that would suit [Britain].'[83]

It is noteworthy nonetheless that the British started examining a possible scenario of Karamanlis' return only in 1973, in juxtaposition to the Americans who had been contemplating it much earlier;[84] even then, such options were not considered very seriously. He was mentioned as 'probably the best and perhaps the only person to bring about an orderly transition to democracy,'[85] but it was otherwise felt that the old political establishment was discredited, defeatist and incapable of joining forces.

Hooper's earlier predictions were quite accurate; 1972 was a rather indecisive year, the British Ambassador describing it as 'quiet' and 'in all essentials so inconclusive',[86] while placing specific emphasis on the 'political non-developments.'[87] Despite the fact that in his end-of-year report, the Ambassador still used the adjective 'inconclusive' on the grounds that it was 'still by no means certain in which direction Greece is heading',[88] the beginning of the following year was far from quiet; in the domain of Anglo–Greek relations it could easily be called 'tumultuous'.

The continuation of 'limited progress towards a good working Anglo–Greek relationship', which was witnessed in 1972, was to be put to the test immediately. The very first British concern expressed at the dawn of the new year unsurprisingly related to Greece's serious preoccupations with the EEC; the Greek officials continually made it amply clear that 'the road to the Ministry of National Economy ran through the Ministry of Foreign Affairs.'[89] British officials, on the other hand, were instructed to tactfully refrain from cultivating the Greek rulers' hopes that the Foreign Office could 'help them overcome the fundamental (i.e. institutional) obstacles in the way of their eventual full membership of the Community.'[90]

It was not only a matter of whether the British could help in this endeavour, but also of whether they might derive any benefit: British officials suggested that any substantial contribution in this direction would not automatically increase their share of civilian public contracts, as the Colonels would have them believe. Britain's share was estimated to be just 10 per cent that of the French, which did not allow much room for optimism. On balance, maintaining normal relations with the Greek rulers seemed to offer the best hope of increasing British commercial dividends in Greece.

Additional and less expected EEC-related issues caused headaches to both governments at the beginning of 1973. For instance, during an official gala attended by the Queen and the Prime Minister celebrating Britain's entry to the EEC, an anonymous caustic letter written by a Greek political prisoner was read by Laurence Olivier. This incident gave rise to a storm of protest from the Greek establishment. The Colonels' response was swift, as the Greek Ambassador called on the Permanent Under-Secretary of State for Foreign Affairs Sir Denis Greenhill, that same day to express his discontent at such an affront. The latter promptly confirmed the British government's unchanged policy towards Greece, while offering reassurances that this incident lacked any governmental 'approval or endorsement'.[91]

In the meantime, the British Foreign Secretary did not miss the opportunity to call the 'letter incident' 'deplorable', while his Foreign Office colleagues called it a 'valuable lesson' and a powerful reminder of 'Greek sensibilities'.[92] All this became all the more expedient, as the 'weakness of the [British] economy during 1973' could hardly escape anybody's attention. The decline of Britain's economy during the 1960s was further exacerbated by international developments too, most strikingly the first oil crisis in 1973. Such was the financial turmoil that Edward Heath was forced to declare a state of emergency five times, a record for a peacetime Prime Minister. The last of these, provoked by a prolonged miner's strike and the ensuing three-day week, triggered an early election in February 1974, which eventually resulted in a hollow victory for the Labour Party.

While the initial flames of this embarrassing incident soon died down, a few peripheral consequences were still felt. These included 'shelving' Hooper's hitherto positively endorsed idea of the British

Army training in Greece on a bilateral basis. This was canvassed in an effort to avert the 'recrudescence of public polemics',[93] which was potentially damaging to British interests, most significantly as regards Marconi's current tender worth £4–5 million (47,5–59,5 millions in today's value) for a ship-to-shore communication centre.

Despite the procrastination regarding bilateral defence cooperation, the Foreign Office did decide in favour of participating at NATO's forthcoming ACE Mobile Force exercise, as it did not want the Greek regime 'to start having doubts about NATO, least of all in this year of CSCE [Conference on Security and Cooperation in Europe] and MBFR [Mutual and Balanced Forces Reduction].'[94] At this point, it is worth mentioning that British forces had never favoured abstaining from NATO visits and exercises that took place on Greek soil. The only reluctance they expressed back in September 1967 during the 'Sunshine Express' exercise was eventually overcome for the sake of the Alliance's stability.[95]

Meanwhile, the normal relations to which the British officials aspired looked to be doomed in light of the rise of a troublesome motion criticising the Colonels' regime in the House of Lords in February 1973. This was the first initiative in either House of Parliament since the Conservatives had come to power and was attributed to criticism mainly relating to Lord Limerick's official visit to Greece.[96] In response, the government hastened to assuage the Colonels by drawing the Greek Ambassador's attention to the 'little significance'[97] of the debate, and the 'limited prestige of the initiator',[98] namely Liberal Party President Lord Beaumont of Whitley; he was already sufficiently unpopular with the Greeks due to the demonstration he had arranged outside the Greek Embassy two months earlier. At the same time, they insisted that it 'was not of our [British government's] choosing and that there has been no change in our policy towards Greece';[99] hence the request on behalf of the British officials to 'play it down'.[100]

Moreover, they also ascertained that there would be a staunch counter-voice during the debate in the shape of Lady Tweedsmuir, whose focus would be on re-emphasising Greece's strategic significance for NATO's underbelly, especially in view of the 'pressures inherent in the Soviet and Bulgarian presence on the frontiers of Turkey and Greece.'[101] Interestingly, British fixation with 'a very real communist threat'[102]

remained significant, further coloured by a number of debatable observations including Hooper's assessment that 'perhaps 60 per cent' of
Greece's 'trouble-making' workers were Communists.[103]

However, Lady Tweedsmuir's speech offered an inadequate palliative
to the Greek regime, whose officials reportedly made 'grudging' noises
about her failure to support the Colonels by fending off the insulting
remarks voiced against them. In addition, they resented the clear distinction she drew between trade and political relations. The British
nonetheless concluded that they had on balance managed 'to come out
of what might have been an awkward situation without losing any
feather or unduly ruffling those of others.'[104]

In the meantime, a number of other complications had come into
play. The first serious trouble for the Greek regime emerged in January
1973 with the student riots at the Athens Polytechnic and escalated
with the occupation of the Law Faculty in late February. The regime
had managed to contain the previous uprisings by allowing student
unions to hold elections the previous November, but this gambit was
unsuccessful. This latest wave of agitation stemmed from a variety of
grievances including the student body's demand to participate in the
drafting of the Charter of Higher Education. The regime's handling of
the protests was regarded as 'predictably clumsy' and resulted in alienating not only academics, but also many ordinary Greeks.[105]

Despite the increasing unpopularity of the regime, the British were
of the opinion that the chances of the 'democratic' opposition posing a
threat to the regime were 'negligible'.[106] Instead, it was prophesied that
'if there were to be an effective challenge to his [Papadopoulos'] control in the near future, it would most probably come from the Army:
from discontented officers, or following a debacle in Cyprus.'[107] So
disquieting had the numerous instances of unrest become that the
secret annual report on the Hellenic Armed Forces drafted on
20 February by Brigadier Baxter, the British Defence Attaché, portrayed them as a possible nemesis for the regime. He specifically and
presciently pointed out that 'student riots with major bloodshed might
be sufficient provocation' for a further military coup.[108]

In light of such events, the British vacillated between improving,
severing or just conserving 'at more or less its present level' their good
working relationship with the regime.[109] The quandary stemmed from

the realisation that their correct, but not wholehearted attitude towards the Colonels—or as they put it 'trying to have the best of both worlds'—so far had yielded no special benefits for them.[110] In view of such quagmires, the next meeting on Greece took place on 4 April. Although its conclusion favoured refraining from making any changes to British policy, the order of priorities certainly signifies a rather different reality. More specifically, Hooper insisted that:

> Important though our commercial interests in Greece are, the need to keep Cyprus quiet thereby preserving the stability of the south-eastern flank of NATO, must be overriding. The Greek role in this is important.[111]

The significance of Greece for NATO was reiterated in a cynical way by claiming that 'from the point of view of Western defence, it is more important (in the short term anyway) that Greece should be stable internally and strong militarily than that she should be free.'[112] It is worth mentioning though that this stance started to foment criticism even among members of the Conservative government, who frequently warned about the repercussions of 'the preparedness of NATO to compromise on the destruction of democracy in a member country of an alliance formed to defend democracy.'[113]

The Soviet naval build-up in the Mediterranean, which had by that time reached its zenith with an average fifty-eight vessels in operation in the area on a daily basis, continued to feed NATO's anxieties.[114] Furthermore, given the 'critical moment in [NATO's] relations with the East' vis-à-vis the discussions on mutual and balanced force reductions and preparatory talks on a possible Conference on Security and Co-operation in Europe, it was deemed essential that 'we should work for cohesion and solidarity in NATO and not indulge in attacks on Greece.'[115] So precarious did NATO's solidarity seem in the early 1970s that even the Scandinavian countries, until then implacable critics of the Greek regime, noticeably tempered their opposition within the Alliance.

With regard to the perplexing issue of Greece and the EEC, Hooper appeared to be pro-active by proposing a more 'sympathetic attitude'. He argued in favour of supporting the Greeks 'on such matters as may arise within the Community affecting their interests but not impinging on important interests of other member states.'[116] As far as the exchange of official visits was concerned, there was unanimous decision that some time should be allowed to elapse before any further arrangements were made. Moreover, the officials adopted no further changes in their policy regarding the sale of arms. Aware of the serious criticism that any relaxation of their basic principles on this issue might cause, as well as the rather shaky condition of the Greek regime, they rejected the offer for the sale of Shorland armoured cars, whose main function was in the context of suppressing riots.[117] The value of this commercial transaction was estimated to be rather small, whereas the political costs would be disproportionally greater. Defence cooperation, cultural relations and bilateral agreements were to continue as normal, as they were 'relatively non-controversial' in Britain.[118]

The gradually stiffening approach of the British government was reflected in the recommendation against 'going too far and too fast.'[119] This mood also informed its decision to postpone an official visit by the British Foreign Secretary, which the Colonels ardently wished for. British officials ruled that they would only consent to it in order 'to mark either a major improvement in Anglo–Greek relations or some significant move by the Greeks towards democracy.'[120] This was also linked to their unease about Greece's internal developments, which led Hooper to conclude that 'real progress towards a restoration of democracy is clearly less likely now than ever';[121] and this, the British officials openly admitted, was causing their government 'grave embarrassment'.[122]

Thus the first months of 1973 were understandably described by the British as a period of 'depressed anxiety'.[123] This desolate climate became entrenched as the months went by leaving the golden era of 1970–71 behind for good—or, more accurately, until the regime's fall from power. Before absolute deadlock was reached, the initial stagnation of 1973 was followed by a short interval characterised as 'the propitious wait'.[124] The following chapter will account for this promising, albeit short-lived, era in Anglo–Greek relations, and the sharp worsening that followed.

7

FROM 'BUSINESS AS USUAL' TO 'DEVELOPING
GOOD AND CONSTRUCTIVE RELATIONS'

Although the omens at the beginning of 1973 were not promising, the second half of 1973 was crowded with developments which were particularly grievous and deeply traumatic for the fabric of Greece. So crucial was the chain of events that year that it sparked off a catastrophic domino effect, leading to unprecedented degrees of repression and abuses of human rights and almost resulting in bringing the country to the brink of war with Turkey. Needless to say, a deterioration in the country's external relations ensued and Anglo–Greek relations were no exception.

The first seminal development of the year was spearheaded by the coup against Papadopoulos staged by a group of naval officers loyal to the King. On 23 May, the destroyer Velos, after withdrawing from a NATO exercise in Italy, refused to return to Greece in an anti-junta protest. The captain, Nikolaos Pappas, six officers, and twenty-five petty officers requested asylum and remained abroad as political refugees. The fallout from this incident, described by the British as 'amateurish and clumsy', although quickly contained by the regime, succeeded in tarnishing Anglo–Greek relations yet again.[1] A large British naval visit fixed for 2 June came under fierce attack 'from the usual quarters in London' on the grounds that the Velos incident had discredited claims of the Greek navy's reliability in the context of

NATO.[2] However, in spite of the flux, the British Ambassador ruled in favour of allowing the visit to proceed as scheduled; not to have done so, he declared, 'would be a public declaration of no confidence, which would be deeply resented here (not only in government circles) and might affect not merely Anglo–Greek relations but also Greek relations with NATO.'[3]

Two interwoven issues, which emerged as a result of the naval mutiny, proved much more challenging for the British government to grapple with. The first related to the abolition of the Monarchy on 1 June on the grounds that the King had conspired against the regime and that in any case his was 'an obsolete legacy from the past.'[6] Indeed, the naval mutiny presented Papadopoulos with the optimal pretext, an opportunity too good to miss; thus he openly accused the King for having behaved 'surreptitiously, and openly as a party leader of adventurers, the bankrupt, the fellow travelers, the saboteurs and even assassins.'[7] In other words, given the traditionally close allegiance of the Greek navy to the King, the Greek Prime Minister used the mutiny as an excuse for ridding the country of its monarchical constitution, despite the fact that the Velos' Captain Pappas had entirely disassociated his undertaking from the self-exiled Monarch on the grounds that 'what the King does is of no interest to us because he has never shown any interest in our problems.'[8]

Papadopoulos' move came as no surprise to the British government, as Hooper evaluated that the use of the Greek King as a scapegoat was tactical to appease his internal critics and safeguard his position. Interestingly enough, though, the British, in view of their professed sympathies for and connections with the royal institution, did not seize the moment 'in order to toughen their stance against the Greek government,' contrary to the Colonels' expectations, and instead faced it 'with realism'.[9]

Immediately following the mutiny, the Foreign Office had stated that 'King Constantine's position, though not hopeless, is a weak one.' It also acknowledged that 'there is certainly pressure within the Greek regime for Papadopoulos to end the Monarchy or depose King Constantine.' At the same time, it reiterated that 'King Constantine's prestige and his chance of returning to Athens have declined markedly and continuously since 1967.'[10] According to an editorial in *The Times*, 'the Monarchy was already unpopular in 1967, and the King can hardly have made it less so by failing to oppose the coup until too late.'[11]

In fact, the British Ambassador in his subsequent, sceptical assessment of the Greek Monarchy highlighted that not being an indigenous institution in Greece, it never 'commanded the almost instinctive respect and affection, which it enjoys in Britain.'[12] Indeed, its history was rather turbulent, as of the previous six kings that had ruled Greece since 1833, only one reigned uninterrupted. In his report, the Ambassador also reflected on the overall passivity, which the Greeks showed upon hearing the news of its abolition. He characteristically noted that 'there has been remarkably little public reaction to it and little sympathy for the King, except among those with personal or sentimental attachments to the royal house.'[13] This apathy he found justifiable on the grounds that he too deemed the Greek monarch 'young, inexperienced, and with few disinterested and competent advisers' and pronounced that he should 'share a measure of responsibility' for the political situation which led to the coup d'état of 21 April 1967.[14]

In light of the aforementioned considerations, the British government displayed a reluctance to lend its official support to King Constantine's causes. This is interesting as many observers of Greek affairs thought that 'the deposing of the King makes any return to a better system more difficult and perhaps more violent.'[15] Several officials did nonetheless carry on keeping their close, but unofficial, channels of communication open, mainly via Lord Mountbatten, and showed continued commitment to advise him occasionally. For instance, after his dethronement, one of the instances when a British official had private dinner with the former King was on 17 November following the suppression of the student demonstrations. At the same time, the British government consented that the King and his family 'should be allowed to stay here [in the UK] without restriction should they wish to do so'—their settlement in London took place a few months later. It recognised that 'to treat a former Head of State with close ties with this country as an ordinary immigrant would expose us to embarrassing and avoidable criticism, not least from supporters of Her Majesty's government.'[16] But this was as far as British officials were prepared to go. In juxtaposition to the long-held view that in the nineteenth century the British were 'King-Makers' in Greece,[17] the Foreign

Office's emphasis centered around safeguarding British interests, not endorsing a seemingly unpopular royal house.

Hence, when the question of how to deal with the abolition of the Monarchy was raised, the British did not vacillate. Despite their realisation that the King had no foreknowledge of, let alone involvement in, the mutiny, they decided to regard their relations with the Greek regime as unchanged. In a revealing statement made after an audience with the Queen about the issue of the Greek Monarchy, Prime Minister Heath declared:

> We naturally much regret the abolition of Monarchy in Greece and sympathise with the plight of King Constantine and his Queen … Unfortunately, there is nothing we can do to help the King. The Greek regime seems firmly in control and would reject any representation from us … The abolition of Monarchy requires a decision on recognition … It would not be desirable to delay recognition, as King Constantine has suggested on Panorama. This could impair Greece's effectiveness as a NATO ally without producing any compensating benefits …[18]

At the same time, Hooper was of the opinion that even if the British wished to interfere, British leverage was too limited; in any case, he concluded that the regime's 'concentration is not much affected by outside critics.'[19] He then prophetically observed that 'the chief threat to the stability of the regime remains, as it was before, a collapse from within, a falling out of members of the junta and to this the royal question is irrelevant.'[20]

The second inexorably interlinked development bore more noticeable repercussions for the British Foreign Office. More specifically, as a remedy to the institutional void created by the abolition of the Monarchy, Papadopoulos announced the establishment of a 'Presidential Parliamentary Republic' and proclaimed that he himself would become President. This was merely the latest addition to a long series of high-level government positions, including that of Regent alongside that of Prime Minister, Minister of Foreign Affairs and Defence, as well as Minister for the Interior that he had acquired over the past six years. Meanwhile, Papadopoulos also promised to present the Greek people with the draft revisions of the 1968 constitution in a month, to invite their judgment on said revisions within two months, and to organise general elections before the end of 1974. But it presented Britain with a further dilemma.

For the third time since the Colonels' assumption of power the British found themselves debating a new act of recognition, as their mission's former accreditation to the Greek King was rendered invalid by the change of the head of state. After lengthy deliberations with their EEC colleagues at the beginning of June (not so much with their NATO partners, hinting at Britain's shifting orientation in matters of foreign policy) they opted to proceed as though no governmental change had taken place at all. Although their assessment had no great distance from the truth, at least from a practical point of view, their decision constituted a clear departure from the British doctrine of recognition; this revealed yet again the relaxation of aspects of set doctrines on occasions when it was thought expedient.

Thus the Foreign Office sent clear instructions to the British Ambassador a few days later that he should inform the Colonels in strict confidence of his government's intention to resume business as usual on 13 June, twelve days after the abolition of the Monarchy.[21] This made Britain the first NATO member to do so—a decision that was attacked by the public as 'premature'.[22] In their communiqué, the British officials highlighted the need for the maintenance of strict confidence as well as 'the fairly low posture' that the Ambassador should follow[23]—'in [a] deadpan manner',[24] as the American Embassy in Athens noted. This was judged essential in view of the growing unpopularity of the British government's business as usual policy towards the ever less likeable Colonels.

Several factors had undoubtedly played a cumulative role in the Greek regime's eroding levels of appeal, to put it mildly, including numerous reports of human rights abuses, mushrooming rumours of widespread corruption, and the mounting budget of the Ministry of Public Order, coupled with the parallel compression of the funding for civilian causes, such as education. To make matters worse, inflated military expenditure (averaging 4.8 per cent between 1967 and 1970, in contrast to NATO members' 3.5 per cent during the same period)[25] was not down to a prodigious increase in arms purchases; instead it was dedicated to the internal security and propaganda needs of the regime, which to a large extent explains the dilapidation of the Army's battle readiness and morale during the Cyprus crisis of July 1974. At the same time, Greek politicians from across the political spectrum began to break their muffled antipathy of the regime and to heal their ideological divisions; indeed, as Thanos Veremis has pointed out, it was then that 'the ground was laid for a post-regime process of civilian renewal.'[26]

The alacrity with which the British government recognised the forcible constitutional change in Greece—compared for instance with the six-week delay following the King's abortive coup in December 1967—further testifies to the relative ease with which the Conservatives dealt with such controversial issues. Such moves of course did not necessarily express the true sentiments of the British government, but certainly revealed a more thoroughgoing business-orientated stance. Interestingly enough, the Foreign Secretary himself unintentionally revealed his personal feelings, when as a result of a slip of the tongue, he referred to the regime in Greece as illegal.[27]

Similarly, the British Ambassador in Athens, in an unusually confessional mode, stated:

> Let me also make it clear, in case anyone thinks I am rooting for the Colonels, that we don't like what goes on any more than anyone does in London—perhaps we like it less, as it is after all we who see the ugly face of Papadopoulism in close-up, and it is our personal friends who are vanishing into gaol or the arms of the military police.[28]

Obviously, the pragmatic Hooper supported the line that his government's policy should try to 'get through the present period with the minimum damage in the long-term to Anglo–Greek relations and [British] interests,' while insisting that a tepid combination of a 'hot and cold policy' was not likely to be profitable.[29] This was the approach followed by their predecessors and was acknowledged to be rather unproductive.

The aspect that most opposition circles criticised was the British readiness to take the lead in extending recognition to Papadopoulos' newly imposed presidential regime. To be sure the regime did organise a referendum as a means of legitimising its unconstitutional changes, but it was widely accepted that the result was rigged. The announced 78 per cent endorsement provoked widespread opprobrium within and outside Greece. The British spoke of a 'good deal of malpractice,' and Hooper affirmed in a rather pessimistic tone that Greece was not yet 'on the road leading back to anything that Western Europe would recognise as democracy.'[30]

Opposition to the British government's decision was expressed both inside and outside Parliament and took many forms, varying from umbrage to outright hostility. The following statement issued by the European-Atlantic Action Committee on Greece is indicative of the prevalent sense of indignation:

> The indecent haste with which the British government recognized the newly declared Greek Republic on 13th June was a gratuitous favour to Papadopoulos and was rightly the subject of critical questioning in the House of Commons by the Opposition's Shadow Secretary. The main beneficiaries did reportedly notice it 'with appreciation'.[31]

At the same time, Ben Whitaker, a Labour MP known for his unflinching opposition to the Colonels, called the regime 'a guttersnipe crew of small-time fascists.'[32]

Meanwhile, knowledgeable commentators elaborated how the recent mutiny and plot came from the regime's power-base, signifying that 'opposition covering a cross section of the Greek population is building up against an unimaginative regime which has lost its initiative and momentum.'[33] As a *Times* editorial put it, 'though he [Papadopoulos] and his colleagues have abandoned their military ranks, they remain a military regime deriving its authority from an act of military force, and as such they must be disturbed by opposition within the armed forces more than from any other quarter';[34] and if there was any seed of truth in the Velos' Captain's allegation that 99 per cent of the Greek Air Force, much the same proportion of the Greek Navy, and about half of the Army were against the regime, then there was very serious cause for concern.[35] This hostile atmosphere continued to develop, fuelled by news of the arrest of the well-respected right-wing politician Evangelos Averoff at the beginning of July on the grounds that he had gathered more than five people at this home without requesting prior authorisation.

On the occasion of Papadopoulos' inauguration as the first President of the new Greek Republic, the British tried to diffuse criticism by issuing a rather lukewarm verbal message, as they cautioned that 'to fail to observe reasonable courtesy and protocol towards the new President and his inauguration would be to risk damaging Anglo–Greek relations.'[36] Hooper, having been directed to convey HMG's 'good wishes', pointed out that such a tepid gesture would come across as 'conspicuously less forthcoming', especially in view of Nixon's message referring to the 'friendly ties between the two countries.'[37] However, the Foreign Office was anxious to forestall any further outburst of public censure and inclined to streamline its policy towards the Colonels with its EEC colleagues, all of whom expressed 'a general lack of enthusiasm.'[38]

There were, of course, other indications of the gradually stiffening British attitudes such as their conscious decision to grant the Greeks favourable treatment only in exchange for tangible gains. It was a shift of accent that induced the Greek Embassy in London to complain that Anglo–Greek relations seemed exclusively confined within NATO and the economic realm.[39] It needs to be emphasised, though, that British officials treated with circumspection calls for further cooling in its stance towards the regime. Hooper argued for a wait-and-see attitude along the following lines:

> the justification for our present policies is the assumption that the regime are here to stay and that while they do so, we must do business with them. Over the next few weeks and months, this assumption is likely to be put to a considerable test; but on the evidence so far available, I would hesitate to say that the position of the regime had yet weakened to an extent which would warrant our hedging our bets by reducing the already rather tenuous content of the 'good working relationship.'[40]

The usual justifications, which the government had employed in the past to disarm its critics, were duly trotted out on this occasion too. The regime was important for NATO, so a good working relationship with it must be maintained. The calls to expel Greece from the Alliance alleging that its Council 'has been obstinately blind to the hypocrisy of keeping an openly Fascist regime in its rank in defiance of the treaty's terms'[41] did not obviously seem to concern them. They also drew attention to the fact that Britain did not adhere to the norm of upholding recognition 'on grounds of moral or political disapproval.'[42] At the same time, when dealing with the Colonels, the British hoped to excuse their more reserved attitudes by arguing that they would 'go along with our allies.'[43] In short, the policy British officials favoured at that particular juncture was yet again a 'quiet policy of wait and see'[44] in order to allow the regime 'either to live up to its professions or condemn itself by its own words and actions.'[45] Not unexpectedly therefore, 'a good deal of confusion'[46] reigned in public perceptions of British foreign policy towards the Colonels.

The 'pretty gruelling' summer of 1973, which saw further naval mutinies—one in the naval base of Salamis near Athens and another involving Ierax, one of the two Greek destroyers visiting the south of France—seemed paradoxically to be coming to a more promising end.[47] President Papadopoulos initiated a series of quasi-liberalising measures, including the lifting of martial law, the announcement of a general amnesty for political detainees, the forthcoming establishment of a civilian government that would lead the country by the end of 1974 to the first parliamentary elections in ten years, and the easing of censorship—all of which caused to the British a 'pleasant surprise both in terms of their significance as well as their unexpected extent.'[48] At the same time, Roger Tomkys suggested that the Greek Embassy in London should seize the opportunity to further improve the impact of such measures by inviting several of its polemicists in London, including Monty Woodhouse and Richard Clogg, to come into communication with them.[49]

Papadopoulos' attempt at liberalisation in order to legitimise his government and cleanse its image as a European pariah seemed to meet the most optimistic expectations. Although there was awareness abroad that they were aimed at principally palliating the EEC's opposition to Greece's bids for full membership, as well as generating confidence for the increase of foreign capital flow, they were still seen as bringing about 'more political developments than the preceding six years,'[50] and leading the country 'further in the direction of liberalisation than observers had thought possible.'[51] They were therefore welcomed by the international community, including the British, who expressed their 'qualified approval'[52] of the new government. However, it was noted with anxiety that such an impressive succession of initiatives was bound to alarm and alienate several of Papadopoulos' colleagues.[53] In other words, the British remarked pessimistically that Papadopoulos' excessive impulses ran the risk of undermining his credibility by causing a bigger rupture with his hardline supporters.

To be sure, the accumulation of quasi-dictatorial powers in the hands of Papadopoulos under the new constitution contributed to the conviction that his regime remained 'totalitarian and basically uncongenial.'[54] While vigilantly monitoring domestic developments, British officials were instructed to make 'encouraging noises' to their Greek opposite numbers. The British Ambassador was specifically briefed about the need to maximise the British advantage in those propitious conditions. In light of this shift towards a more engaging attitude, the Foreign Office recommended that during his first meeting with Greece's new self-appointed President, Hooper should draw the latter's attention to the British government's favourable predisposition towards the resumption of official visits, and towards the enhancement of defence cooperation. It also authorised the Ambassador, among other things, to confirm his government's eagerness to sell frigates to the Greek government. Furthermore, he was asked to express interest in the prospect of a visit by the Chief of the Greek Armed Forces to Britain or a Greek minister in return for a visit to Greece by a British official, most likely Sir Thomas Brimelow. Such an initiative would advance British interests in Greece such as 'selling frigates or earning another public sector contract' and would 'reinforce our limited ability to exercise influence in foreign affairs.'[55]

Despite the fact that this proposal was indeed approved during the routine meeting on Greece, any further gestures, especially with regard to finalising an official British visit, were to be delayed until parliamentary elections took place in Greece. However, it was also noted that 'some modest forward movement is desirable at this stage to embolden the Greeks to continue their liberalising measures and to acknowledge their helpful attitude over Cyprus and an improvement in Anglo–Greek commercial relations.'[56] Hence, the visits of a trade minister and the Chief of the Greek Armed Forces received the seal of approval. At the same time, some sort of endorsement was suggested vis-à-vis Papadopoulos' recent promising policy on Cyprus, including his denouncement of General George Grivas and EOKA and his government's rapprochement with Makarios. In fact, for most of the Colonels' stay in power, the British authorities seemed to be satisfied with the 'prudent and responsible' handling of the Cyprus issue.[57] As far as British policy towards Greece within the EEC was concerned, the Foreign Office advocated the continuation of their 'helpful and sympathetic' approach.

One interesting aspect of the meeting on Britain's policy towards Greece in early October was the decision to resurrect the objective of prodding Greek progress towards democracy, a goal which had been more or less totally neglected since 1972.[58] British officials ruled in favour of it as concerns about the ethical justification of Britain's attitude towards the Greek regime were resurfacing, especially within the context of the EEC but also at home. Moreover, they thought that such a development would reduce the nuisances which currently prevented full and constructive Anglo–Greek relations, a point that had been constantly raised by both British administrations throughout the Colonels' rule. They nonetheless admitted that British leverage on Greek liberalising developments was quite limited.

As a means of redressing the balance of British foreign policy towards Greece, the Head of the Foreign Office's Southern European Department, Alan Goodison, nonetheless pointed out that 'it would be wrong to formulate British policy in terms of democracy in Greece as an end in itself than as a means to furthering British interests.'[59] He also placed emphasis on restraining 'over-activity', as it ran the risk of being translated by the Greek government as 'interference' and ending up having an adverse impact on British objectives.[60] Therefore this newly (re)introduced goal of propelling Greece's democratisation was placed at the bottom of the list of British foreign policy aims, while NATO, Cyprus and commercial interests remained at the top.

This modest, albeit perceptible, shift in British policy undoubtedly constituted a departure from the previous more constrained version of the past. One factor was the recognition that a number of important developments in Anglo–Greek relations had taken place on the commercial side. Aside from the Marconi contract, another public sector contract worth £2.5 million (almost 30 millions in today's value) was signed, won by Standard Telephones and Cables, and an expansion of British banking interests in Greece was noted with satisfaction. In the meantime, British 'exports to Greece were running at an annual rate of just under 100 million (over one billion in today's value) in comparison with the levels of 67 million in 1972 (861 millions in today's value) and 72 million in 1971 (close to one billion in today's value).'[61] It was rather unsurprising, therefore, that the Foreign Office seemed committed to maintaining the 'good working relationship and developing it as fast as seems prudent in view of the influence of the Greek lobby in this country and the consequent danger of increased public polemics if we go too quickly.'[62]

Meanwhile, the eagerly anticipated political amnesty granted by Papadopoulos in August was seen as 'an important victory for those who had been struggling for six years for a restoration of human rights.'[63] In addition, the seeds of optimism, which were already sown in July with the circulation of rumours about Markezinis' coming to power, finally germinated on 8 October. Following the forced resignation of the thirteen military men from the Cabinet, Papadopoulos appointed Spyros Markezinis—a distinguished historian and a former politician known for his 'genuine Anglophilia'—as Greece's new Prime Minister, entrusting him with the task of leading Greece to parliamentary rule.[64] This was a move that many perceived as Papadopoulos' attempt at 'convincing democratic opinion in Europe and America.'[65] A British character sketch described the new Prime Minister as possessing 'a brilliant intellect, demoniac energy,'[66] 'self-confidence and a reputation as an economic wizard';[67] hence the widespread feeling of 'satisfaction'[68] in British circles. Hooper also wrote in his annual review that this positive development deserved 'sympathy as affording a somewhat better prospect of a return to a measure of democracy than any of the likely alternatives.'[69] This latter aspect was particularly highlighted as a response to objections concerning Markezinis' lack of 'a major political following'[70] and 'unpredictability'.[71] Other allegations included 'opportunism' on the grounds that he was the only member of the pre-Colonels' political establishment that kept silent in the preceding years, precisely because he harboured such ambitions.

Opposition circles, although rather less vociferous than before, still considered him as the 'nominee of a dictatorship'[72] and others branded the regime's latest venture 'an unconvincing piece of window-dressing intended to disguise and preserve Papadopoulos's personal power.'[73] Furthermore, the potential incompatibilities between the 'strong, opinionated and highly devious characters'[74] of the two were also noted with concern. It was also argued that at best the outcome of this experiment would be a 'political euphemism: a heavily directed democracy'[75] conveniently giving Papadopoulos the appearance of having fulfilled the promises that he had made through the plebiscite in July. The general conclusion drawn was that the situation was confused and 'fills one with gloom about Greek politics.'[76]

In the aftermath of Markezinis' inauguration and following intra-EEC deliberations, the British government agreed that they could be reasonably forthcoming, especially in the light of other positive developments. These included the return of Xanthopoulos-Palamas to the Foreign Ministry, about which they were 'delighted'.[77] This shift became obvious when the 'fairly encouraging'[78] congratulatory message they sent to Markezinis is compared to that conveyed to Papadopoulos when he became President less than three months earlier. This reflected a general change of trend in most Western governments' attitudes towards the Greek regime. The initial verve felt about Markezinis might also explain the Foreign Office's decision to put into cold storage any initiatives it had contemplated at the beginning of the year about a possible Karamanlis solution. In fact, following Karamanlis' critical message in *Le Monde* on 23 April, the British had started to warm up to the idea of inviting him to London to hold a meeting with either the Prime Minister or the Foreign Minister.[79]

While the recent events in Greece were by and large welcome, hard to ignore doubts were expressed concerning Markezinis' ability to successfully overcome overarching domestic pressures, such as the antipathy with which he was viewed by the old political establishment, which immediately rebuffed his efforts to open a dialogue with him. Rampant inflation, farmers' grudges, increasing labour unrest, the revival of student agitations after a relatively quiet six months and— even worse—the virulent hostility with which Markezinis was treated by Army hardliners continued to cloud foreign governments' optimism. The acuteness of such challenges, as Markezinis predicted accurately, 'would make the current winter a "hot" one.'[80]

In an effort to overcome internal challenges by consolidating his power, Markezinis looked abroad. His focus was directed towards Anglo–Greek relations, which he tried to improve further by highlighting that 'for the first time for many years, Greece had a Prime Minster, who was a whole-hearted friend of Britain,' while expressing his earnest hope that 'Britain would realise this and take full advantage of it.'[81] In the light of such overtures, Hooper reported after meeting Markezinis that the latter regarded the cultivation and intensification of relations with the United Kingdom as one of his principal priorities.

However, Hooper saw in this 'the clear but unspoken implication' that Markezinis wished to find a counterweight to American influence. This of course alarmed the British, who in spite of their fluctuating emphasis on involvement with the EEC at the expense of their traditionally close transatlantic relationship, avowedly opposed being played off against the Americans. A further caveat related to Markezinis' clear determination to extract 'some major manifestation' of British confidence and not just the lukewarm approaches so far received.[82] The British were nonetheless reluctant to concede to his pressures and concluded their meeting on Greece with the conviction that 'though we shall be pressed hard for earnest expression of good will, we have made a reasonable start. Markezinis seems convinced that he needs us and this may up to a point be useful.'[83]

A few days later, Hooper's assessment was distributed to his Foreign Office colleagues:

i) The Markezinis venture is a way—perhaps the only way—back to democracy short of a collapse of ordered government.

ii) It is therefore in British interests that it should succeed.

iii) But (i) there is very little if anything we can do to assure its success, and (ii) it is possible and, given the number of points at which it is under attack, even probable that it may fail.

iv) Since, therefore, we are unable to exert any decisive influence one way or another and will only do ourselves harm and prejudice our position with any successive regime by over-identifying with it, we should do what we can to keep MARKEZINIS happy and on our side by making it clear to him that we wish him well in his efforts while at the same time avoiding any major overt commitment to him.[84]

At the Foreign Office, discussions about the desirable extent of British encouragement shown to Markezinis' government continued unabated, while the British Ambassador maintained his reserved attitude. Hooper reiterated that his government should base any policy change on actions and not just the promises, which they were receiving from Greece's new rulers. He even commented that his colleagues' insistence on a more pro-active stance on the grounds that 'the real achievements (e.g. the amnesty)' should be treated 'as hopeful signs that things are moving in the right direction'[85] was 'veering towards dangerous naivety.'[86] To the reported allegations about Britain's 'backing' of Markezinis, he conceded that 'Mr Tasca [American Ambassador in Athens] is indeed a shade more enthusiastic than we [British] are.'[87] In fact, there can be no doubt about Hooper's sceptical approach towards Markezinis, so much so that the latter was reported to have 'a very poor opinion' of him.[88]

Hooper's Foreign Office colleagues, however, were in favour of a more propitiatory policy as a way of strengthening Markezinis' chances of success—and this, under the current conditions, they deemed it to be in their very best interests too. They expressed the fear 'of missing the bus'[89] if they 'let the Markezinis experiment founder for lack of acceptance abroad.'[90] They also claimed that Markezinis' statements after assuming office were 'much more radically democratic in tone' than expected. They therefore favoured 'a more encouraging, and less cautious, attitude towards Greece than was agreed at the meeting.'[91] In retrospect, it can be argued that Hooper's more restrained stance and lack of overt optimism was better founded compared to the Foreign Office's more eager approach—although it is not clear whether this was due to his personal hostility towards Markezinis or because his political instinct told him that danger lay ahead; and danger of course did lie ahead, thoroughly justifying the Ambassador's scepticism.

The events that precipitated the overthrow of Markezinis' short-lived regime put paid to any hopes for the country's democratisation. They took place primarily in Athens and took the forms of rapidly escalating student protests in tandem with the open hostility of almost every section of political opinion. Ironically, it was this cross-spectrum opposition and the realisation that he could no longer count on his virulent anti-Communist appeal that convinced Papadopoulos of the need to transform his regime into an experimental 'directed democracy'; and whilst attempting to unsuccessfully assuage the public, he enraged even further the only political base he ever enjoyed—his military constituency. This formally removed from the regime both the required military unity (or at least cooperation by intimindation) and 'the civilian clientele necessary for the transformation into authoritarian clientelism.'[92]

Opposition from both parts came to a head during the Athens Polytechnic uprising in the middle of November, which was eventually crushed on 17 November. The Army smashed the iron gates of the building in order to evict the students who had occupied it for three days. The news instantly attracted international publicity; *The Guardian*'s David Tongue reported that in the aftermath 'a funeral air hung over Athens', which witnessed a 'scene of virtual devastation.'[93] The bloody disturbances in Athens unsurprisingly caused widespread alarm as they resulted in loss of life and the re-imposition of martial law. The fact that 'blood was shed in the streets' for the first time since the Colonels came to power was 'bound to have major repercussions'[94] and was considered to be derailing 'the welcome political programme which Papadopoulos initiated last August.'[95]

In Britain, a number of protests in support of the Greek students' struggles took place in front of the Greek Embassy during the crisis.[96] The West German Social Democratic Party condemned the violent suppression of the demonstrations, which just like during the funerals of former Prime Minister George Papandreou a little over five years previously, and that of highly acclaimed poet and Nobel Laureate George Seferis' a year before, had turned into massive protests against the military government. As far as the British government was concerned the blame for the brutal handling of the student riots was ascribed at least in part to the West's consistent refusal to supply the Colonels with the appropriate means of controlling riots, which 'ironically enough, have left the military with no alternative to cracking a nut with a steam hammer.'[97] In its immediate aftermath, British officials expressed concern that Greece was being driven 'towards a state of chaos in which a new army coup may appear as the sole alternative', while promptly realising that hardliner Dimitrios Ioannides was 'the key figure to another army take-over.'[98]

Those turbulent events provoked huge waves of British parliamentary condemnation too. Two motions were tabled and given the emerging atmosphere of uncertainty, the Foreign Office in an unusual agreement with the British Embassy concurred that 'parliamentary attitudes now dictate greater caution.'[99] As the British Ambassador from Athens expressed apprehension about more drastic developments in the offing, the Cabinet discussed the 17 November events during their meeting five days later. In the meantime, Hooper, conscious of the bad press which Papadopoulos' violent reaction had attracted, commented on the increasing hostility of various anti-regime lobbies in London. The Greek Service of the BBC certainly stood out—a particularly unsettling observation in the Ambassador's eyes as he grudgingly pointed out that it was operating on government money.[100]

A single week sufficed to verify Hooper's worse fears. In the early hours of 25 November, Brigadier Dimitrios Ioannnides, the Head of the infamous military police and one of the junta's staunchest hard-liners, took decisive action. He toppled the Markezinis regime by launching a bloodless and effective coup, which was subsequently characterised as the 'most peaceful overthrow of government in his-tory.'[101] Ioannides, who was described by the British inter alia as 'aloof, dedicated, austere and puritanical',[102] felt betrayed by Papadopoulos' liberalisation process and the soaring levels of corrup-tion amongst his entourage. Thus, after staging his coup, he swiftly replaced Papadopoulos with General Phaedon Gizikis as President of the Republic, while Adamantios Androutsopoulos was entrusted with the task of forming a government in lieu of Markezinis.

Proclaiming that they were 'with God and on the side of the peo-ple', the new rulers accused their predecessors as 'lacking in initia-tives and political responsibilities, injured politically and morally' and for having led the country into 'a state of confusion and chaos.'[103] According to the Guardian, 'the new government's stark warning of political austerity is tempered by great stress given to honesty and a fair division of national income.'[104] In fact, several foreign observers remarked that Ioannides was '"sea-green incorruptible" the classical description of Robespierre'; still, though, there seemed to be no doubt that 'he was completely ruthless' against any opposition.[105] The British called it 'a sad day for Greece as we cannot imagine where latest events can lead except to harsher military rule and Greece's further isolation from her allies.'[106]

British officials promptly grasped that General Ghizikis was a mere figurehead and the real force behind the scenes was the 'shadowy figure' of Brigadier Ioannides, hence his characterisation as the 'invis-ible dictator'.[107] In view of their concerns about Ioannides' extremist tendencies and his less than impressive new government, they opted to discuss these developments and their prospects with their NATO colleagues. On the basis of their assessment that 'the attitude already taken by most of our allies [who resumed business with the new regime within a couple of days after it assumed power] effectively deprives them of the means of exerting pressures', they decided to cooperate with the regime. At the same time, publicly they employed the usual justification of the doctrine of de facto recognition as well as the precedent that their business as usual approach to this regime had already established. Soon after, they came to realise that their centuries-long doctrine exposed them to serious criticism; hence, they jettisoned it in favour of the 'state, not governments' approach of their EEC colleagues.[108]

In the meantime, the premature failure of the Markezinis experiment made a number of Foreign Office officials argue with contempt that had the British government embraced it more wholeheartedly, it would have stood a better chance of success. In reply, Hooper claimed that Markezinis' political venture was doomed to fail as it lacked the support of 'too many people [including students, old politicians, the 'extreme left' and 'soldiers'].[109]

Faced with this new complication in the Greek political scene, British officials had no option but to leave aside any romanticising of Markezinis' missed prospects. Instead they had to confront the current reality, which was the assumption of power by a government of 'impotent civilian mediocrities', 'a collection of non-entities';[110] similarly, on another occasion it was noted that '[the] new cabinet distinguishes itself by total absence of any distinguished personality.'[111] Hooper was moved to the jaundiced observation that Papadopoulos' successors may lead people to 'look back to that period with a certain nostalgia.'[112]

In reply to relevant Parliamentary questions raised with regard to the Atlantic Alliance, they argued that 'we have no reason to suppose that the new regime will not continue, like its predecessors, to play an important role in NATO.'[113] In their private conversations, however, they admitted that its 'external political orientation' was 'still not clear'.[114] Only a month earlier, the Greek government's neutral stance 'in conformity with the traditional policy of friendship with the Arabs' during the Yom Kippur War had certainly cajoled the Alliance.[115] It was on the grounds of such worries that both the British Foreign Office and its Embassy in Athens agreed on the need to avoid delaying recognition as 'the possibility of a further reaction within the Armed Forces or by the population at large cannot yet be entirely excluded.'[116]

The British Ambassador drew some comfort from the new Prime Minister's speech of 26 November, whose proclamations regarding

Greece's foreign relations and most importantly Cyprus he found 'reassuring'.[117] The latter was of direct relevance to the British interests; just a month earlier, it was corroborated that 'the SBAs and associated retained sites and installations in Cyprus, will continue to remain of very great importance to the UK and Western defence interests throughout the 1970s.'[118] The British continued to encourage intercommunal negotiations and pressed for flexibility, whilst highlighting at the same time the significance of the Zurich and London Agreement, which guaranteed British privileges of their bases in Cyprus.[119]

Back in London the Foreign Office ruled that the new regime should be recognised 'without undue delay'.[120] This stance was also facilitated by the fact that the coup had been bloodless, an aspect which, in tandem with the domestic unpopularity of the previous regime, contributed to the rather muted public reaction. However, it was generally recommended as expedient for Hooper to wait a little longer before acknowledging the Greek Foreign Minister's note verbale. Uncertain about the realistic prospects of the regime's permanency, several British officials were loath to come across as 'acting with unwarranted haste.'[121]

Hooper seemed to have formed a fairly accurate assessment of the new government's grim outlook and its impact on the standing of Anglo–Greek relations. He commented with consternation that 'the massive purges which followed the recent coup must have thrown the [Greek Armed] forces into a confusion' thus seriously compromising Greece's efficacy as a NATO ally.[122] The future prospects for Anglo–Greek relations looked no less gloomy. With regard to the Cyprus issue, he voiced unease in his memorandum on the fall of Papadopoulos about the fact that 'some of the new military leaders have records of past links with Grivas, which are bound to create misgivings.'[123] Hooper expressed the conviction that the new regime composed of 'inexperienced and largely unsophisticated men with some xenophobic tendencies' would not facilitate any of the British government's objectives.[124]

Thus, it was generally accepted that there existed 'few grounds for optimism about the future [of Greece].'[125] To make matters worse, a few days after the regime had come to power, the British observed that events like the closure of the conservative, though anti-governmental, *Vradyni* newspaper and the detention of approximately 250 people 'had done nothing to strengthen the confidence which Androutsopoulos's statement almost completely destroyed.'[126] Caution was therefore recommended and stress was placed on avoiding the risk 'that with this government, even more than with the previous ones, moral exhortation from above may produce violent and petulant anti-Western reactions, however damaging these may be to Greece's real interests.'[127]

Unwilling to ponder for much longer for fear of 'being left out on a limb',[128] the British Cabinet decided on 4 December to send instructions to their Ambassador 'to take action, which would, in practice, amount to recognition of the regime.'[129] This initiative came only nine days after the coup had taken place, one of the shortest recorded time lapses before accepting a government brought to power by military coup—second only to that following the 21 April 1967 coup.[130]

Meanwhile, 'justifiable concern' about Britain's dealings with the new regime in Greece seemed to be gathering momentum. A number of Parliamentary questions were raised and the Labour Party issued a statement 'deploring our decision to recognise the Greek regime.'[131] Despite this stir, the Foreign Office informed the Ministry of Defence of their approval of the forthcoming Anglo–Greek Staff talks and the visit of the National Defence College. Both initiatives pertained to defence cooperation and were approved before the coup—provided of course that there was to be no escalation occurring in the meantime.[132] The Foreign Office, which admitted the 'very considerable interest' generated by events in Greece, agreed with Hooper's recommendation that British policy objectives remained unchanged.[133] Besides, such initiatives, in view of their clear NATO-association, were not only significant for NATO, but also not expected to provoke serious public reaction.

Caught in the by then commonplace predicament of having to avoid enraging the British public on the one hand and the Greek rulers on the other, British officials acted predictably. In order to abate the public's hostility, they put forward their usual justification, namely that their actions did not in any way imply a moral judgment. In a parallel effort to contain the new Greek regime's retaliation, they continued to show their support for Greece within NATO. Whenever the question of Greece's membership was raised, Britain would take the line that 'whatever we think about the Greek regime, we should not allow feelings about it to threaten the cohesion of the Alliance.'[134] Such a stance clearly reflected the Alliance's asymmetrical relationships. The British, like their American partners, did not seem overly preoccupied about the lack of cohesion caused by the Scandinavians' opposition to the Greek membership.

Britain's determination to promote its interests in Greece is also evidenced by the authorisation granted to the Ministry of Defence by the Foreign Office's Southern European Department to proceed with the sale of small items to Greece, such as smoke bombs and gas masks. Although the rationale used associated such sales with NATO's needs,[135] the agreement was voided a few days later on the grounds that Britain should allow a bit more time to get better acquainted with the regime. What appeared to be the obvious hindrance nonetheless was that these specific weapons might be used to put down civil unrest.

The wait-and-see recommendation by Hooper was made along the following clearly pragmatic lines:

> We cannot at this stage be sure that we shall be able to get along with; but I submit that we and our NATO allies should not be over hasty in assuming that we cannot. We cannot expect to control the reactions of public opinion and I do not suggest that we should try. But at least until the new regime has made its policies more clear, let us not jeopardize our political, strategic, and commercial interests in this area by being over-ready with official censure or admonition.[136]

It had by then become clear that the British government's reluctance to exert pressure on the regime stemmed largely from its pre-monitory fears that 'an inexperienced and unsure government facing awesome difficulties may act unwisely and may not be able to retain power.'[137] This was also evidenced in Britain's wish to mute any opposition within NATO and their reported satisfaction that its December ministerial meeting did not include any controversial discussion of Greece's internal affairs.[138] This stance led George Christoyiannis, the Greek Counsellor, to reciprocate by noting that the British government stood out for its avoidance of pronouncements that could come across as interfering in Greece's domestic affairs. Meanwhile, the Greek Ambassador in London received reassurances about the importance which the British government attached 'to developing good and constructive relations with Greece.'[139]

At the same time, though, the Greek official echoed Greece's customary reservations about Anglo–Greek relations. The wait-and-see policy of the British, the intensification of Labour's attacks against their regime, the lack of any forthcoming official visits, as well as the dearth of progress vis-à-vis British initiatives in favour of Greece within the EEC, all seemed to contribute to the Greek regime's vexation with Britain.[140]

Attacks from a large part of the British public not only continued unabated but intensified even further following Ioannides' coming to power. The Transport and General Workers' Union, representing 1,750,000 workers added 'its voice to the world protests against the brutal repression in Greece by making demarches to both the Greek and British ruling elites.[141] Similar protests in writing were mounted by the National Union of Journalists and the National Union of Teachers, reflecting the strong feelings shared by a very large part of the British public. Indeed, indicative of the very widespread interest in Greek affairs in Britain was the opposition voiced mostly in the form of resolutions sent to the British government by literally tens of unions, ranging from the National Furniture Trade Association to the Draughtsmen and Allied Technicians Association and from the Merchant Navy and Airline Officers' Association to the Society of Graphical and Allied Trades.

It is unsurprising therefore that 1973 was described as another inconclusive year, 'dismal', rife with 'disappointed hopes, political folly and shattered calm.'[142] The end of year was marked by 'a return to the stagnation of early 1973 followed by many question marks and a somewhat mistrustful wait as regarded the direction and the rate of further democratic developments in Greece.'[143] British officials, on the other hand, found nothing more positive to say about 1973, which had seen three Heads of State, three Prime Ministers and three Commanders in chief of the Armed Forces come and go, than that 'the worst has not happened.'[144]

Given the complications in the internal Greek scene and their consequences for the country's external relations, the omens for 1974 did not portend any optimism. The first half of the year witnessed a notable alienation of the regime not only from its domestic public, the vast majority of which never showed any signs of endorsing it, but also from its external allies. In other words, Ioannides' 'increasingly incompetent dictatorship'[145] and its ensuing perplexity made the British comment that they did not contemplate 'any gesture of friendship towards them.'[146] With regard to an exchange of visits, the Foreign Office commented that 'there is nothing in the state of things in Greece or in Anglo/Greek relations' that could grant sound justification for such considerations.[147]

At the same time the British Foreign Office, as if satisfied with its policy's status quo, objected to Hooper's proposal to visit London for an office meeting on Greece.[148] And if such a stance does not sound aggravating in the context of Ioannides' abusive regime, then the classification of the document as 'secret' may quash any doubts. The reasoning offered for their tacit refusal to re-examine their policy related to the fluidity of the conditions in Greece, which made it look inexpedient to revise its principles towards it.[149] British officials did nonetheless express concern at the public outcry against their tolerance of both the new Chilean and Greek governments, to the extent that the possibility of revising its recognition criteria was discussed for the avoidance of 'embarrassments'.[150] British policy towards Greece, it was reaffirmed, needed to rest on the stipulation that it could go 'as far as [possible] within the limits imposed by public and parliamentary opinion.'[151]

FROM A 'GOOD WORKING RELATIONSHIP' TO A 'PROPER WORKING RELATIONSHIP'

While the previous chapter sought to account for the convoluted state of Anglo–Greek relations during 1973, this one will describe the grave challenges experienced in the first half of 1974, which rather unsurprisingly turned out to be another 'difficult year'. It was during this year that conditions under the brutal and incompetent Ioannides regime deteriorated, the Colonels fell from power and the invasion of Cyprus took place—and all these events occurred at a time when political affairs in Britain were developing apace with the return to power of the Wilson Labour government.

In fact, Wilson's victory in the February general election was the major element influencing Anglo–Greek relations. Due to the lack of an outright majority, which produced a hung Parliament, Wilson's mind was tuned more towards winning the next general election in October than to any major foreign policy re-orientations—especially those that would produce no immediate tangible gains for his country's interests. This together with the rapidly worsening circumstances in Greece made it look unclear initially whether the new British government intended 'to work actively for change or whether they wished to revert to something like the policy pursued between 1967 to 1970.'[1] Despite the relative trivialisation of Anglo–Greek relations, a number of meetings took place to discuss the developments in Greece as well as the different policy alternatives.

Harbingers of the new government's less than benign feelings had appeared on many occasions in the few months before the general elections and intensified following Ioannides' abortive coup of 25 November. One of the very first indications manifested itself in the strong disapproval that the Labour leader expressed in response to the Conservatives' decision to resume normal business with the Ioannides regime soon after it assumed power. Labour's distancing from the perceived 'tolerance and support' shown by the Conservatives to the Greek regime was reiterated in several instances. In fact, a Labour Party source even related that Wilson's government was 'on same wavelength as government of Norway',[2] which was one of the regime's staunchest opponents.

Suspicions that such a stance was empty rhetoric for public consumption during the pre-electoral period were temporarily suspended soon after Labour returned to power at the end of February. The following five months, before the regime's demise in July, witnessed a significant degradation in Anglo–Greek relations. This shift was transmitted to the Greek government via the British Ambassador, who was specifically instructed to convey the new government's intentions to circumscribe its contacts with them in a 'business-like' manner.[3] Meanwhile, Alan Goodison admitted to Greek Ambassador Broumas that he expected the new government to 'give pain'[4] to the Greek rulers. In a more diplomatic, though similarly meaningful way, James Callaghan the new Foreign Minister, also confirmed this tendency. He clearly attested that the new government intended to implement overall the same foreign policy as its predecessors with few exceptions, which notably included Greece, about which the British people manifested 'concern', leading the government to be 'less accommodating'.[5]

In other words, the change of faces in Downing Street brought with it a volte-face of British policy towards Greece, at least in terms of emphasis. For instance, the celebration at the Greek Embassy of Independence Day on 25 March was attended on behalf of the government by Roberts, the last in order at the Foreign Office; this move was made more auspicious in view of the fact the Conservatives were represented by former Foreign Secretary Sir Alec Douglas-Home, his Under-Secretary Julian Amery and a few of their MPs.[6]

An even clearer manifestation came with the incoming government's decision to annul the pre-scheduled informal naval visits to Greece, which did come as a surprise. This was the same party which had conducted business as usual with the regime of the Greek Colonels between 1967 and 1970. However, the eventual hardening of the nascent regime's arteries and increasing levels of outspoken disapproval from the international community—a development to which the concurrent revolution in the realm of international human rights had greatly contributed—emboldened the inherent tendencies of a Labour administration to be less tolerant of authoritarianism. As the new Foreign Minister affirmed, 'given the attitude which they [Labour] took while in opposition to the continuing failure to restore democracy in Greece, it would be quite inconsistent to allow a visit of this nature to go forward.'[7] The American Embassy in London reported to the Secretary of State in Washington that the 'cancellation is officially tied to British desire to see democracy restored in Greece', whilst noting that 'we [US government] 'may expect new coolness in British bilateral relationship with Greece.'[8]

As the congratulatory letter of Hugh Greene, Chairman of the European-Atlantic Committee for Democracy in Greece to Callaghan testified,[9] the British decision to cancel the naval visits was heralded with enthusiasm within Britain—though not among Conservative political circles, who expressed contempt for Labour's move.[10] The reactions of several members of the old Greek political establishment revealed the same excitement. For instance, George Mavros, the leader of the Centre Union, endorsed the alleged meddling as 'an international obligation.'[11] Alas, his reward for supposedly inviting foreign intervention in Greek affairs was arrest and detention on an island concentration camp.

In spite of having tried to maintain a distance from the Greek rulers in the recent months, Hooper opposed the idea of being blatantly frank to the Greek rulers about British feelings. He also advised against taking such initiatives not only on the grounds of their inefficacy but also for fear of the likely retaliation against their other interests in connection with Greece. He specifically cautioned that such actions might have a pernicious impact given the regime's 'ultra-nationalist complexion.'[12] He also appeared rather perplexed, if not embarrassed, by the double standards that his government wished to apply to their dealings with the Greek regime—on the one hand proclaiming their wish for a 'business-like relationship' and on the other favouring 'a minimum relationship with the Greek regime as such,'[13] which he found largely incompatible.

In the meantime, he also spurned his government's wishful ideas of imposing positive change on the regime's illiberal complexion, as he repeated that his country's leverage would have very little effect. This assessment provided a clear idea of the relative diminution of British influence on Greek affairs, which becomes even starker once the US' dominant power is added to the equation. Hooper emphatically argued that if pressures exerted on the regime towards its democratisation were to stand a chance, 'the process should begin in Washington' as 'only the US government disposes of sufficient means—strategic, military aid and financial and political involvement—to make pressure effective'; hinting thus at their belief that resolute American interference was the only tangible leverage.[14] Indeed, such evaluations seem to be verified by junior US diplomat in Athens Robert Keely; according to his claim the US 'could topple the regime with no more than a flick of the finger.'[15]

In the light of such concerns, Hooper decided to circumvent Spyridon Tetenes, the new Greek Foreign Minister, who 'was taking a tough line';[16] instead he transmitted his government's decision concerning the cancellation of the naval visits to Aggelos Vlachos, the Secretary General. The latter although showing willingness for cooperation still admitted that the British annulment of the naval visit was 'unethical... and hurt deeply the Greek Armed Forces.'[17] Consequently, it was bound to generate his superiors' resentment on the grounds that 'this was not the behaviour that Greece expected of an ally.'[18] Vlachos' predictions were accurate as only a day later Hooper was reporting to the Foreign Office the strong language the Greek Foreign Ministry used to inveigh against the British decision. The Greek officials chided the British for their 'inadmissible interference in Greece's internal affairs' and for 'seriously jeopardising the Atlantic Alliance.'[19] The Greek Army, which as Hooper noted, believed itself 'to be in the front line against communism' regarded the British decision 'as a poor reward for its whole-hearted commitment to NATO.'[20]

In order to soften the Greek government's reactions, Hooper held a meeting with the Greek Foreign Minister. During their 'very difficult'[21] conversation, the British Ambassador pleaded for patience until the British government could complete the review it had undertaken of its policy towards Greece, but to no avail. In the meantime, the Greek Prime Minister vented his ire by calling a press conference to express his indignation at Britain's unjustifiable interference in Greece's internal affairs.[22]

Overall though, and despite the apparent vitriol and calls for substantial reprisals, including the recall of Ambassadors,[23] the Greek response was not drastic—in part due to the positive influence exerted by the British Ambassador. A few Greek officials too tried to tone down their government's outrage. For instance, the Greek Ambassador in London, showed understanding for the British stance, while the Chief of the Hellenic Navy, which was admittedly less closely associated with the regime than the Army, attested to the solid maintenance of good relations between the two navies.[24]

The Greek regime did try to show its teeth by ceasing to consider Yarrows' tender for frigates estimated to be worth £42 million (almost 430 millions in today's value). The British were not unduly vexed by this, as they had already expressed doubts about the regime's ability to pay such a hefty sum. Other retaliatory measures included the regime's threat to jettison informal and routine visits by the Royal Navy and the Royal Air Force and question certain defence sales, for instance, concerning helicopters.[25] However, it was soon clear that this was as far as the Colonels were prepared to go; there seemed no doubt that they could not afford to alienate themselves entirely. Consequently, despite various calls from a group of young ultra-nationalist officers to spurn NATO patronage, the regime's leaders did not deem such a move in the country's long-term interests.[26]

In addition, during a press conference hosted by Dimitrios Karakostas, the Under-Secretary to the Prime Minister, assiduous efforts were made to restore the balance of Anglo–Greek relations by rebutting 'the suggestion that Greece had entered on a particularly difficult stage in relations with Britain'. Britain's otherwise 'concrete political act' was treated as a mere incident and it was pointed out that 'similar incidents had also occurred in the past but they had not disturbed the relations between the two countries.'[27] The overall feeling that this episode left was best portrayed in Hooper's assessment following his meeting with the Greek Foreign Minister, according to which Greece was not 'angry... only, terribly, terribly hurt' by Britain's alleged 'flagrant interference' in Greek affairs. It was during that same meeting that he was reminded yet again of Greece's tolerance of British wrongdoings in Northern Ireland and Cyprus during past instances.[28]

In the aftermath of this first real crisis in Anglo–Greek relations since Wilson's 'bestialities' remark in June 1968, the British expressed relief that they avoided getting involved in 'a run of mutually damaging demonstrations of hostility or independence.'[29] This reaction clearly signified the demarcation line of British policy limits. Britain's unwillingness to strain their relations with the Greek regime and ostracise it further was also reflected in the decision not to side with the regime's harshest international critics for fear of an even less appealing successor regime. 'Any change was more than likely to be for the worse',[30] Hooper confessed, while Tomkys cautioned that 'a Qaddafist reaction and a further military coup are at least as likely as the restoration of Parliamentary democracy by a chastened and contrite revolutionary junta.'[31] The regime's inability to tackle the mounting financial challenges and muted but real internal dissent further exacerbated such fears.

Although Hooper believed that 'less damage to working relations than might at first have been expected' was inflicted, he still advised against actions which would entangle Britain in 'the impossible and undignified position of damning the Greeks in public and asking them for favours in private'—a precarious policy pursued by Labour towards Greece when last in power.[32] Despite the fact that the incoming Labour government held the Ioannides regime in very low esteem, characterising it as 'a squalid, incompetent shower',[33] they eventually decided not to alter the course of their official business as usual policy towards it. They admitted that 'our [Britain's] own vulnerability in relation to Greece is largely in the commercial field, where we see the contracts which can be lost'[34] as a consequence of the adoption of a more hostile stance towards the new regime. Besides, it was widely accepted that 'HMG acting alone or even in conjunction with those of our NATO and EEC partners who think likewise can exercise very little influence in this [democratic] direction.'[35]

Thus Wilson's government opted for the continuation of diplomatic relations and dealings with Ioannides' otherwise unpalatable regime.

However, it appeared seriously disquieted by the instability that seemed to be spreading over Greece with all the trouble that this portended. The mood was described as 'bleak vergin[g] upon despair'[36] mainly due to the lack of any credible financial programme that could offset the enormous pressures of rising prices and the impact of the worldwide energy crisis. In addition, a press release from the International Commission of Jurists soon reinforced the impression that 'repression during these four months has been more severe than at any time since the military seized power in 1967.'[37] At the same time, the most disturbing factor appeared to be the Armed Forces' factionalism, its loss of morale, effectiveness, integrity and its concomitant discrediting as an institution and a basis for political stability.

After re-evaluating their policy towards Greece, the British government shifted its emphasis from sustaining 'a good working relationship' to a 'proper' one.[38] This shift towards 'coolness' was noted by the Americans too, who nevertheless opined that they did not expect this to translate to any moves to eject Greece from NATO.[39] At the same time, British officials strove to reassure the anxious Greeks that this was a change in terms of appearances and not in substance. The following was indicative of the government's stance:

> This did not mean, however, that there would be any change in our attitude towards Greece in the practical work of the Alliance, where they could expect us to cooperate with them fully... I said that I foresaw no change in 90 percent of our relationship, but the Greek government must expect the British government to be more demonstrative than their predecessors in their criticism of the Greek regime.[40]

An additional irritant in Anglo–Greek relations, which the incoming British government had to deal with, related to the EEC. The issue of the additional protocol was a further complicating factor. In February, just before Labour won the elections, the Greek government announced its willingness to enter into discussions over the protocol with the aim of adapting it to the enlargement of the Community. In view of its realisation that HMG's position in the EEC was not 'one which affords much leverage in relation to Greece',[41] the British Foreign Office recommended passivity while allowing for the appropriate proceedings to take place in Brussels.[42] In the meantime though, when the occasion arose, as for instance during a parliamentary question on 27 March, Roy Hattersley, 'spoke of the need for democracy in Greece before proper negotiations could continue on the relationship between Greece and the community.'[43] This stance mirrored the EEC's position on this issue, which was yet again reflected in a condemnatory statement on 28 March. This confirmed that 'the present situation in Greece remains very far removed from the democratic principles on which the European Community is based' therefore 'the association agreement with Greece must continue to be strictly confined to routine business.'[44]

Meanwhile, and as if the Greek regime did not have enough issues to contend with, the exploitation of oil in the north Aegean ignited anew tensions with its Turkish neighbours, generating fresh concern for Britain. More specifically, the discovery of oil in early 1974, whose importance was deliberately played up by Ioannides for political gains, 'clearly had the makings of major and avoidable Greek/Turkish row', Foreign Office officials noted with unease.[45] In view of the antagonistic Greek–Turkish perceptions pertaining to the Law of the Sea, sea beds, continental shelves and the Hague and Geneva conferences, the Foreign Office diagnosed that the Aegean was threatening to become an area of Greco–Turkish dispute, which the British must avoid being drawn into.[46]

The Aegean claims and counterclaims were reaching uncompromising levels prompting Hooper to warn about the danger that 'a minor incident could escalate into a major one.'[47] The potentially explosive dynamism of this dispute was aggravated by the lack of experience and the nationalistic excitability that Britain thought both governments demonstrated. This acrimonious atmosphere was fuelled by the constant exchange of inflammatory statements. The American Embassy in London reported that the Foreign Office was 'slightly on edge' given that both the Greek and Turkish governments 'do not inspire confidence'.[48] The threat of confrontation voiced by the Turkish government on a regular basis further worsened the situation.[49]

Facing this dilemma, Britain, which according to the American Embassy in London wished 'to avoid taking sides in dispute',[50] changed track and became more pro-active. The first step was to urge Turkey to show forbearance towards Greece for the sake of the stability of the West. Not unexpectedly though, this initiative failed to 'cut much ice', leaving the British pondering about the best course of action.[51] Their second initiative was directed at their American partners. On the grounds that 'the regime depends on the continued tolerance of the United States and the reluctance of the US Administration to work to bring them down',[52] they requested the Americans to urge caution to both sides. The British seemed to believe that 'it may well be that the only hope of avoiding serious trouble lies in the personal interference of US Secretary of State Henry Kissinger',[53] who nevertheless rejected such intervention as unnecessary.[54] His response dissatisfied the British, who reiterated that their influence regrettably continued to be 'very limited'.[55] Kissinger's unambiguous reluctance to become involved was attributed to his almost exclusive focus on the other major challenge the US was facing in the Mediterranean.[56]

The British Foreign Secretary in a renewed effort to try and work out a joint strategy towards Greece made additional representations to his opposite number at the beginning of June. He was of course fully aware that the British could not act unilaterally in the Mediterranean. This was a lesson the British had drawn from the Suez crisis—their hapless military venture in the Eastern Mediterranean in 1956, which lacked American support and was doomed to fail; hence, their insistence on getting the Americans more involved. By the 1970s, ministers were reigned to the fact that 'none of our [British] national interests can be preserved by military intervention on the national level', which helps explain the commitment of nearly all British resources to NATO.[57]

The British Foreign Secretary reasoned that 'the proximity of the next NATO ministerial meeting plus current Greek/Turkish tensions give us a natural opening to do so again.'[58] Both Britain and the United States during their customary regular exchanges of views agreed that the Greek regime was 'singularly unpleasant' and that its instability diminished its value for NATO.[59] Thus they concurred yet again on the need to coordinate their stance towards Greece.[60] However, to Britain's dismay, persistent attempts to secure tangible action failed to find favour within the American administration. Britain was left in no doubt that 'Kissinger would be strongly opposed to any action designed to bring pressure on the present Greek administration.'[61] The US Secretary of State, who by that time was embroiled in the collapse of the Nixon presidency following the Watergate scandal, was prejudiced by 'Britain's qualified support for Makarios and its unconcealed hostility to the Greek regime.'[62]

Meanwhile, one of the most pressing concerns for the British government remained domestic perceptions of and reaction to its policy vis-à-vis the Colonels. Parliament was described as maintaining its 'keen interest'[63] and a number of public protestations were made including those organised by the European–Atlantic Action Committee on Greece. Callaghan remarked that in the light of the 'persistent and continuing criticism in this country of the Greek regime', 'ministers are under pressure from various quarters to do more than they have already done to show their disapproval of the Greek regime.'[64] The calls increasingly appealed for action to be taken within NATO, as it was becoming evident that it was the only organisation that could realistically bring pressure to bear.

This was the one aspect of their relations with Greece that the British government were not prepared to negotiate, however. It is clear that the first pillar of British relations with Greece was the latter's significance for the stability of NATO. James Callaghan, just like his predecessor, had serious reservations about antagonising extensively the Greek regime. This helps account for the new government's aloofness about challenging the Colonels on issues that fell within NATO's ambit. Indeed, as Walter Annenberg American Ambassador in London was reporting, he had received reassurances from Charles Wiggin that 'Callaghan would not plan to propose draconian measures against Greece', whilst acknowledging 'the considerable pressures on HMG to take a strong stand against Greece in NATO.'[65] It was recommended that the Foreign Secretary would wait 'until he had an opportunity to talk to the secretary at Ottawa before formulating any criticisms of the current Greek regime'[66] alluding thus to the hegemonic influences governing the Anglo–American partnership.

In the meantime, the British government continued to emphasise that any concerted international pressure would not necessarily yield any fruits, while at the same time it would run the risk of ostracising the regime and forcing it into extremes. On a number of occasions in the past they had presented similar arguments along the following lines:

> if any change of government did ensue in Greece as a result of heavy
> Western pressure, it would be a still more unpleasant military-based

regime, perhaps Qaddafi-type, or conceivably a period of chaos leading to another totalitarian regime of one [form] or another.[67]

On another occasion, it was highlighted that 'the consequence of Greece leaving NATO and/or pursuing reckless policies over Cyprus and towards Turkey could be very serious.'[68] Such claims seemed rather dubious in light of British efforts to persuade the Americans to intervene. The latter's policy reflected on Ambassador Tasca's testimony before the Rosenthal Committee opted for a 'satisfactory working relationship' after 'having weighed the advantages, disadvantages, and risks involved in all available policy alternatives.'[69]

One immediate concern for the British and Americans centered around the forthcoming NATO ministerial meeting scheduled to take place on 18 and 19 June in Ottawa, which was to celebrate the occasion of NATO's anniversary. The priority the two governments gave to safeguarding Greece's membership was reflected in the eventual omission of discussion on the Greek regime, despite the many protests from a wide spectrum of organisations. The International League for the Rights of Man, an international non-governmental organization affiliated with the United Nations and Council of Europe, sent an appeal on the emblematic occasion of the anniversary urging NATO 'to help restore respect for human rights in Greece.'[70] Alas, as Petra Kelly from the Economic and Social Council of the European Commission and eventual founder of the German Green Party remarked in one of her many protesting letters, 'The Americans who see a danger of the isolation of Greece within the NATO alliance system could go home to Mr Nixon and Mr Agnew in relief. They did not even bring up the problem.'[71]

And although the result of that meeting was not unexpected, as the issue of Greece was only indirectly touched upon, the outcome of another meeting made for some more interesting remarks. The Defence and Overseas Policy Committee conferred with the Cabinet on issues regarding British policy towards politically sensitive countries. It was specifically called with the intention of re-examining Britain's arms sales with a number of dictatorial regimes including the one ruling Greece. The usual policy with regard to forbidding the sale of arms which could be used against the civilian population, was restated, although it was acknowledged that this made Britain less competitive by comparison with other more flexible countries. The concern was explicitly voiced that Britain's reluctance to lift all its restrictions with regard to arms was depriving her of the much-needed capital generated by its arms industry. This was particularly worrisome as Britain was dependent on trade and investments overseas, to which arms sales heavily contributed, generating roughly £500 million (close to 6 billions in today's value) per year and contributing to the British defence industries' overhead costs in sustaining the British Armed Forces. Despite affirming the urgency of vigorously promoting exports, the conclusion reached, one that Wilson found 'generally acceptable',[72] clarified that arms sales should be restricted to cases relating to NATO.[73]

With regard to Greece, it was noted that defence relations, albeit 'friendly and reasonably close', were nonetheless unproductive. The possibility of awarding Yarrows the tender of four or five frigates had resurfaced in view of the Greeks' lack of interest in the front-running American ships. The Foreign Office met this renewed opportunity with clear approval given that the frigates were requested within NATO's framework and were moreover 'badly' needed by the Greek Navy.[74]

In the meantime, the constantly articulated British fears over the escalation of Greek–Turkish antagonism were becoming more pronounced. These flared not so much from the Aegean oil dispute, although they were undoubtedly exacerbated by it, but from the issue of Cyprus irredentism, which was very important for the British. In fact, the troubles, of which the British were always mindful, escalated as the news of the first violent clashes on the island reached London on 15 July.[75] The first indications seemed to verify the British long-held anxieties, namely the staging of a coup by 'Greek contingent/Greek officer elements of National Guard', while special attention was paid on the widely circulating news that Makarios was dead.[76]

The British Foreign Office was immediately put on alert. Callaghan tried to diffuse the rising tensions by urging restraint. In the telegram sent to the Greek Foreign Minister, he encapsulated his grave worry over the unfolding developments by calling them 'undoubtedly very dangerous with serious implications for the stability of the Mediterranean and for the cohesion of the Atlantic Alliance.'[77] At the same time, an urgent call for 'exemplary patience' was directed at his

Turkish counterpart together with the plea that his government would refrain from 'any kind of precipitate action or intervention.'[78]

Parallel efforts were undertaken to consult with Kissinger in order to compare notes and streamline their two countries' actions. Similar initiatives were also directed towards Joseph Luns, NATO's Secretary General. In addition, the British proposed the idea of calling an emergency meeting within the United Nations Peacekeeping Force in Cyprus.[79] However, the latter request did not produce any tangible results, as it failed to secure American commitment on the grounds that it would 'internationalise' the crisis in 'an undesirable manner'.[80] Although the American administration was slow in ratifying British requests by trying to downplay them, the Soviets were quick in offering to send troops to the island in order to restore order—an overture which unsurprisingly met with British opposition.[81]

Meanwhile, in search of realistic solutions, the British rejected calls raised by pro-Makarios Cypriots championing direct intervention.[82] A number of similar requests pressing Britain for a more pro-active stance within the Security Council were made in London. Even Prime Minister Wilson directly inquired about this prospect with his Foreign Office. In fact, his personal engagement was representative of London's high-pitched diplomatic fervour.

However, the reply of the British Foreign Office adhered to the line pursued by their American colleagues, especially in view of the lack of American backing. They ruled against taking any action, which would point the 'finger publicly at Turkey', as they reasoned that this could provoke their armed intervention. Hence, they concluded that 'a Security Council meeting now, while the situation is still very unclear, could encourage the parties concerned to make provocative statements in public, which could make the situation worse, not better.'[83]

In view of the lack of serious external constraints, the emerging conditions in Greece remained in flux, precipitating a number of chain reactions including the resignation of Foreign Minister Spyridon Tetenes and his replacement by Konstantinos Kypreos. Such was the confusion in Greece that the latter, while expressing real sympathy about the extent of British unease, confided to Hooper that he was not fully informed about internal developments.[84]

In the meantime, British officials upon receipt of confirmation that the Cypriot President, Makarios, who was forcibly deposed and replaced by the hardliner Nikos Sampson on 15 July, was still alive, took precautionary action. They strongly recommended that he should leave Cyprus immediately for the fear of an escalation of tensions. At the same time, they admitted that their intervention by force 'was not on the cards at the moment'; instead they favoured a calm wait.[85] In line with this policy they demonstrated determination to rebuff Turkish approaches the following day exploring Britain's willingness to grant tacit acquiescence to a Turkish military intervention.

The widespread concerns materialised only five days later, when the Turkish government authorised the invasion of the northern part of the island using as pretext the need to protect the Turkish Cypriot minority. While the analysis of the diplomatic manoeuvres of the British government prior to and in the aftermath of this seminal event would require another book, these final few pages will concentrate on their reaction to one of the most fundamental repercussions for Greece that the Cyprus crisis precipitated, namely the demise of the Greek Colonels' regime on 23 July 1974.

Amidst the diplomatic agitation resulting from the 'fateful and absorbing period'[86] following the Turkish military provocation and the very strong fears regarding the evolving imbroglio, the British started receiving information about the formation of a civilian government in Greece. Hooper reported the Greek public's reaction as of 'extraordinary jubilation', which intensified when a day later Karamanlis was summoned from Paris and 'returned to a hero's welcome'[87] to assume the post of the Greek Prime Minister with George Mavros as his deputy and in charge of the Foreign Office.

British elation was at commensurable levels. Their excitement over Karamanlis' return to power was evident in the welcoming tone of the Prime Minister's hastily issued congratulatory message, which inter alia stated:

> Please accept my warmest congratulations. I have no doubt that your high reputation as an international statesman and your long experience will make an invaluable contribution at this critical time.[88]

The optimistic tone of the official British reaction constituted a clear departure from the restraint characterising their previous congratulatory messages during the Colonels' seven-year rule. The British were particularly pleased to observe the new government's 'strong pro-NATO, pro-Western Europe bias' and the 'strong anglophil[e]' character of the Ministry of Foreign Affairs. They also noted with delight that the new government was welcomed by supporters of the two main political parties, which had reportedly 'planned the formation of a government including Karamanlis and Mavros since early 1973.'[89]

In spite of admitting that 'the present government is as good as we are likely to get',[90] they advised against becoming 'over-committed'[91] at that very early stage. Hooper argued forcefully that the interim administration was 'far from being the "ecumenical" government which some hoped after the return of Karamanlis.'[92] Additional factors which deepened his concern were the 'bickering and factionalism endemic in Greek politics'[93] to which the reported 'infighting' and 'long-standing differences' testified.[94] He expressed specific trepidation about the possibility of the outbreak of 'clashes between the young left and the new government, particularly if Cyprus goes sour.'[95] The initial British scepticism was shared by the Americans too, who believed that 'Mr Karamanlis was on a narrow ledge.'[96] What is interesting is that as late as 4 September, Hooper in his valedictory dispatch pointed out the ensuing instability of the Greek government due to the Cyprus disaster, the return of 'Andreas Papandreou and other potential trouble-makers', and Greece's 'unhealthy' dependence 'on a few strong personalities, especially the Prime Minister'.[197] This was in sharp contradistinction to his earlier comment that Papadopoulos had brought 'stability of a kind and prosperity.'[98]

However, there is no doubt about the overall relief and satisfaction felt by the British about the demise of the Colonels' regime. This was epitomised in the following note by Callaghan, who commented on the establishment of democratic government in Greece as 'an uncovenanted bonus' of the fateful invasion of Cyprus, one whose consolidation 'Britain did a great deal to assist ... in those first days of uncertainty.'[99] And if this statement was aimed at restoring the record of Britain's policy towards Greece, the following comment made by the retiring Ambassador Hooper, always a strong influence on British attitudes towards the Colonels' regime, may raise eyebrows and bring their intended 'catharsis' into question: 'the day may come when this volatile people will look back on Papadopoulos' first few years as an interlude of internal peace and prosperity in the turbulent history of their country.'[100] As he had put it on an earlier occasion:

> had it not been for the coup d'état of 1967, by now Greece would either have been a country similar to those of Eastern Europe, or a member of the Third World. Neither of these possibilities would have been to the advantage of Western Europe.[101]

EPILOGUE

Michael Stewart, British Foreign Minister between 1968 and 1970, noted with disillusionment in his diary that 'the great difficulty of the world is the moral deficiencies of what should be the free world—Greece, Portugal—Germany distracted, France selfish, ourselves aimless, USA in torment.'[1] It has been the aim of this book to account for and evaluate British policy towards the Greek Colonels' dictatorship. Emphasis was placed on analysing the decision-making process and investigating the impact of specific individuals, whilst highlighting their motives, dilemmas and debates during this complicated seven-year-long phase in Anglo–Greek relations.

The general conclusions certainly corroborate Michael Stewart's lament. The foreign policy formulated by both the Wilson and Heath governments testifies to his assessment, as the limited British attempts at rectifying the 'moral deficiencies' of the Colonels' regime persistently lacked determination and consistency either due to weakness or opportunism. With all its rights and wrongs exposed and discussed, British policy did display consistency in one aspect, which was pragmatism.

It has become amply clear throughout this book that British foreign policy transcended political party boundaries, as it was directed not so much by rhetorical ideologies as by power politics. This assessment is reinforced by the fact that there was no great rancour or glaring disjunction in the policies of either the Labour or the Conservative governments towards the Greek Colonels; rather, their approaches were quite similar and resulted in a remarkable cohesion. It should nonetheless be pointed out that Heath's government showed a greater propensity than Wilson's to facilitate its dealings with the Colonels' regime in an effort to safeguard British interests more effectively. On a number of occasions, the Conservatives were keener to actively promote arms sales and improve their trade prospects with Greece. As they appeared to be more committed to their objectives, they not only were prepared to follow a less reactive stance, but even came forward as more pro-active and accommodating, for example in arranging for the exchange of official visits.

Regardless of their varying degrees of flexibility, it can certainly be argued that all three British governments' policies towards the Colonels' regime were based on realistic assessments of what would be more beneficial for the promotion of British interests with regard to implications for unity within NATO, shared responsibility with Greece over Cyprus, as well as Greece's potentially profitable markets. Influenced by the stringent dictates of the currency devaluation and Cold War era, and buttressed by the American administration, the British governments showed cautious tolerance of the regime's dictatorial methods and implemented policies tantamount to 'business as usual', awkwardly conducted though that business occasionally was. It is on the basis of such motives that all three British governments persistently manifested pusillanimity by avoiding any direct confrontation with the Colonels with only a handful of exceptions.

Although there are no solid grounds to substantiate claims of British complicity in the coming to power of the Greek Colonels, the vast majority of the sources consulted suggest that the British governments did next to nothing to influence the regime's demise—quite the contrary, as it was always feared that the Colonels' fall might precipitate their unwelcome substitution by rulers less sympathetic to British interests. And this finding is rather incriminating in view of the British officials' plethora of reassuring statements that their government was 'firmly committed to the principles of democracy and human rights' and that its stance towards Greece 'takes full account of this.'[2]

It was often reiterated that the British had no right to meddle in the domestic affairs of another country; but the idea of direct intervention in Greece was hardly unfamiliar, as evidenced by British actions as recently as during the Dekemvriana clashes that took place in Athens between late 1944 and early 1945. However, there was one significant difference between the mid-1940s and the late 1960s, namely that Britain's world power status had shrunk considerably and its role as referee in world affairs had been assumed by the United States. Furthermore, and perhaps even more significantly, the Colonels' regime was fiercely opposed to Communism, which had been the raison d'être for British intervention in Greek affairs in the 1940s. In other words, turning a blind eye was clearly in part a reflection of the Manichean Cold War divide; the Colonels were unpleasant, but at least they were on the right side.

Such British motivations might well constitute a legitimate calculation for the protection of British national interests, but it leaves no room for doubt that all three governments' high-minded declarations of their commitment to the Greek regime's rapid democratisation were nothing more than lip service for public consumption. In other words, they served more as a leitmotif in continuing full diplomatic relations and dealings with the Greek regime; while useful for assuaging public opprobrium, they would never be allowed to imperil Britain's vital interests in Greece. As Sir Alec Douglas-Home confessed 'foreign policy and defence is too serious a matter to be conducted on the basis of emotional reactions to aspects of other governments' policies, over which we have no control.'[3]

In fact, throughout the duration of the regime, 'it was the various vehicles of public opinion rather than the executive authorities that sustained the resistance'[4] to the Colonels. Numerous public demonstrations were held in Britain, although at times more regularly than others; a number of resistance organisations sprang up; numberless letters of protest were sent to newspapers and British MPs as well as to the Prime Minister's office; and questions regarding British policy towards Greece were frequently raised during parliamentary debates. The British people's, albeit erroneous, perception of Greece as a bastion of democracy resulted in a far greater degree of public obloquy towards the Greek Colonels' regime compared with, for instance, the military overthrows in Turkey and Pakistan—both significant British military allies—reactions to which were tepid at best. According to Amnesty International's Researcher on Greece, Anne Burley, 'people always knew that nasty things were happening to people in far distant countries, but Greece had a special place in the European imagination.'[5]

The gathering energy of anti-junta protests was aided by the many and active British members of a number of international organisations implacably opposed to the Colonels together with the noticeable concentration of Greek émigrés in London, who believed that the long entrenched liberal democratic political tradition in Britain would better accommodate their struggles for Greece's democratisation. Additionally, a large number of backbenchers who, as a result of being disenfranchised by the governments' policy-making, were free from limitations, repeatedly criticised their own governments' policies of doing business with the military regime in Greece.

Divisions were noted even within the Cabinet itself, especially during the Labour administrations. On one occasion for example, Barbara Castle, the then Secretary of State for employment, spoke of her government's policy as a 'sell-out on Greece'.[6] The most polarising intra-Cabinet issue pertained to the sale of arms to Greece; this was of course not surprising as bitter rivalries over such a politically sensitive issue had occurred during other instances too, most notably in late 1967 over a similar debate about South Africa. The quandary of several Cabinet ministers on this specific issue was expressively epitomised by Tony Benn, who admitted that he was 'torn between detesting the Greek government and feeling that… we should lose a lot of other civil contracts, which would ultimately undermine our economy',[7] if they would refuse to sell arms to Greece.

So all in all, successive British governments faced a welter of censure, either generated from or embedded within its own ranks and its own electorate, as a large swathe of an irate British public, the vast majority of the exiled Greeks, as well as a significant proportion of the British political world characterised the official stance as craven and completely incongruent with an ethical foreign policy. Nevertheless it would have been quite naïve to expect heroism or even moral probity consistently upheld in the foreign policy of any government. According to Sir Alec Douglas-Home, 'while there was a moral content to foreign policy, account had to be had of the physical security of a continent under threat.'[8]

Such strong public interest not only complicated the conduct of British foreign policy, but on a number of instances created friction in

Anglo–Greek relations. In order to harmonise their close, albeit at times frayed, relationship with Greece's illiberal and anachronistic rulers, successive governments employed justifications, which were far from convincing, as has been amply demonstrated. Some critics went a step further by alleging that such arguments were 'at least an illusion or a convenient self-delusion, if not an impromptu and convenient excuse for such a dishonourable inertia and inaction.'[9]

Substantial evidence suggests that all three administrations, and most emphatically the Labour governments, were quite sympathetic to such calls, and were appalled by the undemocratic nature and the repressive methods of the regime in Greece. On several occasions, the British officials themselves described their policy as 'unheroic' at worst and 'correct under the circumstances' at best.[10] Nonetheless it became quickly apparent that neither Labour nor Conservatives could afford to stand up against the regime, in the way for instance that the Scandinavian countries were able to, due to constraints of *Realpolitik*.

In short, British governments' attitudes towards the Greek Colonels during their seven years in power were a synthesis of multi-faceted issues and challenges stemming from various contradictory pressures. This is why, although the motives behind them can be easily spelled out, the policies themselves, in which humanitarian and moral implications often gave way to pragmatism, can be summarised as ambiguous. A British official made a distinction between 'a) what it [British government] says publicly, b) what it says in private and c) what it does in practice.'[11] Interestingly enough, though, the Colonels' administration refused to brand British foreign policy as 'hypocritical', but instead insisted that it was rather 'balanced' in light of the obvious advantages that their regime afforded to them, even if they could not openly admit it.[12]

British governments were faced with the dire predicament of having to choose between public calumny and blackmail by Greece's rulers. By not fully supporting the Greek regime, but equally failing to condemn it, they ended up with a policy that was rather erratic and spineless. As an amalgam of *Realpolitik* disguised with specious allusions to ethical considerations, the policy came across as mercurial; and such a stance was not particularly fruitful at any level. For one thing, at no point did the Colonels seem likely to act on their threats of withdrawing from NATO, nor did Britain benefit to any significant extent from its financial dealings with them; and worse of all, they failed to avert the Cyprus imbroglio.

A senior diplomat in Athens once spread his hands expressively: 'What can we do? I do not know what our role here is. Sometimes the Prime Minister made violent remarks, which he presumed were for back-bench consumption, about barbarities and so on. Then we lose all our contacts—but what do we gain? What are we aiming at?'[13] Given the overall displeasure with the dictatorial features of the Greek regime, as evidenced by comments made by high-ranking officials and diplomats across the British political spectrum and even Prime Minister Wilson, who spoke of the regime's barbarous methods, British policy towards the regime could have been considerably more hostile, had it not been for the protection of the country's vital interests. In fact, almost all British officials found the Colonels' regime personally distasteful and thuggish, but were obliged when acting as officialdom to recognize that Britain alone carried little weight, that the economic benefits to an ailing British economy were too attractive to ignore or sacrifice, that NATO could not afford to alienate Greece (and in any case already had dictatorships in its ranks), that Cyprus was too serious an issue of mutual concern, and that the Greeks themselves were rather disunited, if not docile, in their resistance.

It obviously needs no further elaboration that once in power there are a variety of factors and considerations that a government needs to take into account in formulating foreign policy, and the British governments between 1967 and 1974 were no exception. The case of the Colonels' dictatorial regime undoubtedly bears witness to the classic dilemma between moral correctness and political expediency; and this was not an unknown scenario in most Western countries, who had adopted similarly complaisant policies towards the regime on account of the associated benefits. The undoubted human rights abuses are perhaps the least forgivable aspect and here there is an interesting parallel to be drawn between Anglo–Greek relations and the unethically benign stance adopted by British officials towards the Pinochet regime in the late 1970s and 1980s.

In essence, in trying to steer a course between Scylla (i.e. the damaging consequences of retaliation by the Colonels, such as that which followed Harold Wilson's frank condemnation of the regime in July 1968) and Charybdis (i.e. public outcry fomented by highly critical British press coverage), all three British governments implemented a policy founded on a fair degree of pragmatism and even conservatism. It could be safely argued that the Greek episode fully illustrates the challenges a government always faces when in power, namely a constant clash between the preservation of its values and the safeguarding of the country's interests—an unrelenting struggle between idealism and pragmatism. In the case of the Greek departure from democracy, as in most analogous cases, for instance with the coups in Portugal and Turkey, yet again the expedient course of action ended up prevailing over the morally correct one; and a country with significant power and influence, occupying a pivotal position between Greece and the United States, chose to mind its own business.

NOTES

INTRODUCTION

1. See of instance, Richard Clogg, *Anglo-Greek Attitudes: Studies in History* (2000); Robert Holland and Diana Markides, *The British and the Hellenes: Struggles for Mastery in the Eastern Mediterranean, 1850–1960* (2006); George Pagoulatos (ed.), *UK/Greece: A New Look at Relations* (2000); Konstantina Maragkou, *«Ελληνοβρετανικές σχέσεις κατά τη σύντομη δεκαετία του 1960»* ('Anglo-Greek relations during the "brief decade" of the 1960s') in Manolis Vasilakis (ed.), *From the Unrelenting Struggle to Dictatorship* (2009); G. M. Alexander, *The Prelude to the Truman Doctrine: British Policy in Greece, 1944–47* (1982); Prokopis Papastratis, *British Policy Towards Greece in the Second World War, 1941–1944* (1984); John Koliopoulos, *Greece and the British Connection, 1935–1941* (1977); Konstantina Maragkou, 'British Responses to "The Rape of Greek Democracy"', *The Journal of Contemporary History* (2010); Effie Pedaliu, 'Human Rights and Foreign Policy: Wilson and the Greek Dictators, 1967–1970', *Diplomacy and Statecraft* (2007).
2. George Pagoulatos, *UK/Greece* (2001), p. 9.
3. John Kofas, *Intervention and Underdevelopment: Greece during the Cold War* (1989), p. 7.
4. Yearly Report 1972, Secret, 10 January 1973, Protocol no. 0445/1/155, File no. 1973.3, Diplomatic Archives of the Greek Ministry of Foreign Affairs [hereafter, all references to DAGMFA refer to the Diplomatic Archives of the Greek Ministry of Foreign Affairs].
5. Record of a meeting held at the Greek Ministry of Foreign Affairs on 12 September 1966 between the Chancellor of the Duchy of Lancaster and the Greek Minister of Foreign Affairs, Confidential, 12 September 1966, FO 371/185666, National Archives (hereafter, all references to TNA refer to British National Archives).

6. Regarding the US policy towards the Greek Colonels, see Robert Keeley, *The Colonels' Coup and the American Embassy: A Diplomat's View of the Breakdown of Democracy in Cold War Greece* (2011); James Edward Miller, *The United States and the Making of Modern Greece: History and Power, 1950–74* (2009); Alexis Papahellas, *The Rape of Greek Democracy* (1997); and L. Klarevas, 'Were the Eagle and the Phoenix Birds of a Feather? The United States and the Greek Coup of 1967, *Diplomatic History* (2007). Additional publications on various aspects of the US-Greek connection at the time include the following: Sotiris Rizas, *The United States, the Dictatorship of the Colonels and the Issue of Cyprus, 1967–1974* (2002); Konstantina Maragkou, 'Favouritism in NATO's South-Eastern Flank: The Case of the Greek Colonels, 1967–1974', *Cold War History* (2009); John Sakkas, 'The Greek dictatorship, the USA and the Arabs', *The Journal of Southern Europe and the Balkans* (2004); and Konstantina Maragkou, 'The Relevance of Détente to American Foreign Policy: The Case of Greece, 1967–1979', *Diplomacy & Statecraft* (2014).

7. Letter, John Spraos, Chairman of the Greek Committee against Dictatorship, to Michael Stewart, Foreign Secretary, 22 April 1968, Modern Greek Archives (MGA) correspondence, II, Birmingham Branch of League for Democracy in Greece, King's College London, Archives and Special Collections [KCLA hereafter].

8. Half-yearly Report 1972, Greek Ambassador to Greek Ministry of Foreign Affairs, 29 June 1972, Protocol no. 0445/15/1312, File no. 1973.3, DAGMFA.

9. Interviews with Stylianos Pattakos and Nickolaos Makarezos.

10. Memorandum by Sir Michael Stewart, UK Policy towards Greece, Confidential, 17 February 1969, FCO 9/871, TNA.

11. Exceptions include the following articles: Konstantina Maragkou, 'British Responses to "The Rape of Greek Democracy"' (2010); Effie Pedaliu, 'Human Rights and Foreign Policy' (2007); and Helen Conispoliatis, 'Facing the Colonels: How the British Government Dealt With the Military Coup in Greece in April 1967', *History* (2007).

12. For a comprehensive analysis of British foreign policy in the late 1960s and early 1970s, see Jonathan Hollowell (ed.), *Britain Since 1945* (2003); David Childs, *Britain Since 1945: A Political History* (2012); John W. Young, Effie Pedaliu, Michael D. Kandiah (eds), *Britain in World Politics: From Churchill to Blair*, Vol. 2 (2013); S. Dockrill, *Britain's Retreat from East of Suez: The Choice between Europe and the World* (2002); Stuart Ball and Anthony Seldon (eds), *The Heath government, 1970–74*, (1996); and Glen O'Hara and Helen Parr (eds), *The Wilson governments, 1964–1970 Reconsidered* (2014).

13. Telegram, Athens 4797, Phillips Talbot, American Embassy in Athens, to Department of State, Secret, Priority, 21 April 1967, Department of State, Central Files, POL 23–9 Greece, American National Administration of Records and Archives, College Park, MD [hereafter 'NARA'].

14. Georgios Hristopoulos and Ioannis Bastias, *Istoria tou Ellinikou Ethnous* (*'History of the Greek Nation'*), Vol. 16, (2000), p. 266.

15. For an account of Greece's history in the 1960s, see John S. Koliopoulos and Thanos Veremis, *Modern Greece: A History Since 1821* (2009); Richard Clogg, *A Concise History of Greece* (2013), Kostis Kornetis, *Children of the Dictatorship: Student Resistance, Cultural Politics and the Long 1960s in Greece* (2013). See also David H. Close, *Greece since 1945* (2002).

16. *Kathimerini*, 21 April 1967, front page (Εξξεράγη στρατιωτικόν κίνημα— συνελήφθησαν πολιτικοί άνδρες την 2:30 πρωινήν δύναμις τεθωρακισμένων κατέλαβεν το κέντρον των Αθηνών. Υπό τα έκπληκτα βλέμματα ολίγων Αθηναίων που εκυκλοφόρουν, την προκεχωρημένην αυτήν ώρα, τεθωρακισμένα απέκλεισαν τα Παλαιά Ανάκτορα, ενώ στρατιωτικαί δυνάμεις κατελάμβανον τον ΟΤΕ τους ραδιοφωνικούς θαλάμους του ΕΙΡ εις το Ζάππειον και τα υπουργεία).

17. S. Gregoriades, *The History of the Dictatorship*, Volume 1 (1975), p. 99.

18. *The Guardian*, 14 December 1967, p. 9.

19. *The Times*, 24 April 1967, p. 9.

20. For a comprehensive account of the history of the military establishment in Modern Greece, see Thanos Veremis, *The Military in Greek Politics: From Independence to Democracy* (1997) and Dimitris Charalambes, *Stratos kai Politike Exousia* (*'The Military and Political Power'*) (1985).

21. Interview with Ben Whitaker.

22. *The Times*, 22 April 1967, front page.

23. *The Daily Telegraph*, 22 April 1967, front page.

24. *The Guardian*, 24 April 1967, front page.

25. *The Guardian*, 22 April 1967, front page.

26. 'Conclusions of a Meeting on Greece', N. J. Barrington, Confidential, 17 February 1969, FCO 9/871, TNA.

27. Telegram Athens 4797, Phillips Talbot, American Embassy in Athens to Department of State, Secret, Priority, 21 April 1967, Department of State, Central Files, POL 23–9 Greece, NARA.

28. P. Mangold, *Success and Failure in British Foreign Policy: Evaluating the Record, 1900–2000* (2001), pp. 8–11.

29. John W. Young, 'Britain and "LBJ's War", 1964–68', in *Cold War History* (2002), p. 88.

30. For an account of Anglo-American relations at the time, see J. Dumbrell, *A Special Relationship: Anglo-American Relations in the Cold War and After* (2001), J. Hollowell (ed.), *Twentieth Century Anglo-American Relations* (2001), and John Baylis, *Anglo-American Defence Relations, 1939–1984: The Special Relationship* (1984).

31. Goodman, *Awkward Warrior: Frank Cousins, His Life and Times*, p. 493, quoted in John W. Young, 'Britain and "LBJ's War", 1964–68' (2002), p. 88.

32. Harold Wilson, *The Labour Government, 1964–1970: A Personal Record* (1971), p. 439.

33. J. W. Young, *Britain and European Unity, 1945–1992* (1993), pp. 172–3.

34. On British entry in the European Community see, among others: Oliver J. Daddow, *Britain and Europe Since 1945: Historiographical Perspectives on Integration* (2004); Stephen George, *An Awkward Partner: Britain in the European Community* (1990); David Gowland and Arthur Turner, *Reluctant Europeans: Britain and European Integration, 1945–1998* (2000); Hugo Young, *This Blessed Plot: Britain and Europe from Churchill to Blair* (1999).

35. See, George Kazamias, 'Britain in the Cyprus Crisis of 1974', *GreeSE Paper No 42*, Hellenic Observatory Papers on Greece and Southeast Europe, December 2010; Vassilis Fouskas, 'Uncomfortable Questions: Cyprus, October 1973–August 1974', in *Contemporary European History*, Volume 14, Issue 1; Jan Asmussen, *Cyprus At War: Diplomacy and Conflict During the 1974 Crisis* (2008); Polyvios Polyviou, *Η Διπλωματία της Εισβολής ['The Diplomacy of the Invasion']* (2010).

1. FROM 'EXTREME RESERVE' TO 'BUSINESS AS USUAL'

1. *Greek Observer*, March 1969, p. 24.
2. K. Maragkou, 'The Foreign Factor and the Greek Colonels' coming to power on 21 April 1967', in *Southeast European and Black Sea Studies* (2006), pp. 427–443.
3. Foreign and Commonwealth Office Brief prepared for Prime Minister Wilson, Secret, 19 June 1969, PREM 13/2697, TNA.
4. Telegram, Sir Patrick Dean to FCO, 26 April 1967, FCO 9/125, TNA.
5. Telegram 276, Sir Ralph Murray Athens to FCO, Confidential, 21 April 1967, FCO 9/124, TNA.
6. Letter, P. L. O'Keeffe British Embassy to A. E. Palmer FCO, Secret, 4 February 1971, FCO 9/1385, TNA.
7. Cabinet Conclusions (67) 28th meeting, 4 May 1967, CAB 128/42, TNA.

8. Telegram, State 187449, Rusk, Department of State to American Embassy in Athens, Secret, 3 May 1967, Department of State, Central Files, POL 15 Greece, NARA.

9. Harold Wilson, *The Labour Government, 1964–1970: A Personal Record*, (1971), p. 685.

10. Parliamentary Debates, House of Commons, vol. 750, 20 July 1967.

11. Telegram, State 180756, Katzenbach, Department of State to American Embassy in Athens, Secret, 23 April 1967, Department of State, Central Files, POL 15–1 Greece, NARA.

12. *The Times*, 25 April 1967, p. 5.

13. Telegram, State 180756, Katzenbach, Department of State to American Embassy in Athens, Secret, 23 April 1967, Department of State, Central Files, POL 15–1 Greece, POL Greece-UK, NARA.

14. Cabinet Conclusions (67), 28th meeting, 4 May 1967, CAB 128/42, TNA.

15. Parliamentary Records, House of Commons, vol. 745, 24 April 1967, c. 1160.

16. Parliamentary Records, House of Commons, vol. 746, 11 May 1967.

17. Telegram, London 8978, American Embassy in London to Sec State, Limited Official Use, 29 April 1967, Department of State, Central Files, POL 23–9 Greece, NARA.

18. Parliamentary Records, House of Lords, vol. 283, c. 515, 8 June 1967.

19. Report on a visit to Greece, M. K. Macmillan, MP and A. Gregory, MP to House of Commons, 18 May 1967, PREM 13/1690, TNA.

20. Ibid.

21. Greece, George Brown to Harold Wilson, 1 May 1967, Secret, FCO 9/164, TNA.

22. Robert McDonald, 'The Colonels' Dictatorship', in Marion Sarafis and Martin Eve (eds), *Background to Contemporary Greece*, p. 266.

23. Sotiris Rizas, *The Rise of the Left in Southern Europe: Anglo-American Responses* (2012), p. 57.

24. *The Times*, 23 December 1967, p. 6.

25. Ms.Eng.c.5019, Modern Political Papers, Bodleian Library, Oxford.

26. Alan Davidson to Hohler, Confidential, 26 April 1967, FCO 9/125, TNA.

27. Telegram, Sir Ralph Murray to FCO, 26 April 1967, FCO 9/124, TNA.

28. Cabinet Paper: Greece, A. E. Davidson to Hohler, Confidential, 15 May 1967, FCO 9/164, TNA.

29. R. Keeley, *The Colonels' Coup and the American Embassy: A Diplomat's View of the Breakdown of Democracy in Cold War Greece* (2011).

30. Intelligence Memorandum, Subject: Military take-over in Greece (Situation Report Number 2–1130 EST), CIA, Directorate of Intelligence, 21 April 1967, NSF, Country File, Middle East, Memos & Miscellaneous, Vol. III, Lyndon B. Johnson Library Archives, Austin, Texas [LBJ hereafter].

31. Telegram, Sir Patrick Dean to FO, 21 April 1967, FCO 9/125, TNA.

32. Yiannis Valinakis, 'The US Bases in Greece: The Political Context', in Thanos Veremis, US Bases in the Mediterranean (1989), p. 33.

33. Ibid.

34. Ibid.

35. Letter from Sir Michael Stewart to Hohler, Confidential, 3 August 1967, FCO 9/172, TNA.

36. John W. Young, The Labour Governments: 1964–1970, Vol. 2 (2003), p. 135.

37. Cabinet, Memorandum by the Secretary of State for Foreign Affairs, An Anglo-American balance sheet, CP 64 164, 2 September 1964, Secret, TNA CAB 129/118.

38. Ibid.

39. Ennio di Nolfo, 'The Transformation of the Mediterranean, 1960–1975', in Odd Arne Westad and Melvyn P. Leffler (eds), The Cambridge History of the Cold War (2010), p. 245.

40. John Sakkas, 'The Greek Dictatorship, the USA and the Arabs, 1967–1974', in The Journal of Southern Europe and the Balkans, (2004), p. 252.

41. Peter Murtagh, The Rape of Greece: The King, the Colonels and the Resistance (1994), p. 155.

42. Record of a meeting held at the Greek Ministry of Foreign Affairs on 12 September 1967, between the Chancellor of the Duchy of Lancaster and the Greek Minister of Foreign Affairs, Confidential, Foreign Office and Whitehall Distribution, 12 September 1967, FO 371/185666, TNA

43. Ibid.

44. 1967 Reports, Memos, Cabinet JIC series, Soviet policies in the Middle East and North Africa and their likely development, CAB 158/66, TNA.

45. R. W. James, Foreign Office to W. J. Luscombe Office of the Minister without Portfolio, Anglo-Greek relations, 4 August 1966, FCO 371/185666, CE 1052/5, TNA.

46. Telegram, H. A. F. Hohler to George Brown, Confidential, 21 April 1967, FCO 9/125, TNA.

47. Telegram, George Brown to Washington, Confidential, 25 April 1967, FCO 9/125, TNA.

48. Telegram, Sir Ralph Murray to Sir Michael Stewart, Confidential, 2 June 1967, FCO 9/170, TNA.

49. Speaking notes, The new Greek government, Confidential, FCO 9/125; Conclusions of a meeting of the Cabinet, Secret, CC(67)23, CAB 128/42, TNA.

50. Amendments to C.O.S. 1591/9/3/64, DEFE 11/445, undated in Alan James, Keeping the Peace in the Cyprus Crisis of 1963–1964, (2002), p. 58.

51. Signed in 1955—known as the Baghdad Pact until 1959—by Iran, Iraq, Turkey, Pakistan and the UK in an effort to contain the Soviet Union by forming a line of strong states along its south-western frontier.

52. Joint Memorandum by the Secretary for Foreign Affairs and the Secretary of State for Commonwealth Affairs, Subject: British interest in Cyprus, OPD (67) 65, 29 June 1967, FCO 28/67, TNA.

53. DO 161/5, dispatch no. 8 from Sir A. Clark, High Commissioner to CRO, para. 31, 23 November 1962 in Alan James, *Keeping the Peace in the Cyprus crisis of 1963–1964*, p. 44.

54. Christos Xanthopoulos-Palamas, *Diplomatic Triptych* (1979), p. 220.

55. *The Times*, 4 September 1967, p. 3.

56. Greece, George Brown to Harold Wilson, 1 May 1967, Secret, FCO 9/164, TNA.

57. Restricted Saving Telegram, FO to UK Director IMF/IBRD, Washington, UK/Greek Intergovernmental debt, 3 November 1967, T 312/1866, TNA.

58. C. C. Lucas to Owen, 6 October 1967, T 334/144, TNA.

59. Brief for the Financial Secretary, The Situation in Greece, R. S. Symons to Hay, 5 June 1967, T 312/1867, TNA.

60. Phillips to Gorham, Secret, 14 June 1968, FCO 9/172, TNA.

61. Restricted Saving Telegram, FO to UK Director IMF/IBRD, Washington, UK/Greek Intergovernmental debt, 3 November 1967, T 312/1866, TNA.

62. R. W. James, Foreign Office to W. I. Luscombe, Office of the Minister without portfolio, 4 August 1966, FCO 371/185666, CE 105215, TNA.

63. FO to UK Director IMF/IBRD, Washington, 3 November 1967, T 312/1866, TNA.

64. Memorandum of Conversation, Subject: Greek Situation, Secret, 24 April 1967, Department of State, Central Files, POL 23–9, NARA.

65. Record of a meeting between the Foreign Secretary and H.M. Ambassador in Athens, Confidential, 3 May 1967, FCO 9/126, TNA.

66. Cabinet Conclusions (67) 28th meeting, 4 May 1967, CAB 128/42, TNA.

67. Ms. Wilson. c.889, 8 May 1967, Modern Political Papers, Bodleian Library.

68. Alexander Kazamias, 'Antiquity as Cold War Propaganda: The Political Uses of the Classical Past in Post-Civil War Greece', in Dimitiris Tziovas (ed.), *Re-imagining the Past: Antiquity and Modern Greek Culture* (2014), p. 39.

69. *The Guardian*, 9 April 1970, p. 4.

70. Interview with Roger Williams.

71. *The Guardian*, 9 April 1970, p. 4.

72. For an account of the anti-Colonels' campaign in London, see Maria Karavia, *The London Diary (To Imerologio tou Londinou)*, (2007).

73. *The Times*, 23 December 1967, p. 6.

74. Greece, George Brown to Harold Wilson, 1 May 1967, Secret, FCO 9/164, TNA.

75. Cabinet Conclusions, 23(67), 23d meeting, 27 April 1967, CAB 128/42, TNA.

76. Ibid.

77. Ibid.

78. Telegram, London 8713, Bruce, American Embassy in London to Secretary of State, Subject: Greek coup, Secret, Priority, 24 April 1967, Department of State, Central Files, POL 23–9 Greece, NARA.

79. Telegram, State 183175, Department of State to American Embassy in Athens, Secret, Flash, 27 April 1967, Department of State, Central Files, POL Greece-UK, POL Greece-US, NARA.

80. Ms. Wilson.c.889, 8 May 1967, Modern Political Papers, Bodleian Library.

81. Ibid.

82. Guidance No 96, Foreign and Commonwealth Office to Certain Missions, Confidential, Priority, 9 May 1967, FCO 9/227, TNA.

83. *The Times*, 24 November 1967, p. 4.

84. *The Times*, 23 November 1967, front page.

85. *The Times*, 22 November 1967, p. 4.

86. Memorandum on Greece, Alan Davidson to Private Secretary, 20 December 1967, FCO/139, TNA.

87. OPD (68) 13th meeting, Memorandum by the Foreign Secretary on Policy towards Greece, 12 July 1968, CAB 148/35, TNA.

88. *The Times*, 14 December 1967, p. 10.

89. Interview with Stylianos Pattakos.

90. Ms.Eng.c.5018, Motion 393 & 394, Party Conference at Scarborough, p. 49, Bodleian Library, Modern Political Papers.

91. Ibid.

92. Ms.Eng.c.5019, Modern Political Papers, Bodleian Library.

93. Ibid.

94. Clive Ponting, *Breach of Promise: Labour in Power, 1964–1970*, (1989), p. 321.

95. Ibid., p. 183.

96. Telegram, Verykios to Greek Ministry of Foreign Affairs, Secret, 20 October 1967, Protocol no. 5904/ST/2, File no. 1968/3.2, DAGMFA.

97. I. T. M. Lucas to H. A. F. Hohler, Confidential, 16 August 1967, FCO 9/227, TNA.

98. Telegram, Bonn 3878, McGhee (American Embassy in Bonn) to Secretary of State, Confidential, 6 October 1967, Department of State, Central Department, POL 23–9 Greece, NARA.

99. Airgram-1901, Bohlen (American Embassy in Paris) to Dept of State, Confidential, 5 June 1967, Department of State, Central Department, POL 23–9 Greece, NARA.

100. Telegram, American Embassy in Ankara to Dept of State, 17 August 1967, Department of State, Central Files, POL 23–9, NARA.

101. Ibid.

102. Telegram, Morris (American Embassy in Berlin) to Dept of State, 10 June 1967, Department of State, Central Files, POL 23–9, NARA.

103. Ibid.

104. USG Memorandum, Subject: Future US Policy towards Greece, H. Daniel Brewster to Rockwell, 27 April 1967, Department of State, Central Files, POL 1 Greece—US, NARA.

105. *The Washington Post*, 29 April 1967, p. A12; for a full account of the US policies towards the Greek Colonels, see James Edward Miller, *The United States and the Making of Modern Greece: History and Power, 1950–1974* (2009) and Robert V. Keely, *The Colonels' Coup and the American Embassy: A Diplomat's View of the Breakdown of Democracy in Cold War Greece* (2011).

106. For a full account of NATO's policy towards the Greek Colonels' regime, see Maragkou, Konstantina (2009) 'Favouritism in NATO's Southeastern flank: The case of the Greek Colonels, 1967–74', *Cold War History*, 9: 3, 347–366

107. Verykios to Greek Ministry of Foreign Affairs, 12 September 1967, Protocol no. 4941/ST/2-A/1, File no. 1967/2.4, DAGMFA.

108. Telegram, NATO 74, US Mission NATO to Secretary of State, Secret, 23 October 1967, Department of State, Central Files, POL Greece, NARA.

109. Telegram, A-9, American Consulate General in Strasbourg to Depart-

ment of State, Limited Official Use, 2 August 1967, Department of State, Central Files, NARA.

110. http://www.nato.int/nato_static_fl2014/assets/pdf/stock_publications/20120822_nato_treaty_en_light_2009.pdf.

111. Consultative Assembly, Order no. 256 (1967) on the general policy of the CoE, Provisional edition, CoE Archives, Strasbourg, GA 353, Greece, Correspondence, Press Cuttings, Documentation, President of the Assembly, 1967.

112. De Freitas Press conference—CoE—Directorate of Information President of the Council of Europe's Assembly, 28 April 1967, Oxford University, Bodleian Library, Manuscripts & Rare Books, De Freitas Collection, Box 17.

113. Denmark, Norway and Sweden against Greece, Directorate of Information, 20 September 1967, p. 1, GA 352, Consultative Assembly, Council of Europe Archives.

114. Telegram, A-9, American Consulate General in Strasbourg to Department of State, Limited Official Use, 2 August 1967, Department of State, Central Files, NARA.

115. Letter, George Brown, Foreign Office to Eric Baker, Amnesty International, 6 June 1967, Amnesty International File 1179, Correspondence, International Institute for Social History Archives, Amsterdam [IISH hereafter].

116. Arne Treholt, *Europe and the Greek Dictatorship*, in Richard Clogg and George Yannopoulos (eds), *Greece Under Military Rule* (1972), p. 213.

117. Telegram A-177, Unclassified, 28 May 1967, Department of State, Central Files, POL 23–9 Greece, NARA.

118. Telegram Guidance no. 10, Greece and the Council of Europe, Foreign and Commonwealth Office to certain missions, 21 January 1969, FCO 9/870, TNA.

119. Ibid.

120. Letter, Lord Shawcross to Michael Stewart, 19 March 1968, UDCL/348/3, Archives of the International Commission of Jurists, Hull History Centre.

121. Ms.Eng.c.5018, Greece: Anglo-Greek relations, Bodleian Library, Modern Political Papers.

122. Hood to Central Department, Greece and the Council of Europe, Confidential, 23 June 1967, FCO 9/227, TNA.

123. Ibid.

124. Michael Stewart (British Embassy in Athens) to A. E. Davidson (Foreign Office), 27 July 1967 Department of State, Central Files, NARA.

125. Ibid.

126. Daily Bulletin, no. 2674, Euratom et Marché Commun, Agence International d' information pour la Presse, Mr Mercy, 3 May 1967, T 312/1867, TNA.

127. Van Coufoudakis, 'The European Economic Community and the 'Freezing' of the Greek Association, 1967–74', in *The Journal of Common Market Studies*, Vol. XVI, no. 2, (December 1977), p. 118.

128. Stephen Xydis, 'Coups and Counter-coups in Greece', in *Political Science Quarterly* (1974), p. 519.

129. For an overview, see Konstantina Maragkou, *International politics and the Greek Colonels (1967–74): any role for Human Rights?*, and *The Council of Europe's first test: Greece and the Colonels' regime, 1967–69*, both forthcoming articles

130. Airgram A-413, Tubby (US Mission Geneva) to Department of State, Unclassified, 18 May 1967, Department of State, Central Files, POL 23–9 Greece, POL 5–2 NATO, NARA.

131. International Commission of Jurists, Press Release, The rule of law abrogated in Greece, Urgent, 9 May 1967, Adamantia Pollis Collection, IV. Vertical File, Miscellaneous, DF 853.c63q—Carton 15, Department of Rare Books and Special Collections, Princeton University Library [PULA thereafter].

132. Circular no. 24/67 to Member States, Greece, Socialist International, London, 8 May 1967, Socialist International Archives.

133. Letter, H. C. Beckh (International Committee of the Red Cross) to Stephen Sedley (Haldane Society), 7 August 1967, B AG 225 084–074, Archives of the International Committee of the Red Cross, Geneva [ICRC hereafter].

134. 24th meeting of the Executive Committee, Commission of the Churches on International Affairs, 31 July—4 August, Cambridge, Annexe 10, Greece, Country Files and Correspondence 1946–1995, Europe, 42.3.050, World Council of Churches General Secretariat Archives [WCC hereafter].

135. Telegram, American Embassy in Athens to Dept. of State, 11 December 1967, Department of State, Central Files, Department of State, Central Files, NARA.

136. Letter, S. C. Silkin to George Brown, 1 August 1967, FCO 9/227, TNA.

137. Ibid.

138. Letter, Fred Mulley to S. C. Silkin, 13 June 1967, FCO 9/227, TNA.

2. FROM 'WRESTLING WITH THE QUESTION OF RECOGNITION' TO 'WORTHY COMPETITORS OF JUDAS ISCARIOT'

1. *The Times*, 14 December 1967, p. 10.
2. Ibid.
3. Memorandum for the President, Subject: Your meeting with King Constantine of Greece, Secret, 7 September 1967, Department of State, Dean Rusk, Briefing Book Files, LOT 69D533, NARA.
4. Ibid.
5. Arne Treholt, *Europe and the Greek Dictatorship* (1972), p. 219.
6. Stewart to Foreign Office, 26 October 1967, PREM 13/2139 TNA.
7. Peter Calvocoressi, *World Politics Since 1945* (1996), p. 270.
8. Thanasis Diamantopoulos, *Kostas Mitsotakis: A Political Biography* (1989), p. 306.
9. *The Times*, 15 December 1967, p. 9.
10. Ibid.
11. Ibid.
12. *Daily Telegraph*, 16 December 1967.
13. Letter from Greek Prime Minister Papadopoulos to US President Johnson, 6 January 1968, NSF, Special Head of State Correspondence File, Box: 20 [1 of 2], Greece, LBJ Library.
14. *The Times*, 15 December 1967, front page.
15. *The New York Times*, 15 December 1967, p. 19.
16. Telegram, London 4787, Bruce, American Embassy in London to Secretary of State, Subject: Greece, Secret, Immediate, 14 December 1967, Department of State, Central Files, POL 2 Greece, NARA.
17. Ibid.
18. Telegram, London 4852, Bruce, American Embassy in London to Secretary of State, Confidential, Priority, 15 December 1967, Department of State, Central Files, POL 23–9 Greece, NARA.
19. Parliamentary Records, House of Commons, Vol. 756, c. 377, 19 December 1967.
20. Letter, Downing Street to Mrs Pym, 11 January 1968, MGA, Correspondence, Members of Parliament, (K-Z), KCLA.
21. Telegram, Athens 3188, Talbot, Confidential, 16 January 1967, POL 23–9 Greece, Central Files, Department of State, NARA.
22. Research memorandum REU-68, Subject: Western Europe and Canada confront the Greek situation, George C. Denney to Rusk, Confidential, 27 December 1967 POL 23–9 GR, Central Files, Department of State, NARA.
23. Telegram, Bonn 6323, McGhee, American Embassy in West Germany to Secretary of State, Confidential, 15 December 1967, Department of State, Central Files, POL 16 Greece, NARA.

24. Telegram, Ankara 2893, American Embassy in Ankara to Secretary of State, Confidential, 16 December 1967, Department of State, Central Files, POL 16 Greece, NARA.
25. Airgram A-1067, Subject: Wait and see French policy on Greece, American Embassy in Paris to Department of State, Confidential, 26 December 1967, Department of State, Central Files, POL 23–9, NARA.
26. Telegram, London 4787, Bruce, American Embassy in London to Secretary of State, Subject: Greece, Secret, Immediate, 14 December 1967, Department of State, Central Files, POL 2 Greece, NARA.
27. Verykios, London to Greek Ministry of Foreign Affairs, 30 December 1967, Protocol no. 8071/ST/2, File no. 1967/2.1, DAGMFA.
28. Memorandum by the Minister of Overseas Development, OECD Consortium Aid to Greece, 12 September 1968, OPD (68) 16th meeting, CAB 148/35, TNA.
29. Telegram, London 4818, Bruce, American Embassy in London to Secretary of State, Confidential, Priority, 14 December 1967, Department of State, Central files, POL 23–9 Greece, NARA.
30. *The New York Times*, 15 December 1967, p. 19.
31. Ibid.
32. Background Note, Confidential, FCO 9/1217, TNA.
33. Interview with John Fraser.
34. *The New York Times*, 15 December 1967, p. 19.
35. Telegram, London 4995, Bruce, American Embassy in London to SecState, Confidential, 22 December 1967, Department of State, Central Files, POL 23–9 Greece, NARA.
36. *The Times*, 2 January 1968, p. 3.
37. Telegram, Athens 3220, Talbot, American Embassy in Athens to Secretary of State, Secret, Exdis, 17 January 1968, Department of State, Central Files, POL Greece-US, NARA.
38. Telegram, Athens 4320, Talbot, American Embassy in Athens to Secretary of State, Confidential, 28 December 1967, Department of State, Central Files, NARA.
39. Ibid.
40. Telegram, London 5140, American Embassy in London to Secretary of State, Confidential, 2 January 1968, Department of State, Central Files, POL 23–9 Greece, NARA.
41. Parliamentary Records, House of Commons, Vol. 757, c. 177–8, 25 January 1968.
42. Ibid.
43. Parliamentary Records, House of Commons, Vol. 756, c. 633, 14 December 1967.

44. *The Times*, 19 April 1968, p. 8.

45. Resolution to the Greek Prime Minister sent to the editor of the *Birmingham Post*, 18 February 1968, MGA correspondence, II, Birmingham Branch of League for Democracy in Greece, KCLA.

46. *The Times*, 25 January 1968, p. 4.

47. Resolution to the Greek Prime Minister sent to the editor of the *Birmingham Post*, 18 February 1968, MGA correspondence, II, Birmingham Branch of League for Democracy in Greece, KCLA.

48. Additional information, Tourism from *The Financial Times*, 9 March 1970, Greece 1970 correspondence, PAK, 1970, Box. 642, Socialist International Archives, Amsterdam.

49. *Hellenic Review*, Vol. 1, no. 1, June 1968, p. 4.

50. *The Times*, 26 April 1968, p. 6.

51. For a full account of its organisation, results and plans, see Maurice Fraser Associate Report, Mid-June 1968, Adamantia Pollis Collection, III. Inter-American Federation for Democracy in Greece, DF 853. c63q—Carton 12, PULA.

52. *The Times*, 22 April 1968, p. 10.

53. Ibid.

54. Summary of the report of the Human Rights Commission on the Greek Case, 25 November 1969, p. 25, 42.3.050, WCC General Secretariat Archives.

55. See Reports by Amnesty International, Subject: Situation in Greece, 27 January 1968 & Subject: Torture of Political Prisoners in Greece, 6 April 1968, Amnesty International Archives, File 431, International Institute for Social History Archives, Amsterdam.

56. Parliamentary Records, House of Commons, Vol. 762, c. 1647, 11 April 1968.

57. Statement on Greece by the President of the CoE Assembly, Information, 24 April 1968, GA 362, Greece, Correspondence, Memoranda, Documentation, Council of Europe Archives, Strasbourg.

58. Parliamentary Records, House of Commons, Vol. 762, c. 1662, 11 April 1968.

59. A. E. Davidson to Beith, Greece: Council of Europe, Attitude of HMG to the Scandinavian Initiative and action taken by HMG, 29 March 1968, FCO 9/230, TNA.

60. Telegram from Kirk to the Foreign Office, Council of Europe's debate on the situation in Greece, 8 May 1968, FCO 9/230, TNA.

61. Parliamentary Records, House of Commons, Vol. 760, c. 351, 14 March 1968.

62. Ibid.

63. Arne Treholt, *Europe and the Greek Dictatorship* (1972), p. 214.

64. OPD (68), Minutes of the 13th meeting, Defence and Oversea Policy Committee, 12 July 1968, CAB 148/35, TNA.
65. OPD (68), Minutes of the 15th meeting, Defence and Oversea Policy Committee, 1 August 1968, CAB 148/35, TNA.
66. Ibid.
67. Clucas to Owen, Sale of nuclear reactor to Greece, 31 March 1969, T 334/144, TNA.
68. OPD (68), Minutes of the 15th meeting, Defence and Oversea Policy Committee, 1 August 1968, CAB 148/35, TNA.
69. Ibid.
70. Ibid.
71. Parliamentary Records, House of Commons, Vol. 762, c. 1665, 11 April 1968.
72. Greece: Draft DOP Committee Paper, K. D. Rogers to Church, 15 January 1969, BT 333/16, TNA.
73. C. C. Lucas to Owen, Sale of nuclear reactor to Greece, 31 March 1969, T 334/144, TNA.
74. Ibid.
75. Letter, J. E. C. Macrae FCO to D. K. Bolton, 8 May 1969, MGA correspondence, II, Birmingham Branch of League for Democracy in Greece, KCLA.
76. Clucas to Owen, Sale of nuclear reactor to Greece, 31 March 1969, T 334/144, TNA.
77. OPD (68) Minutes of the 16th meeting, Greece: OECD Consortium Aid, 17 September 1968, CAB 148/35, TNA.
78. Ibid.
79. Van Coufoudakis, 'Greek Foreign Policy, 1945–1985: Seeking Independence in an Interdependent World' in Kevin Featherstone and Dimitris Katsoudas (eds), *Political Change in Greece, Before and After the Colonels* (1987), p. 233.
80. OPD (68) 48th meeting, Memorandum by the Secretary of State for Foreign Affairs, 2 July 1968, CAB 148/37, TNA.
81. Ibid.
82. *The Times*, 27 April 1968, p. 5.
83. Memorandum by the Minister of Overseas Development, OECD Consortium Aid to Greece, 12 September 1968, OPD (68) 16th meeting, CAB 148/35, TNA.
84. Interview.
85. Telegram, Rome 6692, Ackley, American Embassy in Rome to Secretary of State, Confidential, 19 June 1968, Department of State, Central Files, POL 30–2 Greece, NARA.

86. Parliamentary Records, House of Commons, Vol. 767, c. 241, 25 June 1968.

87. *The Times*, 28 June 1968, p. 7.

88. Ibid.

89. Foreign Secretary to the Prime Minister, 27 June 1968, PREM 13/2141, TNA.

90. John W. Young, 'The Diary of Michael Stewart as British Foreign Secretary, April–May 1968', in *Contemporary British History* (2005), p. 483.

91. Foreign Secretary to the Prime Minister, 27 June 1968, PREM 13/2141, TNA.

92. Ibid.

93. Ibid.

94. Telegram No 496, Sir Michael Stewart to FO, Confidential, Priority, 1 July 1968, PREM 13/2141, TNA.

95. OPD (68), 48th meeting, Memorandum by the Secretary of State for Foreign Affairs, 2 July 1968, CAB 148/37, TNA.

96. Parliamentary Records, House of Commons, Vol. 768, c. 27, 8 July 1968.

97. Telegram, London 10623, American Embassy in London to Secretary of State, Limited Official Use, 5 July 1968, State Department, Central Files, POL Greece-UK, NARA.

98. Parliamentary Records, House of Commons, Vol. 767, c. 1501, 3 July 1968.

99. Telegram, London 10623, Kaiser (American Embassy London) to Department of State, Limited official use, 5 July 1968, Department of State, Central Files, POL Greece-UK, NARA.

100. Ibid.

101. Telegram, Athens 5664, American Embassy in Athens to Secretary of State, Talbot, Confidential, 5 July 1968, Department of State, Central Files, POL Greece-UK, NARA.

102. OPD (68) 48, Greece, Memorandum by the Secretary of State for Foreign Affairs, 2 July 1968, CAB 148/37, TNA.

103. Ibid.

104. *Le Monde*, 16 September 1970 in Pollis Collection, VIII. Resistance Organisations, DF 853.c63q, carton 21, PULA.

105. 'Athenian', *Inside the Colonels' Greece* (1972), p. 142.

106. OPD (68) 48, Greece, Memorandum by the Secretary of State for Foreign Affairs, 2 July 1968, CAB 148/37, TNA.

107. Barbara Castle, *The Castle Diaries* (1984), p. 484.

108. Richard Crossman, *The Crossman Diaries: Selections from the Diaries of a Cabinet Minister*, Vol. 3 (1979), p. 132.

109. OPD (68), Minutes of the 13th meeting, July 1968, CAB 148/35, TNA.
110. Parliamentary Records, House of Commons, Vol. 796, c. 267, 23 July 1968.
111. Ibid.
112. OPD (68) 16th meeting, OECD Consortium Aid to Greece, Memorandum by the Minister of Overseas Development, 12 September 1968, CAB 148/35, TNA.
113. Memorandum of Conversation, Subject: British observations on Greek Constitution and Cyprus, Confidential, 1 August 1968, Department of State, Central Files, POL 15–5 Greece, NARA.
114. *The Times*, 22 January 1968, p. 8.
115. Peter Leuprecht, 'Max van der Stoel: A Tireless Defender of Greek Democracy' in *Security and Human Rights*, no. 3 (2011).
116. *The Times*, 9 May 1968, p. 5.
117. *The Times*, 18 July 1968, p. 4.
118. *The Times*, 20 March 1968, p. 5.
119. Council of Europe, Doc. 2467, Appendix, Opinion of three legal experts on the democratic character of the draft Greek Constitution published in Athens on 10 July 1968, p. 47, 5 September 1968, 42.3.049, WCC Secretariat Archives; Legal Affairs Committee, The situation in Greece, p. 1, Consultative Assembly, 6 September 1968, GA 352, Council of Europe Archives.
120. Intelligence Note—254, US Department of State, Director of Intelligence and Research, Thomas L. Hughes, Secret, No Foreign Dissemination, Limited Distribution, 11 April 1968, Department of State, Central Files, POL 15 Greece, NARA.
121. *The Times*, 19 September 1968, p. 4.
122. Ibid.
123. Ibid.
124. Interview with Brigadier Baxter.
125. Interview with John Fraser.
126. Telegram 257714, Dept. of State to American Embassy in Athens, Confidential, Priority, 18 October 1968, Department of State, Central Files, DEF 19–8, US-Greece, NARA.
127. *The Times*, 24 April 1967, p. 9.
128. Michael Stewart to the Prime Minister, Greece: the supply of arms, 19 June 1969, FCO 9/887, TNA.
129. *The Times*, 23 September 1968, p. 6.
130. OPD (68) 16th meeting, 12 September 1968, CAB 148/35, TNA.
131. Yearly Report 1970, Sorokos to Greek Ministry of Foreign Affairs,

Secret, 31 December 1970, Protocol no. 6261/ST/2, File no. 1973.3, DAGMFA.

132. Ibid.

133. Extract from the *New York Herald Tribune*, 25 May 1968, FCO 9/214, TNA.

134. Derek Dodson (British Embassy in Athens) to R. H. G. Edmonds (Southern European Department), UK Policy towards Greece, Confidential, 1 November 1968, FCO 9/870, TNA.

135. Ibid.

136. Conclusions of a meeting in the Secretary of State's room, Policy towards Greece, 3 July 1969, FCO 9/871, TNA.

137. Southern European Department, Greece: The Secretary's of State meeting with Sir Michael Stewart on 7 November 1968, FCO 9/870, TNA.

138. *Greek Observer*, June 1969, p. 7.

139. Sir Hugh Greene, *The Third Floor Front: A View of Broadcasting in the Sixties* (1969), p. 66.

140. Ibid., p. 97.

141. Ibid., p. 135.

142. OPD (69) 3, Defence and Overseas Policy Committee, Greece, Memorandum of the Secretary of State for Defence and the Secretary of State for Foreign and Commonwealth Affairs, Confidential, 24 January 1969, FCO 9/870, TNA.

143. Konstantina Maragkou, *Activists without borders: The Beckets vs the Colonels in the 'long 1960s'* in Constantine Arvanitopoulos, Evanthis Hatzivassiliou, Antonis Klapsis, Effie G. H. Pedaliu (eds.), *The Greek Dictatorship and the International System: A Case Study of Southern European Military Juntas*, forthcoming, Routledge, Cold War History Series.

144. Letter, Cedric Thornberry to Tom Sargeant, London, 20 September 1967, DJU11/24, International Commission of Jurists Archives, Hull History Centre [HCC hereafter].

145. Letter, Rustan Thoren to Hans Janitschek, London, 26 June 1969, File 642, Socialist International Archives.

146. Defensive Speaking Notes for the Secretary of State's talk with the Greek Foreign Minister during a NATO meeting in Brussels, Edmonds to Beith, 12 November 1968, FCO 9/870, TNA.

147. Ibid.

148. OPD (69) 3, Defence and Oversea Policy Committee, Greece, Memorandum of the Secretary of State for Defence and the Secretary of State for Foreign and Commonwealth Affairs, Confidential, 24 January 1969, FCO 9/870, TNA.

3. FROM 'LOW-EBB', BACK TO NORMAL, AND THEN TO THE 'LOW-EST-EBB'

1. Southern European Department, Greece: The Secretary's of State meeting with Sir Michael Stewart on 7 November 1968, FCO 9/870, TNA.
2. Record of a conversation between Sir Denis Greenhill and the Greek Foreign Minister on 28 November 1968, Confidential, 1 December 1968, FCO 9/870, TNA.
3. Ibid.
4. Ibid.
5. Greece: Supplementary brief on development in Anglo-Greek relations for the Secretary of State for Foreign and Commonwealth Affairs' meeting with Sir Michael Stewart on 18 November 1968, 14 November 1968, FCO 9/870, TNA.
6. Michael Stewart to British Embassy in Athens, Confidential, 17 December 1968, FCO 9/870, TNA.
7. R. A. Sykes to D. Healey, Confidential, 4 December 1968, FCO 9/870, TNA.
8. Derek Dodson to R. Edmonds, Confidential, 4 December 1968, FCO 9/870, TNA.
9. Greece: Memorandum by the Secretary of State for Defence and the Secretary of State for Foreign and Commonwealth Affairs, Confidential, 24 January 1969, FCO 9/870, TNA.
10. Ibid.
11. Brief for the President, Memorandum by the Secretary of State for Defence and the Secretary for Foreign and Commonwealth Affairs. Confidential, 29 January 1969, BT 333/16, TNA.
12. Military Aid to Greece, Indiana Senator Vance Hartke, 8 June 1970, Konstantinos Mitsotakis Archives [KKA hereafter].
13. Note for the Record, meeting on Policy towards Greece on 19 November 1968, D. S. D. Maitland, 22 November 1968, FCO 9/885, TNA.
14. R. A. Sykes to Mr Edmonds, Confidential, 4 December 1968, FCO 9/870, TNA.
15. Sir Michael Stewart to FCO, telegram no. 10, Priority, Confidential, 4 January 1969, BT 333/16, TNA.
16. P.L.P. Foreign Affairs Group's meeting on Greece, 18 February 1969, FCO 9/887, TNA.
17. Ibid.
18. Letter, George Thomson, FCO to Lord Milford, 22 January 1970, MGA correspondence, II, Birmingham Branch of League for Democracy in Greece, KCLA.

19. Letter, A. E. Palmer FCO Southern European Department to C Martin, Camden Trades Council, February 1970, MGA correspondence, II, Birmingham Branch of League for Democracy in Greece, KCLA.

20. Derek Dodson to Edmonds, tel. no 763, Training for Greek policemen, Confidential, Priority, 5 November 1968, FCO 9/870, TNA.

21. Parliamentary Records, House of Commons, Vol. 777, c. 882, 10 February 1969.

22. Parliamentary Debates, House of Commons, Vol. 778, c. 1278–79, 25 February 1969.

23. *Greek Report*, February 1969, p. 16.

24. Sir Charles Cunningham (Atomic Energy Authority) to Mr Norman, Immediate, Confidential, 22 August 1969, T 334/144, TNA.

25. Letter, John MacDonald to Michael Stewart, Secretary for Foreign Affairs, 28 April 1969, MGA correspondence, II, Birmingham Branch of League for Democracy in Greece, KCLA.

26. Parliamentary Records, House of Commons, Vol. 783, c. 26, 5 May 1969.

27. R. H. G. Edmonds to Bendall, Memorandum on Policy towards Greece, Confidential, 6 January 1969, FCO 9/885, TNA.

28. Parliamentary Records, House of Commons, Vol. 778, c. 11, 17 February 1969.

29. Parliamentary Records, House of Commons, Vol. 778, 25 February 1969.

30. Parliamentary Records, House of Commons, Vol. 781, c. 231, 1 April 1969.

31. R. H. G. Edmonds to Bendall, Memorandum on Policy towards Greece, Confidential, 6 January 1969, FCO 9/885, TNA.

32. Ibid.

33. Record of a meeting on Policy towards Greece: The supply of Arms to Greece, Confidential 19 June 1969, FCO 9/871, TNA.

34. Ibid.

35. Ibid.

36. Ibid.

37. Parliamentary Debates, House of Commons, Vol. 783, c. 25, 5 May 1969.

38. Ibid., c. 26.

39. *Greek Observer*, June 1969, p. 25.

40. *The Times*, 12 September 1969, p. 5.

41. *The Guardian*, 30 August 1969, p. 2.

42. Ibid.

43. Parliamentary Records, House of Commons, Vol. 783, c. 26, 5 May 1969.

44. OPD (69) 3, Defence and Overseas Policy Committee, Greece, Memorandum of the Secretary of State for Defence and the Secretary of State for Foreign and Commonwealth Affairs, Confidential, 24 January 1969, FCO 9/870, TNA.
45. Draft Memorandum for the Cabinet Defence and Overseas Policy, 21 January 1969, FCO 9/870, TNA.
46. Ibid.
47. Ibid.
48. Confidential Note, David V. Bendall agreeing on the Confidential Note on Greece by Reginald L. Secondé, Confidential, 15 July 1970, FCO 9/1216, TNA.
49. 'Er tat mid leid, Griechenland: Koenig', Der Spiegel, 14 April 1969.
50. Airgram CA-3684, Department of State to American Embassy in Athens, Subject: King Constantine's concern about a possible move to depose him, 27 June 1969, State Department, Central Files, NARA.
51. Ibid.
52. Ibid.
53. Meeting on Policy towards Greece, Confidential, 3 July 1969, FCO 9/871, TNA.
54. Telegram, Athens 3866, American Embassy in Athens to Secretary of State, Confidential, 3 September 1969, McClelland, State Department, Central Files, Pol 23–9 Greece, NARA.
55. Telegram, State 150055, Richardson Dept of State to American Embassy in Athens, Confidential, 5 September 1969, State Department Files, Central Files, POL 23–9, NARA.
56. Sir Michael Stewart to R. H. G. Edmonds, British Policy towards Greece, Confidential, 28 May 1969, FCO 9/871, TNA.
57. Ibid.
58. Ibid.
59. Ibid.
60. Ibid.
61. Parliamentary Debates, House of Commons, Vol. 785, c. 463, 18 June 1969.
62. P.L.P. Foreign Affairs Group's meeting on Greece, 18 February 1969, FCO 9/887, TNA.
63. Parliamentary Records, House of Commons, Vol. 785, c. 463, 18 June 1969.
64. Parliamentary Records, House of Commons, Vol. 787, c. 1716–17, 23 July 1969.
65. Parliamentary Records, House of Commons, Vol. 785, c. 463, 18 June 1969.

66. P.L.P. Foreign Affairs Group's meeting on Greece, 18 February 1969, FCO 9/887, TNA.

67. Sir Michael Stewart to Michael Stewart, Greece: Information Policy Report '69, Confidential, 26 June 1969, FCO 26/267, TNA.

68. Parliamentary Reports, House of Commons, Vol. 787, c. 1717, 23 July 1969.

69. Meeting on Policy towards Greece, 20 October 1969, FCO 9/885, TNA.

70. Ibid.

71. Sir Charles Cunningham to Mr Norman (UKAEA negotiator), 22 August 1969, T 334/144, NA.

72. Michael Stewart to Prime Minister, Confidential, 23 July 1969, FCO 9/887, TNA.

73. Letter, Diana Pym to PM Harold Wilson, 27 January 1969, MGA Correspondence IV, Members of Parliament, (K-Z), KCLA.

74. Meeting on Policy towards Greece, 19 June 1969, TNA, FCO 9/871, TNA.

75. Parliamentary Records, Commons, Vol. 783, c. 25, 5 May 1969.

76. Ibid.

77. Sorokos to Greek Ministry of Foreign Affairs, 22 April 1970, Protocol no. 1953/ST/Z, File no. 1970/4.1, DAGMFA.

78. Conclusions of a meeting on Greece, N. J. Barrington, 17 February 1969, FCO 9/871, TNA.

79. Meeting on Policy towards Greece, 19 June 1969, FCO 9/871, TNA.

80. Meeting on Policy towards Greece, 3 July 1969, FCO 9/871, TNA.

81. Telegram, Department of State to all NATO capitals, State 149124, Confidential, 4 September 1969, Department of State, Central Files, NARA.

82. Record of a meeting on Policy towards Greece, Confidential, 3 July 1969, FCO 9/871, TNA.

83. R. H. G. Edmonds to R. S. Gorham, 17 January 1969, FCO 9/844, TNA.

84. Conclusions of a meeting held at the FCO, 17 February 1969, FCO 9/871, TNA.

85. Record of a meeting on Policy towards Greece, Confidential, 19 June 1969, FCO 9/871, TNA.

86. Parliamentary Records, House of Commons, Vol. 791, c. 826, 7 November 1969.

87. PLP Foreign Affairs Group's meeting on Greece, 18 February 1969, FCO 9/887, TNA.

88. *Greek Report*, October 1969, p. 8.

89. Ibid., p. 6.

90. *The Times*, 1 December 1969, p. 9.
91. Telegram, London 9187, Richardson, American Embassy in London to Secretary of State, Secret, 8 November 1969, Department of State, Central files, POL 23–9 Greece, NARA.
92. *The Times*, 22 November 1969, p. 4.
93. *The Times*, 2 December 1969, front page.
94. Ibid., p. 8.
95. Ibid.
96. P. L. O'Keeffe (British Embassy in Athens to J. M. Snodgrass (Southern European Department), Human Rights Commission Report, Confidential, 5 January 1970, FCO 9/1199, TNA.
97. *The Times*, 2 December 1969, p. 8.
98. Ibid.
99. *The Times*, 4 December 1969, p. 8.
100. Meeting on Policy towards Greece, 2 October 1969, FCO 9/885, TNA.
101. The Committee of Ministers

Considering that Greece has seriously violated Article 3 of the Statute;

Noting the situation in Greece as described in Recommendation 547 of the Consultative Assembly, adopted on 30th January 1969;

Noting further that the Greek government, as required in paragraph 7 of this Recommendation, have declared their withdrawal from the Council of Europe under Article 7 of the Statute.

1. Understands that the Greek government will abstain from any further participation in the activities of the Council of Europe as from today;
2. Concludes that on this understanding there is no need to pursue the procedure for suspension, under Article 8 of the Statute;
3. Charges the Ministers' Deputies to settle the administrative and financial consequences of this situation;
4. Expresses the hope of an early return in Greece of conditions which will enable her to resume full membership of the Council of Europe.

4. 'A SERIES OF SHIFTS AND JOLTS, WITH OCCASIONAL SUNNY INTERVALS'

1. Greece: Annual Review for 1970, Diplomatic report no. 16/71, Sir Michael Stewart to FCO, FCO 9/1388, TNA.
2. Greece and the Council of Europe: Reports of the European Commission of Human Rights, R. L. Secondé (Southern European

Department) to Mr Bendall, Confidential, 12 January 1970, FCO 9/1199, TNA.

3. Greece and the Council of Europe, A. E. Palmer to Mr Snodgrass, Confidential, 13 January 1970, FCO 9/1199, TNA.

4. Ibid.

5. Yearly Report 1970, Sorokos to Greek Ministry of Foreign Affairs, Secret, 31 December 1970, Protocol no. 6261/ST/2, File no. 1973.3, DAGMFA.

6. Ibid.

7. Ibid.

8. Ibid.

9. Letter, Diana Pym to PM Harold Wilson, 27 January 1969, MGA Correspondence IV, Members of Parliament, (K-Z), KCLA.

10. Yearly Report 1970, Sorokos to Greek Ministry of Foreign Affairs, Secret, 31 December 1970, Protocol no. 6261/ST/2, File no. 1973.3, DAGMFA.

11. Record of a meeting on Policy towards Greece, Confidential, 17 December 1969, FCO 9/871, TNA.

12. Ibid.

13. Yearly Report 1970, Sorokos to Greek Ministry of Foreign Affairs, Secret, 31 December 1970, Protocol no. 6261/ST/2, File no. 1973.3, DAGMFA.

14. Record of a meeting on Policy towards Greece, Confidential, 17 December 1969, FCO 9/871, TNA.

15. Memorandum by the Southern European Department, Greece, Internal Situation, Confidential, 28 June 1970, FCO 9/1216, TNA.

16. Telegram 133, Edwin McAlpine to Prime Minister Wilson, 5 March 1970, PREM 13/3247, TNA.

17. Record of a meeting on Policy towards Greece, Confidential, 17 December 1969, FCO 9/871, TNA.

18. Telegram, State 150055, Richardson, Dept. of State to American Embassy in Athens, Confidential, 5 September 1969, State Department Files, Central Files, POL 23–9, NARA.

19. Record of a meeting on Policy towards Greece, 17 December 1969, FCO 9/871, TNA.

20. Notes for Supplementaries, George Thompson, Parliamentary Questions, 2 February 1970, FCO 9/1199, TNA.

21. Greece: Prime Minister's talks in Washington, 22 January 1970, PREM 13/3246, Prime Minister PM/70/9, TNA.

22. Ibid.

23. Parliamentary Debates, House of Commons, Vol. 793, c. 1139, 16 December 1969.

24. Greece Military Cooperation, 17 December 1969, FCO 9/885, TNA.
25. Director of Intelligence and Research, Intelligence Note 878, Subject: USSR-Greece: Moscow wants good relations with present regime, INR-George C. Denney to the Secretary, Secret/No foreign dissemination, 30 December 1969, Department of State, Central Files, POL Greece-USSR, NARA.
26. See Sotiris Walldén, *Unseemly partners: Greek Dictatorship, Communist regimes and the Balkans, 1967–1974* (2009).
27. C. M. Woodhouse, *The Rise and Fall of the Greek Colonels* (1985), p. 299.
28. Ibid.
29. Ibid.
30. *The Times*, 25 September 1967, front page.
31. The Greek Armed Forces, Sir Michael Stewart (British Embassy) to Mr Stewart (Foreign Office), Confidential, 19 November 1969, FCO 9/1229, TNA.
32. Record of a meeting on British Policy towards Greece, Confidential, 6 January 1970, FCO 9/1215, TNA.
33. Ibid.
34. Michael Stewart to Prime Minister, Greece: Prime Minister's talks in Washington, Confidential, 22 January 1970, PREM 13/3246, TNA.
35. Ibid.
36. Greece and the Council of Europe: Reports of the European Commission of Human Rights, R. L. Secondé (Southern European Department) to Mr Bendall, Confidential, 12 January 1970, FCO 9/1199, TNA.
37. Thomas Brimelow to Mr Secondé, Record of a Conversation with the Greek Ambassador on 11 February 1970: Consequences of the action taken against Greece in the Council of Europe, Confidential, 11 February 1970, FCO 9/1199, TNA.
38. Telegram no. 109, Sir Michael Stewart to FCO, Confidential, Priority, 6 March 1970, FCO 9/1200, TNA.
39. Thomas Brimelow to Mr Secondé, Record of a Conversation with the Greek Ambassador on 11 February 1970: Consequences of the action taken against Greece in the Council of Europe, Confidential, 11 February 1970, FCO 9/1199, TNA.
41. Telegram no. 82, Sir Michael Stewart to FCO, Greece and the Council of Europe, Confidential, Priority, 23 February 1970, FCO 9/1200, TNA.
42. R. L. Secondé to Sir T. Brimelow, Anglo-Greek relations, Confidential, 25 February 1970, FCO 9/1216, TNA.
43. Greece and the Council of Europe: Reports of the European Commission of Human Rights, R. L. Secondé (Southern European

Department) to Mr Bendall, Confidential, 12 January 1970, FCO 9/1199, TNA.

44. Telegram no. 49, Sir M. Stewart to Foreign and Commonwealth Office, Anglo-Greek relations, Confidential, 2 February 1970, FCO 9/1199, TNA.

45. Telegram no. 71, Sir Michael Stewart to FCO, Confidential, 17 February 1970, FCO 9/1199, TNA.

46. Extract, GMV (70) 2nd meeting, 3 March 1970, PREM 13/3246, TNA.

47. Ibid.

48. R. L. Secondé to Sir T. Brimelow, Anglo-Greek relations, Confidential, 25 February 1970, FCO 9/1216, TNA.

49. Parliamentary Records, House of Commons, Vol. 795, 2 February 1970.

50. See Peter Murtagh, *The Rape of Greece: The King, the Colonels and the Resistance* (1994), pp. 209–220.

51. A. E. Palmer to Mr Snodgrass and Secondé, Difficulties in Anglo-Greek relations, Secret, 23 June 1970, FCO, TNA.

52. Ibid.

53. Telegram no. 120, Sir Michael Stewart to FCO, Priority, Confidential, 12 March 1970, FCO 9/1200, TNA.

54. Ibid.

55. Telegram no. 121, Sir Michael Stewart to FCO, Priority, Confidential, 12 March 1970, FCO 9/1200, TNA.

56. Ibid.

57. Telegram no. 101, Michael Stewart to British Embassy in Athens, Confidential, 9 April 1970, FCO 9/1200, TNA.

58. Ibid.

59. N. A. I. French (Western Organisations Department) to D. J. Robey (UK permanent representative to the Council of Europe), Confidential, 13 May 1970, FCO 9/1202, TNA.

60. Ibid.

61. Sir Michael Stewart to FCO, Greece: Annual Review for 1970, Diplomatic Report no. 16/71, FCO 9/1388, TNA.

62. R. L. Secondé to Sir Michael Stewart, Personal and Confidential, 26 June 1970, FCO 9/1217, TNA.

63. Sir Michael Stewart to R. L. Secondé, Policy towards Greece, Personal and Confidential, 7 July 1970, FCO 9/1217, TNA.

64. D. V. Bendall agreeing on a confidential note from R. L. Secondé, 16 July 1970, FCO 9/1216, TNA.

5. FROM 'UNWARRANTED EXPECTATIONS OF GREATER SYMPA- THY' TO 'SATISFACTORY' RELATIONS

1. Yearly Report 1970, Sorokos to Greek Ministry of Foreign Affairs, Secret, 31 December 1970, Protocol no. 6261/ST/2, File no. 1973.3, DAGMFA.
2. P. L. Secondé to Sir Michael Stewart, Personal and Confidential, 26 June 1970, FCO 9/1217, TNA.
3. Letter from O'Keefe, Athens to Snodgrass, FCO, 19 June 1970, FCO 9/1205, TNA.
4. Telegram no. 318, Sir Michael Stewart to FCO, 20 June 1970, FCO 12/17, TNA.
5. Sorokos to Greek Ministry of Foreign Affairs, 17 July 1970, Protocol no. 3361/ST/20, File no. 1970/3 DAGMFA.
6. Brief note, Diamantopoulos, London, 19 June 1970, File no. 1970/3.5, DAGMFA.
7. Note from a meeting with Secondé at the Foreign Office, London, 26 June 1970, File no. 1970/3.5, DAGMFA.
8. David V. Bendall agreeing on Confidential Note on Greece from Reginald Secondé, 15 July 1970, FCO 9/1216, TNA.
9. Ibid.
10. Sir Michael Stewart to Secondé, 7 July 1970, FCO9/1193, TNA.
11. J. E. Powell-Jones, British Embassy Athens to Southern European Department, Policy towards Greece, Confidential, 24 July 1970, FCO 9/1217, TNA.
12. Note from a meeting with Secondé at the Foreign Office, London, 26 June 1970, File no. 1970/3.5, DAGMFA.
13. Letter, Michael Stewart, British Embassy in Athens, to R. L. Secondé, FCO, Policy towards Greece, Private and Confidential, 7 July 1970, FCO 9/1217, TNA.
14. A. E. Palmer to Mr Snodgrass and Mr Secondé, Difficulties in Anglo-Greek relations, Secret, 23 June 1970, FCO 9/1217, TNA.
15. Sir Michael Stewart to Secondé, 7 July 1970, FCO9/1193, TNA.
16. Policy towards Greece by J. E. Powell-Jones, Athens to Southern European Department, Confidential, 24 July 1970, FCO 9/1217, TNA.
17. DBC Logan to Tickell, 5 April 1971, FCO 9/1404, TNA.
18. Call by the Greek Ambassador on the Secretary of State for Foreign Affairs, Confidential, 11 June 1971, FCO 9/1385, TNA.
19. Sorokos to Broumas, 5 October 1970, File no. 1972/4.1, DAGMFA.
20. Southern European Department to J. E. Powell-Jones, British Embassy in Athens, Policy towards Greece, Confidential, 24 July 1970, FCO 9/1217, TNA.

21. Greece: Arms supplies, Secondé to Wiggin, 2 April 1971, FCO 9/1404, TNA.
22. Hooper to Secondé, 6 July 1971, FCO 9/1401, TNA.
23. *The Times*, 21 July 1970, p. 5.
24. Michael Stewart to Alec Douglas-Home, 2 September 1970, FCO 9/1198, TNA.
25. Diplomatic report, No 441/70, Greece as military ally, Sir Michael Stewart to Michael Stewart, Confidential, 11 September 1970, FCO 9/1229, TNA.
26. Bibliographical note on Xanthopoulos-Palamas, November 1971, FCO 9/1410, TNA.
27. Ibid.
28. Powell-Jones, Athens to Secondé, 27 October 1970, FCO 9/1208, TNA.
29. Diplomatic report 441/70, by Sir Michael Stewart, 11 September 1970, FCO 9/1229, TNA.
30. Ibid.
31. See, Alexandros Nafpliotis, 'The 1971 Re-establishment of Diplomatic Relations Between Greece and Albania: Cooperation and Strategic Partnership Within Cold War Bipolarity, in Othon Anastasakis, Dimitar Bechev, Nicholas Vrousalis (eds), *Greece in the Balkans: Memory, Conflict and exchange* (2009).
32. Greece, Memorandum by Southern European Department, the Internal situation, Confidential, 28 September 1970, FCO 9/1216, TNA.
33. Greece 1967–71, no. 122/71, Michael Stewart to FCO, Confidential, 25 January 1971, FCO 9/1385 TNA.
34. Telegram Athens 5727, Tasca to Dept. of State, Secret, 14 October 1970, POL Greece-UK, NARA.
35. Letter, Robin W. J. Hooper, British Embassy Athens to R. L. Secondé, FCO, Confidential, 30 June 1971, FCO 9/1401, TNA.
36. D. V. Bendall agreeing on a confidential note on Greece by R. L. Secondé, 16 July 1970, FCO 9/1216, TNA.
37. Palmer's comment on Greece: Sir Michael Stewart's dispatch of 25 January, 3 February 1971, FCO 9/1385, TNA.
38. Ibid.
39. Policy towards Greece, report drafted by R. L. Secondé, Southern European Department, FCO, 26 June 1971, FCO 9/1219, TNA.
40. Record of a conversation between the Foreign and Commonwealth Secretary and the Greek Under-Secretary for foreign affairs in the FCO, Confidential, 20 September 1970, FCO 9/1401, TNA.
41. Monitoring of BBC Greek Service, 22 September 1971, FCO 9/1391, TNA.

42. Lagakos, Memorandum of a meeting between Christos Xanthopoulos-Palamas and Sir Alec Douglas-Home, London, 3 November 1970, Protocol no. CA30–61, File no. 1970/3.6, DAGMFA.
43. Record of a meeting between Brimelow and the Greek Under-Secretary for Foreign Affairs, 23 September 1971, FCO 9/1391, TNA.
44. Stewart to Douglas-Home, 9 December 1970, FCO 9/1229, TNA.
45. Lagakos, Memorandum of a meeting between Christos Xanthopoulos-Palamas and Sir Alec Douglas-Home, London, 3 November 1970, Protocol no. CA30–61, File no. 1970/3.6, DAGMFA.
46. Letter, Michael Stewart, British Embassy in Athens, to R. L. Secondé, FCO, Policy towards Greece, Private and Confidential, 7 July 1970, FCO 9/1217, TNA.
47. Peter Murtagh, *The Rape of Greece* (1994), p. 146.
48. Leonidas Papagos, *Notes, 1967–1977* (1999), p. 231.
49. Ibid., pp. 293–94.
50. Yearly Report 1971, Sorokos to Greek Ministry of Foreign Affairs, Secret, 20 December 1971, Protocol no. 6350/ST/2, File no. 1973.3, DAGMFA.
51. Secondé to Wiggin, 7 June 1971, Confidential, FCO 9/1414, TNA.
52. Report by R. L. Secondé, Visit to Greece: 7–13 December, Confidential, 22 December 1970, TNA.
53. Greece: Annual review for 1970, no. 16/71, by Stewart, 1 January 1971, FCO9/1388, TNA.
54. Ibid.
55. Telegram, Athens 5727, Tasca to Department of State, Secret, Exdis, 14 October 1970, Department of State, Central Files, POL Greece-UK, NARA.
56. Telegramme, MFA to Greek Embassy, London, 21 October 1970, Protocol no. CA30–56, File no. 1970/3.6, DAGMFA.
57. FCO Memorandum, Policy towards Greece, 11 June 1971, FCO 9/1415, TNA.
58. Call by the British Ambassador on the Secretary of State for Defence, Greece: the internal situation, and Anglo-Greek relations, Confidential, 11 June 1971, FCO 9/1385, TNA.
59. Ibid.
60. Robin Hooper's summary to Sir Alec Douglas-Home, Confidential, 30 June 1971, FCO 9/1385, TNA.
61. *The Times*, 14 June 1971, p. 5.
62. Leonidas Papagos, *Notes, 1967–1977* (1999), p. 366.
63. Diplomatic report no. 122/71, Greece, 1967–71, by the British Ambassador in Greece to Secretary of State for Foreign and

Commonwealth affairs, Confidential, 25 January 1971, FCO 9/1385, TNA.

64. Ibid.
65. Telegram Athens 6414, Tasca to Dept. of State, Secret, 9 November 1972, RG-59, POL 15–1 Greece, NARA.
66. Diplomatic report no. 122/71, Greece, 1967–71, by the British Ambassador in Greece to Secretary of State for Foreign and Commonwealth affairs, Confidential, 25 January 1971, FCO 9/1385, TNA.
67. Letter, Robin W. J. Hooper, British Embassy Athens to R. L. Secondé, FCO, Confidential, 30 June 1971, FCO 9/1401, TNA.
68. Personal Message, Papadopoulos to Douglas-Home, 24 March 1971, FCO 9/1415, TNA.
69. Secondé to Wiggin, 7 June 1971, FCO 9/1414, TNA.
70. O'Keefe, Athens to J. H. Moore, 11 November 1971, FCO 9/1392, TNA.
71. *The Times*, 'The Embarrassing Regime in Greece', 22 April 1971.
72. European–Atlantic Action Committee on Greece, Declaration, Modern Greek Archives, Correspondence II, King's College London Archives [KCLA].
73. Letter, R. L. Secondé to Wiggin and Goodenough, Greece and NATO, Confidential, 13 December 1971, FCO 9/1392, TNA.
74. Ibid.
75. Telegram no. 216, Hooper to FCO, FCO 9/1385, 4 June 1971, FCO 9/1385, TNA.
76. Background, Confidential, FCO 9/1526, TNA.
77. Call by the Greek Ambassador on the Secretary of State for Foreign Affairs, Confidential, 11 June 1971, FCO 9/1385, TNA.
78. Greece: Annual Review by R. W. J. Hooper to FCO, Confidential, 31 December 1971, FCO 8/1388, TNA.
79. Annual Report on the Hellenic Armed Forces, 1970, H. J. P. Baxter. British Embassy Athens to the Deputy Chief of the Defence Staff (Intelligence), Secret, February 1972, TNA.
80. Telegram Athens 6505, Tasca American Embassy Athens to Department of State, Subject: US Military assistance for Greece, Secret, 1 December 1970, DEFE 19 US-Greece, Department of State, Central files, NARA.
81. Record of a meeting between Brimelow and the Greek Under-Secretary for Foreign Affairs, 23 September 1971, FCO 9/1391, TNA.
82. Sorokos to Greek Ministry of Foreign Affairs, 10 March 1972, N. 4111.4/3/67, 1974/5.11. DAGMFA.

83. Annual Report on the Hellenic Armed Forces, 1970, H. J. P. Baxter British Embassy Athens to the Deputy Chief of the Defence Staff (Intelligence), Secret, February 1972, TNA.

84. Sorokos to Greek Ministry of Foreign Affairs, Yearly Report 1971, Secret, 20 December 1971, Protocol no. 6350/ST/2, File no. 1973.3, DAGMFA.

85. Ibid.

86. Ibid.

87. Yearly Report 1971, Sorokos to Greek Ministry of Foreign Affairs, Secret, 20 December 1971, Protocol no. 6350/ST/2, File no. 1973.3, DAGMFA.

88. Policy towards Greece, report drafted by R. L. Secondé, Southern European Department, FCO, 26 June 1971, FCO 9/1219, TNA.

89. Hooper, Athens to Secondé, FCO, 6 July 1971, FCO 9/1401, TNA.

90. Leonidas Papagos, *Notes* (1999), p. 366.

91. Parliamentary Debates, House of Commons, Vol. 858, c. 1628, 27 June 1973.

92. Ibid.

93. Greece: Annual Review for 1971 by R. W. J. Hooper to FCO, Confidential, 31 December 1971, FCO 8/1388, TNA.

94. Palmer to Wilberforce and Secondé, 7 July 1971, FCO 9/1386, TNA.

6. 'A POLICY OF "DOING GOOD BY STEALTH"'

1. Lord's debate on Greece, 15 February: Talking points, in confidence, FCO 9/1731, TNA.

2. Telegram, Sorokos to Greek Foreign Ministry, 31 January 1972, Protocol no no. 4111.4/1/AS7, File no. 1974/5.11, DAGMFA.

3. *The Times*, 22 March 1972, p. 14.

4. Telegram, Broumas to Greek Ministry of Foreign Affairs, Secret, 22 May 1973, Protocol no. 4111.4/5/AS100, File no. 1974/5.11, DAGMFA.

5. 'The Hardliners', J. F. R. Martin to R. F. Cornish, Confidential, 30 August 1973, FO 286/1458, TNA.

6. 'Greece: Escape by the Red Carpet', *Time Magazine*, US edition, Vol. 99, no. 8, 1 May 1972.

7. Greece: The internal political situation, C. D. Wiggin to Logan, Confidential, 30 November 1972, FCO 9/1526, TNA.

8. Wiggin to Hitch, 22 August 1972, FCO 9/1526, TNA.

9. Topics for discussion at Mr Royle's office meeting on 6 September 1972, Secret, FCO 9/1827, TNA.

10. Annual Review for 1972, no. 56/74, Hooper to Douglas-Home, Confidential, 2 January 1973, FCO 9/1709, TNA.

11. Defence Report by Brigadier Baxter, Secret, 2 March 1972, FCO 9/1530, TNA.
12. Telegram, Sorokos to Greek Ministry of Foreign Affairs, 2 May 1972, no. 4111.4/11/133, 1974/5.11 DAGMFA.
13. Yearly Report 1972, Greek Ambassador in London to Greek Ministry of Foreign Affairs, Secret, 10 January 1973, Protocol no. 0445/1/155, File no. 1973.3, DAGMFA.
14. Defence Report by Brigadier Baxter, 2 March 1972, FCO 9/1530, TNA.
15. Hooper to Douglas-Home, 2 March 1972, FCO 9/1530, TNA.
16. Defence Report by Brigadier Baxter, 2 March 1972, FCO 9/1530, TNA.
17. Hooper to Douglas-Home, 2 March 1972, FCO 9/1530, TNA.
18. Ibid.
19. Hooper to Wiggin, 19 January 1972, FCO 9/1532, TNA.
20. Ibid.
21. Ibid.
22. Supplementary briefs to 'Visit by Lord Limerick to Greece, A. Brooke Turner to Brimelow, 12 October 1972, FCO 9/1520, TNA.
23. WSG 1/2, Diplomatic Report no 27/73, Greece: Annual Review for 1972, Hooper to FCO, Confidential, 2 January 1973, FCO 9/1709, TNA.
24. Telegram, Athens 957, Subject: Cyprus: Discussion with UK Embassy, Tasca to Dept. of State, Secret, 16 February 1972, RG-59, POL Greece-UK, NARA.
25. Topics for discussion at Mr Royle's office meeting on 6 September 1972, Secret, FCO 9/1527, TNA.
26. Possible ministerial visits, Brooke to Brimelow, 8 February 1971, FCO 9/1532, TNA.
27. Ibid.
28. Palmer to Fearne, Wilberforce, Wiggin, 13 January 1972, FCO 9/1514, TNA.
29. Annual Review for 1972, no. 56/74, Hooper to Douglas-Home, Confidential, 2 January 1973, FCO 9/1709, TNA.
30. Greece: Record of office meeting in Parliamentary Under-Secretary's office, 11 February 1972, FCO 9/1728, TNA.
31. Hooper, Athens to Brook Turner, London, 9 March 1972, FCO 9/1532, TNA.
32. Greece: Record of office meeting in parliamentary Under-Secretary's office, 6 September 1972, FCO 9/1728, TNA.
33. Ibid.

34. British Policy towards Greece, Mr Royle's meeting with HM Ambassador at Athens 20 September 1973, FCO 9/1733, TNA.
35. A. Royle to Anthony Grant, 23 February 1972, FCO 9/1526, TNA.
36. Hooper, Athens to Brook Turner, London, 9 March 1972, FCO 9/1532, TNA.
37. Record of conversation between the Parliamentary Under-Secretary and the Greek Under-Secretary for foreign affairs, 2 May 1972, FCO 9/1526, TNA, DAGMFA.
38. Annual Report on the Hellenic Armed Forces—1972, by Baxter, 20 February 1973, FCO 9/1738, TNA.
39. Hooper to Brooke Turner, Confidential, 3 January 1971, FCO 9/1734, TNA.
40. Telegram, Sorokos to Greek Ministry of Foreign Affairs, 2 May 1972, no. 4111.4/11/133, 1974/5.11.
41. Wiggin on Palmer to Wiggin, 27 June 1972 FCO 9/1526, TNA.
42. R. J. Andrew to Lord Bridges, 5 July 1972, FCO 9/1526, TNA.
43. Telegram no. 178, Hooper to FCO, 30 May 1973, FO 286/1456, TNA.
44. Telegram Athens 1210, Tasca to Secretary of State, Secret, 26 February 1973, POL Greece-UK, NARA.
45. Palmer to Wiggin, 20 June 1972, FCO 9/1526, TNA.
46. Wiggin to Palmer, handwritten note by Brooke Turner, 27 June 1972, FCO 9/1526, TNA.
47. Greece, meeting at the office of the Parliamentary Under-Secretary, Secret, 6 September 1972, FCO 9/1527, TNA.
48. Greece: Record of office meeting in Parliamentary Under-Secretary's office, 6 September 1972, FCO 9/1728, TNA.
49. Briefs for Defence Secretary's visit to Athens, FCO to Cullen, 29 August 1972, FCO 9/1533, TNA.
50. Telegram no. 471, Powell-Jones to FCO, 7 September 1972, FCO 9/1533, TNA.
51. Telegram to Greek Ministry of Foreign Affairs, 14 June 1972, Protocol no. 4111.4/15/1197, File no. 1974/5.11, DAGMFA.
52. Powell-Jones to Douglas-Home, 13 September 1972, FCO 9/1533, TNA.
53. Topics for discussion at Mr Royle's office meeting on 6 September 1972, Secret, FCO 9/1527, TNA.
54. Telegram no. 471, Powell-Jones to FCO, 7 September 1972, FCO 9/1533, TNA.
55. Greece: Record of office meeting in Parliamentary Under-Secretary's office, 6 September 1972, FCO 9/1728, TNA.

56. Telegram no. 470, Powell-Jones to FCO, 7 September 1972, FCO 9/1533, TNA.
57. Powell-Jones to Douglas-Home, 13 September 1972, FCO 9/1533, TNA.
58. Booke Turner to Powell-Jones, 21 September 1972, FCO 9/1533, TNA.
59. Text of Lord Carrington's interview with the BBC, 16 October 1972, FCO 9/1533, TNA.
60. Topics for discussion at Mr Royle's office meeting on 6 September 1972, Secret, FCO 9/1527, TNA.
61. Draft, Defensive Speaking Note, Lord debate on Greece, 15 February, Speech by Lady Tweedsmuir, Confidential, FCO 9/1731, TNA.
62. Brooke Turner to Brimelow, General Political Brief, 12 October 1972, FCO 9/1534, TNA.
63. Ibid.
64. Record of conversation between Lord Limerick and Makarezos, 2 November 1972, FCO 9/1534, TNA.
65. Telegram no. 581, Hooper to FCO, 3 November 1972, FCO 9/1534, TNA.
66. Statement of Lord Limerick on departure from Greece, 3 November 1972, FCO 1535, TNA.
67. Hooper to Douglas-Home, Lord Limerick's visit to Greece, 8 November 1972, FCO 9/1534, TNA.
68. Record of a conversation at the Greek Foreign Ministry, 1 November 1972, FCO 9/1535, TNA.
69. Telegram no. 581, Hooper to FCO, 3 November 1972, FCO 9/1534, TNA.
70. Lord Limerick's visit to Greece, Hooper to Douglas-Home, 8 November 1972, FCO 9/1534, TNA.
71. Ibid.
72. Telegram Athens 6414, Tasca to Dept of State, Secret, 9 November 1972, RG-59, POL 15–1 Greece, NARA.
73. Hooper to Douglas-Home, Lord Limerick's visit to Greece, 8 November 1972, FCO 9/1534, TNA.
74. WSG 1/2, Diplomatic Report no 56/72, Greece: Annual Review for 1972, Hooper to Douglas-Home, Confidential, 2 January 1973, FCO 9/1709, TNA.
75. Tomkys, Athens to Prendergast, 19 October 1972, FCO 9/1526, TNA.
76. Ibid.
77. The Greek View of the British Political Situation and our commercial prospects, Brooke Turner to Wiggin and Royle, 29 November 1972, FCO 9/1526, TNA.

78. 'Athenian', *Inside the Colonels' Greece* (1972).

79. Richard Clogg and George Yannopoulos (eds), *Greece Under Military Rule* (1972).

80. WSG 1/2, Diplomatic Report no 56/72, Greece: Annual Review for 1972, Hooper to Douglas-Home, Confidential, 2 January 1973, FCO 9/1709, TNA.

81. Ibid.

82. WSG 1/2, Diplomatic Report no. 56/72, Greece: Annual Review for 1972, Hooper to Douglas-Home, Confidential, 2 January 1973, FCO 9/1709, TNA.

83. Hooper to Brooke Turner, Confidential, 3 January 1971, FCO 9/1734, TNA.

84. Konstantina Maragkou, *Anglo-American Attitudes Towards Konstantinos Karamanlis During the Greek Colonels' Regime'* (2009), pp. 278–293.

85. Note by R. W. Hooper on a record conversation between Ms Byatt and Athanasiades held on 10 January 1973, Confidential 18 January 1973, FO 286/1455, TNA.

86. Telegram no. 27/73, Greece: Annual Review for 1972 by Hooper, Confidential, 2 January 1973, FCO 9/1709, TNA.

87. Ibid.

88. WSG 1/3, Diplomatic Report no. 56/74, Greece: Annual review from 1973, R. J. W. Hooper to FCO, Confidential, 7 January 1974, FCO 9/1998, TNA.

89. Brooke Turner to Wiggin, Confidential, 3 January 1973, FCO 9/1731, TNA.

90. Hooper to Brooke Turner, Confidential, 3 January 1973, FCO 9/1734, TNA.

91. Telegram no. 3, Douglas-Home to Athens, Confidential, 5 January 1973, FCO 9/1729, TNA.

92. Brooke Turner to Hooper, Confidential, 11 January 1973, FCO 9/1729, TNA.

93. Memorandum, Defence relations with Greece, by Brooke Turner, 8 January 1973, FCO 9/1737, TNA.

94. Wiggin to Goodison, 5 March 1973, FCO 9/1719, TNA.

95. Konstantina Maragkou, 'Favoritism in NATO's Southern Flank' (2009), p. 360.

96. A. Brooke Turner to Wiggin, Policy towards Greece, Confidential, 3 January 1973, FCO 9/1731, TNA.

97. Call on Royle by Broumas, 14 February 1973, FCO 9/1731, TNA.

98. Telegram, Broumas to MFA, 14 February 1973, Protocol no. 8314/11/32, File no. 1974/5.12, DAGMFA.

99. Your telegram no. 59, Lords' Debate on Greece, Wiggin, Logan, Goodenough, FCO 9/1731, TNA.
100. Telegram, Broumas to MFA, 14 February 1973, Protocol no. 8314/11/32, File no. 1974/5.12, DAGMFA.
101. Draft, Speech, Lord Debate on Greece, 15 February, speech by Lady Tweedsmuir, FCO 9/1731, TNA.
102. Lord's Debate on Greece, 15 February, in Confidence, FCO 9/1731, TNA.
103. Record of conversation, Thomas Brimelow to R. Baker, Confidential, 21 January 1974, FCO 9/2013, TNA.
104. Martin to Prendergast, 29 March 1973, FCO 9/1732, TNA.
105. Greece, Topics for discussion at Mr Royle's Office meeting on 4 April 1973, Confidential, FCO 9/1732, TNA.
106. Ibid.
107. Ibid.
108. Annual Report on the Hellenic Armed forces—1972, Brigadier Baxter to the deputy Chief of the Defence Staff (intelligence), 20 February 1973, FCO 9/1738.
109. Telegram no. 103, Hooper to FCO, Confidential, 29 March 1973, FCO 9/1732, TNA.
110. Ibid.
111. Hooper's comments on Goodison to Logan, Confidential, 30 March 1973, FCO 9/1732, TNA.
112. Hooper to Douglas-Home, 21 February 1973, Secret, FCO 9/1738, TNA.
113. Press Release, PEST (The Progressive Tory Pressure Group), 26 July 1973, File no. 1974/5.12, DAGMFA.
114. Konstantina Maragkou, 'Favouritism in NATO's Southern Flank: The Case of the Greek Colonels, 1967–1974' in Cold War History, Vol. 9, Issue 3 (2009), p. 361.
115. Draft, Speech, Lord Debate on Greece, 15 February 1973, speech by Lady Tweedsmuir, FCO 9/1731, TNA.
116. Hooper's comments on Goodison to Logan, Confidential, 30 March 1973, FCO 9/1732, TNA.
117. Prendergast to Tomkys, 16 January 1973, FCO 9/1735, TNA.
118. Greece, Topics for discussion at Mr Royle's Office meeting on 4 April 1973, Confidential, FCO 9/1732, TNA.
119. Record of a meeting on Greece, 4 April 1973, FCO 9/1732, TNA.
120. Hooper's comments attached to Goodison to Logan, 30 March 1973, FCO 9/1732, TNA.
121. Ibid.

122. Record of a conversation between Royle and Broumas, 21 May 1973, FCO 9/1729, TNA.
123. Broumas to Greek Ministry of Foreign Affairs, Greek-British relations, Part III, Secret, 14 January 1974, Protocol no. 0445/1/90, File no. 1973.3, DAGMFA.
124. Ibid.

7. FROM 'BUSINESS AS USUAL' TO 'DEVELOPING GOOD AND CONSTRUCTIVE RELATIONS'

1. Internal Political Situation by Martin, 5 June 1973, FO 286/1456, TNA.
2. Telegram no. 173, Hooper to FCO, 29 May 1973, FO 286/1456, TNA.
3. Ibid.
6. *The Guardian*, 2 June 1973, p. 1.
7. *The Times*, 2 June 1973, front page.
8. *The Times*, 28 May 1973, front page.
9. 1st Trimester Report, Greek Embassy London to Greek Ministry of Foreign Affairs, 30 June 1973, Protocol no. 0455/16/2206, File no. 1973.3, DAGMFA.
10. Foreign Office to British Embassy (Tehran) 31 May 1973, FCO 9/1742 TNA.
11. *The Times*, 25 May 1973, p. 19.
12. Hooper to Douglas-Home 14 June 1973, FCO 9/1713, TNA.
13. Ibid.
14. Ibid.
15. *The Guardian*, 2 June 1973, p. 12.
16. The former King of the Hellenes, 31 July 1973, FCO 9/1742 TNA.
17. Hatzivassiliou, Evanthis, '*Heirs of the King-Makers: The British Embassy in Athens, 1951–1961*' in Diplomacy & Statecraft, Volume 18, Issue 3, September 2007, pp. 573–591.
18. Prime Minister's Audience with the Queen: Abolition of Greek Monarchy, 5 June 1973, FCO 9/1713, TNA.
19. Hooper to Douglas-Home 14 June 1973, FCO 9/1713, TNA.
20. Ibid.
21. Telegram no. 163, Douglas-Home to Athens, 10 June 1973, FO 286/1456, TNA.
22. Letter, Errington Thubron, League for Democracy in Greece to Sir Alec Douglas-Home, Secretary of State for Foreign Affairs, 14 June 1973, MGA correspondence, II, Birmingham Branch of League for Democracy in Greece, KCLA.

23. Anglo-Greek relations, J. B. Denson to A. C. Goodison, Confidential, 12 July 1973, FCO 9/1730, TNA.

24. Telegram London 6594, ref: Athens 3606, 3646, Annenberg, Athens to American Embassy London, Limited Official use, 6 June 1973, POL 16 Greece, POL Greece-UK, RG 59, NARA.

25. John Pesmazoglou, 'The Greek Economy After 1967', in Richard Clogg and George Yannopoulos (eds), *Greece Under Military Rule* (1972), p. 181.

26. Thanos Veremis, *The Military in Greek Politics: From Independence to Democracy* (1997), p. 165.

27. Parliamentary Records, House of Commons, Vol. 859, No. 126, 13 June 1973.

28. Hooper to Goodison, 21 June 1973, FCO 9/1714, TNA.

29. Ibid.

30. Report no. 6/73, The Greek Referendum of 1973, Hooper to Douglas-Home, 9 August 1973, FCO 9/1714, TNA.

31. Anglo–Greek relations, J. B. Denson to A. C. Goodison, Confidential, 12 July 1973, FCO 9/1730, TNA.

32. Parliamentary Records, House of Commons, Vol. 859, No. 141, 4 July 1973.

33. *The Guardian*, 29 May 1973, p. 14.

34. *The Times*, 25 May 1973, p. 19.

35. *The Times*, 28 May 1973, front page.

36. Inauguration of President Papadopoulos, A. C. Goodison to Sir T. Brimelow, Confidential, 14 August 1973, TNA.

37. Telegram 304, Denson to FCO, 23 August 1973, FO 286/1458, TNA.

38. Telegram no. 292, Denson Athens to FCO, 10 August 1973, FCO 9/1730, TNA.

39. Hitch to Tomkys, 30 May 1973, FCO 9/1729, TNA.

40. Telegram no. 178, Hooper to FCO, 30 May 1973, FO 286/1456, TNA.

41. *The Guardian*, 29 May 1973, p. 14.

42. Royle to Hugh Dykes, London, 18 June 1973, FCO 9/1714, TNA.

43. Goodison to Hooper, 15 June 1973, FCO 9/1714, TNA.

44. Abolition of the Greek Monarchy, Hooper to Douglas-Home, 14 June 1973, Confidential, FCO 9/1732, TNA.

45. Hooper to Goodison, 19 July 1973, FCO 9/1714, TNA.

46. Goodison to Hooper, 29 June 1973, FCO 9/1714, TNA.

47. Hooper to Goodison, 10 July 1973, FCO 9/1714, TNA.

48. Note, G. Christogiannis for the attention of the Ambassador, Secret, 1 September 1973, File no. 1974/5.11, DAGMFA.

49. Ibid.

50. Annual Review for 1973, no. 56/74, Hooper to Douglas-Home, 7 January 1974, FCO 9/1998, TNA.
51. Denson to Goodison, 6 September 1973, FCO 9/1732, TNA.
52. Ibid.
53. Annual Review for 1973, no. 56/74, Hooper to Douglas-Home, 7 January 1974, FCO 9/1998, TNA.
54. Abolition of the Greek Monarchy, Hooper to Douglas-Home, 14 June 1973, Confidential, FCO 9/1732, TNA.
55. Denson to Goodison, 6 September 1973, FCO 9/1732, TNA.
56. Meeting on Greece at Mr Royle's office on 20 September 1973, Confidential, FCO 9/1733, TNA.
57. Sorokos to Greek Ministry of Foreign Affairs, 5 October 1972, no. 4111.4/22/343, 1974/5.11. DAGMFA.
58. Objectives of HMG's Policy towards Greece, A. C. Goodison to J. B. Denson, 5 October 1973, FCO 9/1733, TNA.
59. Goodison to Wiggin, 28 September 1973, FCO 9/1733, TNA.
60. Ibid.
61. Anglo-Greek relations, J. B. Denson to A. C. Goodison, Confidential, 6 September 1973, FCO 9/1732, TNA.
62. Policy towards Greece, A. Brooke Turner to Wiggin, Goulding, 3 January 1973, FCO 9/1731, TNA.
63. *The Times*, 12 October 1973, p. 21.
64. Anglo-Greek relations, C. D. Wiggin to A. C. Goodison, 24 October 1973, FCO 9/1733, TNA.
65. *The Times*, 12 October 1973, p. 21.
66. Hooper to Goodison, Confidential, 25 October 1973, FCO 9/1712, TNA.
67. R. W. J. Hooper to Goodison, Confidential, 15 November 1973, FCO 9/1712, TNA.
68. Broumas to Greek Ministry of Foreign Affairs, Greek-British Relations, Secret, 14 January 1974, Protocol No. 0445/1/90, File No. 1973.3, DAGMFA.
69. Annual Review for 1973, no. 56/74, Hooper to Douglas-Home, 7 January 1974, FCO 9/1998, TNA.
70. Denson to Goodison, Confidential, 6 September 1973, FCO 9/1732, TNA.
71. R. W. J. Hooper to Goodison, Confidential, 15 November 1973, FCO 9/1712, TNA.
72. Tomkys to Cornish, 11 October 1973, FCO 9/1716, TNA.
73. Hooper to Goodison, Confidential, 25 October 1973, FCO 9/1712, TNA.

74. Ibid.
75. *The Guardian*, 2 October 1973, p. 14.
76. The Internal Political debate, J. F. R. Martin to R. F. Cornish, 25 October 1973, FCO 9/1712, TNA.
77. Hooper to Goodison, Confidential, 16 October 1973, FCO 9/1730, TNA.
78. Telegram no. 263, Douglas-Home to Athens, 9 October 1973, FCO 9/1716, TNA.
79. For an account of Britain's stance towards the 'Karamanlis solution', see Konstantina Maragkou, 'Anglo-American Attitudes Towards Konstantinos Karamanlis During the Greek Colonels' Regime' in Konstantinos Svolopoulos, Konstantina E. Botsiou, Evanthis Hatzivassiliou (eds), *Konstantinos Karamanlis in the Twentieth Century* (2009), p. 290.
80. *The Times*, 11 October 1973, p. 18.
81. Hooper to Goodison, 16 October 1973, FCO 9/1730, TNA.
82. Ibid.
83. Ibid.
84. R. W. J. Hooper, Secret, 30 October 1973, FCO 9/1733, TNA.
85. Goodison to Wiggin, Confidential, 1 November 1973, FCO 9/1733, TNA.
86. Cornish to Baker, 7 November 1973, FCO 9/1733, TNA.
87. R. W. J. Hooper, Confidential, 20 November 1973, FO 286/1460, TNA.
88. C. D. Wiggin, Confidential, 6 November 1973, FCO 9/1733, TNA.
89. Ibid.
90. Goodison to Wiggin, Confidential, 1 November 1973, FCO 9/1733, TNA.
91. Ibid.
92. Thanos Veremis, *The Military in Greek Politics: From Independence to Democracy* (1997), p. 168.
93. *The Guardian*, 19 November 1973, front page.
94. Telegram no. 398, Hooper to FCO, Confidential, 20 November 1973, FCO 9/1712, TNA.
95. Greece, Draft minute, Goodison to Secretary of State, 13 November 1973, FCO 9/1733, TNA.
96. Maria Karavia, *To imerologio tou Londinou*, photo caption 72.
97. Memorandum no. 516/73, Praxicopematics: or the fall of Papadopoulos, Hooper to FCO, 6 December 1973, FCO 9/1717, TNA.
98. Press Gossip, H. Byatt, Confidential, 26 October 1973, FCO 286/1459, TNA.

99. Goodison to Hooper, 23 November 1973, FCO 9/1733, TNA.

100. WSG 1/3, Diplomatic Report no. 56/74, Greece: Annual review for 1973, Hooper to FCO, 7 January 1974, FCO 9/1998, TNA.

101. Telegram, Gauvin, Aftermath of new coup in Greece, 25 November 1973, FCO 9/1717, TNA.

102. Memorandum no. 516/73, Praxicopematics: or the fall of Papado-poulos, Hooper to FCO, 6 December 1973, FCO 9/1717, TNA.

103. *The Guardian*, 29 November 1973, p. 2.

104. Ibid.

105. Letter, Christopher King to Philip Potter, The IRCR and Greece, Strictly confidential, 18 March 1974, 42.3.050, WCC Secretariat Archives.

106. Telegram, Gauvin, New coup in Greece, 25 November 1973, FCO 9/1717, TNA.

107. WSG 1/3, Diplomatic Report no. 56/74, Greece: Annual review for 1973, Hooper to FCO, 7 January 1974, FCO 9/1998, TNA.

108. Doctrine of recognition employed by ECC States, R. F. Cornish to Wright, Confidential, FCO 9/1717, TNA.

109. WSG 1/3, Diplomatic Report no. 56/74, Greece: Annual review for 1973, Hooper to FCO, 7 January 1974, FCO 9/1998, TNA.

110. Diplomatic report no. 56/74, Annual review for 1973, Hooper to FCO, Confidential, 7 January 1974, FCO 9/1998, TNA.

111. Telegram, Gauvin, Aftermath of new coup in Greece, 25 November 1973, FCO 9/1717, TNA.

112. Memorandum no. 516/73, Praxicopematics: or the fall of Papadopoulos, Hooper to FCO, 6 December 1973, FCO 9/1717, TNA.

113. Notes for supplementaries, Goodison to Wiggin, 26 November 1973, FCO 9/1733, TNA.

114. Telegram no. 416, Hooper to FCO, 27 November 1973, FCO 9/1717, TNA.

115. John Sakkas, 'The Greek Dictatorship, the USA and the Arabs, 1967–1974' in *The Journal of Southern Europe and the Balkans*, Vol. 6 No. 3 (2003), p. 254.

116. Telegram no. 416, Hooper to FCO, 27 November 1973, FCO 9/1717, TNA.

117. Telegram no. 426, Hooper to FCO, 29 November 1973, FCO 9/1717, TNA.

118. Chiefs of Staff Committee, The importance to the United Kingdom of Military facilities in Cyprus, Report by the Defence Policy Staff, Top Secret, 8 October 1973, FCO 46/1017, TNA.

119. Broumas to Greek Ministry of Foreign Affairs, Greek-British relations, Part III, Secret, 14 January 1974, Protocol no. 0445/1/90, File no. 1973.3, DAGMFA.

120. WSG ¼, Greece: Recognition memorandum, Goodison, 29 November 1973, FCO 9/1717, TNA.

121. Ibid.

122. Memorandum no. 516/73, Praxicopematics: or the fall of Papadopoulos, Hooper to FCO, 6 December 1973, FCO 9/1717, TNA.

123. Ibid.

124. Ibid.

125. Cabinet meeting 59 (73), 4 December 1973, CAB 128/53, TNA.

126. Greek Internal Situation, J. F. R. Martin to R. F. Cornish, Confidential, 6 December 1973, FCO 9/1717, TNA.

127. Memorandum no. 516/73, Praxicopematics: or the fall of Papadopoulos, Hooper to FCO, 6 December 1973, FCO 9/1717, TNA.

128. Telegram no. 416, Hooper to FCO, 27 November 1973, FCO 9/1717, TNA.

129. Cabinet meeting 59 (73), 4 December 1973, CAB 128/53, TNA.

130. Recognition, R. F. Cornish to Baker, Restricted, 6 December 1973, FCO 9/1717, TNA.

131. Defence cooperation with Greece, A. C. Goodison to Wiggin, Confidential, 17 December 1973, FCO 46/965, TNA.

132. Telegram no. 320, Douglas-Home to Athens, 27 December 1973, FCO 9/1737, TNA.

133. Goodison to Hooper, Confidential, 19 December 1973, FCO 286/1461, TNA.

134. Background note to House of Lords question, 11 December 1973, FCO 9/1717, TNA.

135. WSG 10/2, Greece: Arms sales, Goodison to Wiggin, 14 December 1973, FCO 9/1735, TNA.

136. Memorandum no. 516/73, Praxicopematics: or the fall of Papadopoulos, Hooper to FCO, 6 December 1973, FCO 9/1717, TNA.

137. Goodison to Wiggin, 12 December 1973, FCO 9/1717, TNA.

138. Points to be made, Call by the Greek Ambassador on the Parliamentary Under-Secretary of Staff on Tuesday 22 January 1974, Secret, FCO 9/2013, TNA.

139. Ibid.

140. Broumas to Greek Ministry of Foreign Affairs, Greek-British relations, Part III, Secret, 14 January 1974, Protocol no. 0445/1/90, File no. 1973.3, DAGMFA.

141. Letter, S. Miranda to E. Thubron, 21 November 1973, MGA, Correspondence, Trades Unions, KCLA.

142. Diplomatic report no. 56/74, Annual review for 1973, Hooper to FCO, Confidential, 7 January 1974, FCO 9/1998, TNA.
143. Ibid.
144. Ibid.
145. Memorandum, Greece: Annual review 1974, S. T. Corcoran, 10 March 1975, FCO 9/2226, TNA.
146. Goodison to Wiggin, 25 January 1974, FCO 9/2015, TNA.
147. Background note, Mr Ridley's parliamentary question on Greece: 2 April, Confidential, FCO 9/2015, TNA.
148. Visit to London of HM Ambassador Athens, Goodison to Wiggin, Confidential, 25 January 1974, FCO 9/2015, TNA.
149. Goodison to Hooper, 22 January 1974, FCO 9/1998, TNA.
150. Diamantopoulos to MFA, 21 December 1973, Protocol no. 4111.41/44/4276, File no. 1974/5.12, DAGMFA.
151. Cornish to Baker, 14 January 1974, FCO 9/1998, TNA.

8. FROM A 'GOOD WORKING RELATIONSHIP' TO A 'PROPER WORKING RELATIONSHIP'

1. Telegram no. 57, Hooper (British Embassy London) to FCO, Confidential, 14 March 1974, FCO 9/2015, TNA.
2. THE HA 01692, American Embassy at the Hague to the Secretary of State, Limited Official Use, April 1974, Department of State Archives Online Repository, NARA online.
3. Telegram no. 49, Callaghan to Athens, 13 March 1974, FCO 9/2005, TNA.
4. Broumas to MFA, 18 April 1974, Protocol no. 4111.4/10/AS876, File no. 1974/5.11, DAGMFA.
5. Ibid.
6. Broumas to Athens, 26 March 1974, Protocol no. 4111.4/5/AS74, File no. 1974/5.11, DAGMFA.
7. Telegram no. 49, Greece and NATO, Callaghan to Athens, Confidential, 13 March 1974, FCO 9/2015, TNA.
8. Telegram London 03333, from AmEmbassy London to SecState Washington, Subject: Cancellation of British ship visit to Greece, March 1974, Confidential, NARA online.
9. Greene to Callaghan, 19 March 1974, FCO 9/2004, TNA.
10. Broumas to Athens, 26 March 1974, Protocol no. 4111.4/5/AS74, File no. 1974/5.11, DAGMFA.
11. Telegram no. 66, Hooper to FCO, 16 March 1974, FCO 9/2015, TNA.

12. Telegram no. 56, Hooper to FCO, 14 March 1974, FCO 9/2005, TNA.
13. Telegram no. 57, Hooper to FCO, 14 March 1974, FCO 9/2005, TNA.
14. Ibid.
15. R. Keeley, *The Colonels' Coup and the American Embassy: A Diplomat's View of the Breakdown of Democracy in Cold War Greece* (2011), p. 121.
16. Greek reactions to cancellation of HM Ship visit, A. C. Goodison to Wiggin, Secret, 18 March 1974, FCO 9/2015, TNA.
17. Telegram, Greek Foreign Ministry to Greek Embassy Athens, Secret, 15 March 1974, 4111.4/6/AS419, 1974/5.11. DAGMFA.
18. Telegram no. 58, Hooper to FCO, 14 March 1974, FCO 9/2015, TNA.
19. Telegram no. 63, Hooper to FCO, 15 March 1974, FCO 9/2015, TNA.
20. Telegram no. 73, Hooper to FCO, Confidential, 19 March 1974, FCO 9/2015, TNA.
21. Goodison to Goulding, 18 March 1974, FCO 9/2015, TNA.
22. Telegram no. 66, Hooper to FCO, 16 March 1974, FCO 9/2015, TNA.
23. Greek reactions to cancellation of HM Ship visit, A. C. Goodison to Wiggin, Secret, 18 March 1974, FCO 9/2015, TNA.
24. Goodison to Hooper, 13 March 1974, FCO 9/2015 and Hooper to MoD, 18 March 1974, FCO 9/2015, TNA.
25. Background note, Mr Ridley's parliamentary question on Greece: 2 April, Confidential, FCO 9/2015, TNA.
26. Ibid.
27. Telegram no. 75, Hooper to FCO, 20 March 1974, FCO 9/2015, TNA.
28. Hooper to Goodison, 2 April 1974, FCO 9/2015, TNA.
29. Tomkys to Baker, 20 March 1974, FCO 9/2015, TNA.
30. Hooper to Goodison, 29 May 1974, FCO 9/2013, TNA.
31. Tomkys to Baker, 20 March 1974, FCO 9/2015, TNA.
32. Hooper to Goodison, 2 April 1974, FCO 9/2015, TNA.
33. Diplomatic Report no. 340/74, Valedictory Dispatch, Confidential, 4 September 1974, FCO 9/2024, TNA.
34. Letter from W. R. Tomkys (British Embassy in Athens) to R. H. Baker (Southern European Department, FCO, 20 March 1974, Confidential, FCO 9/2015, TNA.
35. Telegram no. 57, Hooper (British Embassy London) to FCO, Confidential, 14 March 1974, FCO 9/2015, TNA.

36. Telegram, Athens 0512, Subject: Greece after Euphoria, ExDis, January 1974, NARA online.
37. Press Release, International Commission of Jurists, Subject: Disrespect for the rule of law in Greece, 25 March 1974, Pollis Collection, IV. Vertical File Miscellaneous, DF. 853.c63q, carton 15, PULA.
38. Anglo-Greek relations, Goodison to Hooper, 22 April 1974, FCO 9/2015, TNA.
39. London 03333 151700Z, American Embassy in London to Secretary of State Washington, Confidential, March 1974, NARA online.
40. Anglo-Greek relations, Goodison to Hooper, 22 April 1974, FCO 9/2015, TNA.
41. Letter from W. R. Tomkys (British Embassy in Athens) to R. H. Baker (Southern European Department, FCO, 20 March 1974, Confidential, FCO 9/2015, TNA.
42. Greece and the EEC, Braithwaite to Butler, 8 July 1974, FCO 9/2016, TNA.
43. Anglo/Greek relations, A. C. Goodison to Robin Hooper, Confidential, 22 April 1974, FCO 9/2015, TNA.
44. EC BRU 01896 282255Z, US Mission at the EEC in Brussels to Secretary of State, Unclassified, March 1974, NARA online.
45. 'Oil exploration in the Aegean', Tomkys to Cornish, 21 February 1974, FCO 9/2009, TNA.
46. 'Turkish-Greek relations: the Aegean and oil', R. A. Fyjis-Walker to Tomkys, 26 February 1974, FCO 9/2009, TNA.
47. Telegram no 113, Callaghan to UKDEL NATO, 20 May 1974, FCO 9/2010, TNA.
48. Telegram, London 06114, AmEmbassy London to SecState Washington, Subject: British assessment of current Greek-Turkish tensions, Secret, May 1974, NARA online.
49. Turkish-Greek relations, H. Phillips Ankara to Wiggin, FCO, 13 May 1974, FCO 9/20102, TNA.
50. Telegram, London 06114, AmEmbassy London to SecState Washington, Subject: British assessment of current Greek-Turkish tensions, Secret, May 1974, NARA online access.
51. Turkish-Greek relations, H. Phillips Ankara to Wiggin, FCO, 13 May 1974, FCO 9/2012, TNA.
52. Anglo-Greek relations, W. R. Tomkys to R. H. Baker, Confidential, 20 March 1974, FCO 9/2015, TNA.
53. Turkish/Greek relations, H. Phillips Ankara to Wiggin, 13 May 1974, FCO 9/2010, TNA.
54. 'Greek/Turkish relations', Baker to Wiggin, 19 April 1974, FCO 9/2010, TNA.

55. Telegram no. 1240, Callaghan to Washington, 31 May 1974, FCO 9/2015, TNA.
56. Telegram no. 1991, Ramsbotham to FCO, 4 June 1974, FCO 9/2010, TNA.
57. Quote from Effie Pedaliu, 'We Were Always Realistic': The Heath Government, the European Community and the Cold War in the Mediterranean, June 1970–February 1974', in J. W. Young, E. G. H. Pedaliu and M. D. Kandiah (eds), *Britain in Global Politics: From Churchill to Blair*, Volume 2 (2013), p. 161.
58. Telegram no. 1240, Callaghan, 31 May 1974, FCO 9/2015, TNA.
59. Record of conversation, Hattersley and Hartman, 13 May 1974, FCO 9/2015, TNA.
60. M. I. Goulding to Baker, 16 May 1974, FCO 9/2015, TNA.
61. Hooper to Wiggin, Confidential, 6 June 1974, FCO 9/2015, TNA.
62. Keith Kyle, 'British Policy on Cyprus, 1974–2004' in Hubert Faustman and Nicos Peristianis (eds) *Britain in Cyprus: Colonialism and Post-colonialism, 1878–2006* (2006), p. 586.
63. Record of conversation, Thomas Brimelow to R. Baker, Confidential, 21 January 1974, FCO 9/2013, TNA.
64. Telegram no. 1240, Callaghan to Washington, 31 May 1974, FCO 9/2015, TNA.
65. Telegram, London 07057, Annenberg, AmEmbassy London to SecState Washington, Subject: Greek issue at NATO ministerial, Confidential, June 1974, NARA online.
66. Ibid.
67. Wiggin to Goulding, 23 April 1974, FCO 9/2004, TNA.
68. Memorandum OPD (74) 18, Relations with politically sensitive countries, Hunt, Smith and Roberts, 3 June 1974, FCO 9/2019, TNA.
69. Telegram, State 048279, SecState Washington to AmEmbassy Athens, Subject: Ambassador's appearance before Rosenthal committee, Limited Official Use, NARA online.
70. The International League for the Rights of Man, Subject: Human Rights violations in Greece scored on NATO's 25th Anniversary, 26 June 1974, Pollis Collections, IV. Vertical File, Miscellaneous, DF 853.c63q, carton 15, PULA.
71. Letter, Dr. Petra Kelly to the Editor, 13 June 1973, Petra Kelly Archives, File no. 1914 Archives of the Green Party, Berlin.
72. WSG 21/1, Frigates for the Greek Navy, Goodison to Wiggin, 9 July 1974, FCO 9/2022, TNA.
73. Memorandum OPD (74) 18, Relations with politically sensitive countries, Hunt, Smith and Roberts, 3 June 1974, FCO 9/2019, TNA.

74. Goodison to Wiggin, 9 July 1974, FCO 9/2022, TNA.

75. Telegram no. 178, Olver to FCO, 15 July 1974, FCO 9/1890, TNA.

76. Telegram no. 180, Olver to FCO, 15 July 1974, FCO 9/1890, TNA.

77. Telegram no. 129, Callaghan to Athens, Ankara, Washington, UKDEL, UKMIS NY, 15 July 1974, FCO 9/1890.

78. Ibid.

79. Ibid.

80. Telegram no. 283, Ramsbotham, Washington to FCO, 15 July 1974, FCO 9/1890, TNA.

81. Telegram no. 184, Olver to FCO, 15 July 1974, FCO 9/1890, TNA.

82. Telegram no. 190, Olver to FCO, 15 July 1974, FCO 9/1890, TNA.

83. Call by the Cyprus High Commissioner, Goodison to Private Secretary, 15 July 1974, FCO 9/1890, TNA.

84. Telegram no. 196, Hooper to FCO, 15 July 1974, FCO 9/1890, TNA.

85. Goulding to Goodison, 16 July 1974, FCO 9/2006, TNA.

86. James Callaghan, *Time and Change* (1987), p. 356.

87. WSG 25/2, Diplomatic Report, 340/74, Valedictory Despatch, R. W. J. Hooper to FCO, Confidential, 4 September 1974, FCO 9/2024, TNA.

88. Telegram no. 191, Callaghan to Athens, 24 July 1975, FCO 9/2003, TNA.

89. Greek government, J. F. R. Martin to Goodison, Confidential, 24 July 1974, FCO 9/2003, TNA.

90. Telegram no. 339, Hooper to FCO, Confidential, 25 July 1974, FCO 9/2003, TNA.

91. Government changes in Cyprus and in Greece, W. R. Tomkys to Goodison, 24 July 1974, FCO 9/2003, TNA.

92. Telegram no. 339, Hooper to FCO, Confidential, 25 July 1974, FCO 9/2003, TNA.

93. Ibid.

94. Ibid.

95. Telegram no. 339, Hooper to FCO, Confidential, 25 July 1974, FCO 9/2003, TNA.

96. Greece, meeting between Dr Kissinger and Sir John Killick on Tuesday 27 August 1974 in the Department of State, Washington, Secret, FCO 9/1947, TNA.

97. Ibid.

98. WSG 25/2, Diplomatic Report, 340/74, Valedictory Despatch, R. W. J. Hooper to FCO, Confidential, 4 September 1974, FCO 9/2024, TNA.

99. James Callaghan, *Time and Change* (1987), p. 356.

100. WSG 25/2, Diplomatic Report, 340/74, Valedictory Dispatch, R. W. J. Hooper to FCO, Confidential, 4 September 1974, FCO 9/2024, TNA.

101. Record of conversation, Thomas Brimelow to R. Baker, Confidential, 21 January 1974, FCO 9/2013, TNA.

EPILOGUE

1. John W. Young, 'The Diary of Michael Stewart as British Foreign Secretary, April–May 1968', in *Contemporary British History* (2005), p. 491.

2. Letter, A. E. Palmer FCO Southern European Department to Alfred Lomas, London Cooperative Society Political Committee, 17 August 1970, MGA correspondence I, Co-operational organisations, KCLA.

3. Telegram to MFA, 28 June 1973, Protocol no. 4111.41/33/127, File no. 1974/5.12, DAGMFA.

4. C. M. Woodhouse, *The Rise and Fall of the Greek Colonels*, (1985), p. 40.

5. Interview with Anne Burley.

6. Barbara Castle, *The Castle Diaries, 1964–1970* (1984), p. 514.

7. Tony Benn, *Office Without Power, Diaries 1968–72* (1988), p. 96.

8. Telegram to MFA, 28 June 1973, Protocol no. 4111.41/33/127, File no. 1974/5.12, DAGMFA.

9. Jean Meynaud, *Political Forces in Greece* (2002), p. 525.

10. Conclusions of a meeting held at the FCO, 17 February 1969, FCO 9/871, TNA.

11. Telegram, Broumas to Greek Ministry of Foreign Affairs, 6 July 1973, Protocol no. 4111.4/13/AS135, File no. 1974/5.11, DAGMFA.

12. Sorokos to Greek Ministry of Foreign Affairs, Yearly Report 1971, Secret, 20 December 1971, Protocol no. 6350/ST/2, File no. 1973.3, DAGMFA.

13. *Greek Observer*, March 1969, p. 24.

BIBLIOGRAPHY

A) Archives

British National Archives, Kew Gardens, Richmond, Surrey (TNA)

Class: Foreign Office (FO) & Foreign and Commonwealth Office (FCO)

Files: 9/75, 9/76, 9/120, 9/124, 9/125, 9/126, 9/132, 9/133, 9/136, 9/139, 9/148, 9/165, 9/166, 9/172, 9/209, 9/214, 9/221, 9/224, 9/227, 9/228, 9/229, 9/230, 9/231, 9/286, 9/634, 9/793, 9/830, 9/835, 9/838, 9/844, 9/845, 9/846, 9/847, 9/848, 9/849, 9/850, 9/858, 9/870, 9/871, 9/872, 9/874, 9/877, 9/878, 9/880, 9/883, 9/885, 9/887, 9/908, 9/1162, 9/1192, 9/1193, 9/1194, 9/1198, 9/1199, 9/1200, 9/1202, 9/1205, 9/1206, 9/1208, 9/1213, 9/1215, 9/1216, 9/1217, 9/1229, 9/1233, 9/1234, 9/1383, 9/1384, 9/1385, 9/1386, 9/1388, 9/1389, 9/1390, 9/1391, 9/1392, 9/1396, 9/1397, 9/1398, 9/1400, 9/1401, 9/1404, 9/1410, 9/1414, 9/1415, 9/1514, 9/1520, 9/1526, 9/150, 9/1532, 9/153, 9/1534, 9/1535, 9/1709, 9/1714, 9/1716, 9/1717, 9/1719, 9/1723, 9/1728, 9/1729, 9/1730, 9/1731, 9/1732, 9/1733, 9/1734, 9/1735, 9/1737, 9/1738, 9/1740, 9/1741, 9/1742, 9/1817, 9/1860, 9/1890, 9/1998, 9/2004, 9/2005, 9/2009, 9/2010, 9/2013, 9/2014, 9/2015, 9/2016, 9/2019, 9/2022, 9/2226, 13/13, 13/92, 19/73, 22/307, 25/502, 26/266, 26/267, 27/68, 27/118, 28/67, 28/159, 28/1520, 53/85, 53/86, 53/87, 55/79, 55/80, 55/81, 55/308, 55/309, 67/23, 67/30, 67/227, 371/169070, 371/169081, 371/179948, 371/179981, 371/185666, 371/185667, 371/185677, 371/187613, 372/7827, 953/2121.

Class: Treasury (T)

Files: 312/1867, 334/144, 317/1477, 312/1674, 312/1866, 312/1867, 312/2601, 312/1859, 334/144.

BIBLIOGRAPHY

Class: Board of Trade (BT)

Files: 333/16, 241/1485, 241/1486

Class: United Kingdom Atomic Energy Authority (AB)

Files: 42/42, 48/313, 38/503, 38/43, 38/772, 59/223

Class: Cabinet Conclusions

CAB 128(42)—Files: 67/23, 67/28, 67/30, 67/67, 67/70, 67/74
CAB 128(43)—Files: 68/9
CAB 128(44)—Files 69/55
CAB 128(52)—Files 73/35
CAB 128(53)—Files 73/57, 73/59
CAB 128(54)—Files 74/3
CAB 128(55)—Files 74/35

Class: Cabinet, Joint Intelligence Committee Meetings (CAB 158)

Files: 37, 45

Class: Cabinet, Joint Intelligence Committee Series (CAB 159)

File: 66

Class: Cabinet Defence and Oversea Policy Committee (CAB 148)

Files: OPD(68) 37: 13th and 16th Meetings, OPD(68) 48: 13th and 15th
    Meetings, OPD(68) 56: 16th Meeting, OPD(69) 3, OPD(91) 2.

Class: Premier Papers (Prem)

Files: 11/4841, 13/92, 13/1690, 13/2139, 13/2140, 13/2141, 13/2696,
    13/2697, 13/3246, 13/3247, 15/44, 15/672

Class: Mediterranean Department (DO)

File: 220/169

Diplomatic Archives of the Greek Ministry for Foreign Affairs, Athens,
    Greece (DAGMFA)

Class: London Embassy

Files: 1967/2.1, 1967/2.4, 1969/5.1, 1970/3.4, 1970/4.1, 1970/4.4,
    1971/12.3, 1972/3.2, 1972/4.1, 1973/2.7, 1973/3.7, 1973/3.8,
    1974/5.11

National Archives and Records Administration, College Park, M.D.
Record Group 59, Records of the Department of State

BIBLIOGRAPHY

Class: Central Files

Files: POL GREECE-US, POL 1 GREECE-US, POL 2 GREECE, POL 2–1
GREECE, POL 7 GREECE, POL 12–6 GREECE, POL 14 GREECE, POL
15–1 GREECE, POL 17 GREECE-UK, POL 23–9 GREECE, POL 30–2
   GREECE, POL 33
GREECE-US, POL GREECE-UK

Class: LOT Files

Files: 66 D 110, 66 D 347, 67 D 586, 68 D 453, 69 D 182, 69 D 533 65 D
   330, 70 D
265, 71 D 6, 72 D 318
Record Group 84, Records of Diplomatic and Consular Posts
Athens Post Files: LOT 71 A 2420, LOT 72 A 5030

INR (Bureau of Intelligence and Research)

Central Intelligence Agency
Lyndon B. Johnson Library, Austin, Texas

Class: National Security Files (NSF)

Files: Country File, National Security Council Meetings File, Memos to the
   President, National Intelligence Estimates, National Security Action
   Memorandums (NSAMS), Files of the Special Committee of the National
   Security Council, Name File (Komer Memos, Vol. 1 & McCone Memos),
   Agency File (UN), Files of McGeorge Bundy, Files of Robert Komer, Files
   of Harold Saunders, Special Head of State Correspondence File.

Class: White House (WHCF)

Files: Central Files, Confidential File, Appointment File.
Class: Office Files of the White House Aids.
Class: Personal Papers.
Class: Recordings and Transcripts of Conversation.
Class: Vice-President Security File.
Class: Oral Histories Collection.

Private and institutional archives

Adamantia Pollis, Princeton University Library, Special Collections &
   Archives, NJ, USA.
Amnesty International, Columbia University Rare Books and Manuscripts
   Library, NY, USA.
Amnesty International, International Institute of Social History, Amsterdam,
   The Netherlands.

BIBLIOGRAPHY

Antonio Solaro, Princeton University Library, Special Collections & Archives, NJ, USA.

Archives of the Council of Europe, Council of Europe, Strasbourg.

Council of Europe online archives.

Geoffrey de Freitas Collection, Oxford University, Bodleian Library, Manuscripts & Rare Books.

Harold Wilson, Modern Papers Collection, Bodleian Library, Oxford (Ms Wilson), UK.

International Commission of Jurists Archive, Hull History Centre, Hull, UK.

International Red Cross Archives, Geneva, Switzerland.

Konstantinos Karamanlis, Konstantinos Karamanlis Archive, Athens, Greece.

Konstantinos Mitsotakis, Konstantinos Mitsotakis Archive, Athens, Greece.

League for Democracy in Greece, King's College London Archives, UK.

Lord George-Brown, Modern Papers Collection, Bodleian Library, Oxford (Ms.Eng.), UK.

Maria Becket Personal Archive, Becket Family, Athens & Geneva.

Modern Greek Archives, King's College London Archives, UK.

Petra Kelly Archives, Archives of the Green Party, Berlin, Germany.

Socialist International, International Institute of Social History, Amsterdam, The Netherlands.

Stephen Rousseas Files, Columbia University Rare Books and Manuscripts Library, NJ, USA.

Sir Michael Stewart, Churchill Archives Centre, Cambridge, UK.

World Federation of Churches Archives, Geneva, Switzerland.

B) Printed Primary Sources

Parliamentary Debates, House of Commons & House of Lords, Fifth Series, (HMSO: London), Vols.: 745–793, 850.

Council of Europe, Consultative Assembly, 19th session.

International Labour Office, Official Bulletin, Volumes: 51, 52, 53.

EEC Bulletin, no. 7 (July 1967).

Overseas Review, British Conservative Party, Issues: 21–37.

Department of Sate: Foreign Relations of the US, Volumes: XV (1960–63) & XVI (1964–68), Cyprus, Greece and Turkey.

The Committee on Foreign Relations, United States Senate, Greece: February 1971, A Staff Report, 92nd Congress, 1st Session, 4 March 1971.

Hearings before the Sub-Committee on Europe of the Committee on Foreign Affairs, House of Representatives: Greece, Spain and the Southern NATO Strategy.

Foreign Relations of the United States (FRUS), Volumes: XVI: Foreign

BIBLIOGRAPHY

Relations, 1964–68, Cyprus, Greece, Turkey & XXX: Foreign Relations, 1969–1976, Greece, Cyprus, Turkey.

National Statistics of Greece.

C) Printed Works

I. Books

Alexander, G. M., *The Prelude to the Truman Doctrine, British Policy in Greece, 1944–47*, (Oxford: Clarendon Press, 1982).

Alikaniotes, Dionysios, *Texts of P. Kanellopoulos From his Struggle Against the Dictatorship, 1967–74* (Athens: D. Gialleles, 1987) [In Greek].

Andrews, Kevin, *Greece in the Dark, 1967–74* (Amsterdam: Adolf Hakkert, 1980).

Asmussen, Jan, *Cyprus at War: Diplomacy and Conflict During the 1974 Crisis* (London and New York: I.B. Tauris, 2008).

'Athenian', *Inside the Colonels' Greece*, (London: Chatto & Windus, 1972).

Ball, Stuart, and Anthony Seldon (eds), *The Heath Government, 1970–74: A Reappraisal* (Abingdon: Routledge, 2015).

Barkman, Karl, *Ambassador in Athens* (London: The Merlin Press, 1989).

Barlett, C. J., *British Foreign Policy in the Twentieth Century* (London: Macmillan Education Ltd, 1989).

Baylis, John, *Anglo-American Defence Relations, 1939–84* (London: Palgrave Macmillan, 1984, 2nd ed.)

Benn, Tony, *Out of the Wilderness, Diaries 1963–67* (London: Hutchinson Ltd, 1987).

Benn, Tony, *Office Without Power, Diaries 1968–72* (London: Arrow Books, 1988).

Callaghan, James, *Time and Change* (Glasgow: William Collins Sons and Co Ltd, 1987).

Calvocoressi, Peter, *World Politics Since 1945* (Abingdon: Routledge, 1996, 7th edition).

Campbell, J. and Sherrard, P., *Modern Greece* (London: Ernest Benn, 1968)

Castle, Barbara, *The Castle Diaries, 1964–1970* (London: George Weidenfeld & Nicolson Ltd, 1984).

Catris, John, *Eyewitness in Greece: The Colonels Come to Power* (St. Louis: Missouri, New Critics Press, 1971).

Charalambes, Dimitris, *Stratos kai Politike Exousia* ('The Military and Political Power'), (Athens: Exantas, 1985) [In Greek].

Chelmis, George, *The Troubled Two-Year Period, 1973–74: From the Personal Diary of an EyeWitness* (Athens: Kastaniotis, 2006) [In Greek].

Childs, David, *Britain Since 1945: A Political History* (London: Routledge, 2000).

Clogg, Richard and George Yannopoulos (eds), *Greece Under Military Rule* (London: Secker & Warburg, 1972).

BIBLIOGRAPHY

Clogg, Richard, *Greek to Me: A memoir of Academic Life*, (London: IB Tauris, 2018).

Clogg, Richard, *Anglo-Greek Attitudes: Studies in History* (London: Macmillan, 2000).

Close, David, *Greece Since 1945: Politics, Economy and Society* (London: Pearson Education Ltd, 2002).

Coker, Christopher, 'Foreign and Defence Policy' in Jonathan Hollowell (ed.), *Britain since 1945* (Oxford: Blackwell Publishers, 2003).

Coufoudakis, Van, *Cyprus: A Contemporary Problem in Historical Perspective* (Minneapolis: Modern Greek Studies, University of Minnesota, 2006).

Coufoudakis, Van, 'Greek Foreign Policy, 1945–1985: Seeking Independence in an Interdependent World' in Kevin Featherstone and Dimitris Katsoudas (eds), *Political Change in Greece, Before and After the Colonels* (London: Croom Helm, 1987).

Couloumbis, Theodore, John Petropoulos and Harry Psomiades, *Foreign Intervention in Greek Politics: A Historical Perspective* (New York: Pella Publishing, 1976).

Couloumbis, Theodoros, *...71...74 Notes of an Academic* (Athens: Pattakis, 2002) [In Greek].

Crossman, Richard, *The Crossman Diaries: Selections from the Diaries of a Cabinet Minister* (London: Hamish Hamilton Ltd and Jonathan Cape Ltd, 1979).

Daddow, Oliver J., *Britain and Europe Since 1945: Historiographical Perspectives on Integration* (Manchester: Manchester University Press, 2004).

di Nolfo, Ennio, 'The Cold War and the Transformation of the Mediterranean, 1960–1975', in Odd Arne Westad and Melvyn P. Leffler (eds), *The Cambridge History of the Cold War* (Cambridge: Cambridge University Press, 2010).

Diamantopoulos, Thanasis, *Kostas Mitsotakis: A Political Biography*, Vol. 2, (Athens: Papazeses, 1989) [In Greek].

Dilks, David, *Retreat from Power: Studies in Britain's Foreign Policy of the Twentieth Century* (London: Macmillan, 1981).

Dismukes, Bradford and James McConnell (eds), *Soviet Naval Diplomacy*, (New York: Pergamon Press, 1979).

Dockrill, Saki, *Britain's Retreat from East of Suez: The Choice Between Europe and the World* (New York: Palgrave, 2002).

Donoughue, Bernard, *Downing Street Diary: With Harold Wilson in No. 10* (London: Pimliko, 2006).

Dumbrell, John, *A Special Relationship: Anglo-American Relations from the Cold War to Iraq* (London: Palgrave, 2006, 2nd ed.)

Elliniki Etairia Politices Epistemes (Hellenic Association of Political Sciences), *The Dictatorship, 1967–1974*, (Athens: Kastaniotis, 1999) [In Greek]

Faustman, Hubert and Nicos Peristianis (eds) *Britain in Cyprus: Colonialism and Post-Colonialism, 1878–2006* (Mannheim & Mohnesee: Bibliopolis, 2006).

BIBLIOGRAPHY

Foley, Charles and W. Scobie, *The Struggle for Cyprus* (Stanford: Hoover Institution Press, 1975).

Frederika, Queen, *A Measure of Understanding* (London: Macmillan, 1971).

Gaddis, John Lewis, *We Now Know: Rethinking Cold War History* (Oxford: Oxford University Press, 1998).

George, Stephen, *An Awkward Partner: Britain in the European Community* (Oxford: Oxford University Press, 1990).

Gowland, David and Arthur Turner, *Reluctant Europeans: Britain and European Integration, 1945–1998* (London: Longman, 2000).

Green, Sir Hugh, *The Third Floor Front: A View of Broadcasting in the Sixties* (London: The Bodley Head, 1969).

Gregoriades, Solon, *The History of the Dictatorship*, 3 Volumes (Athens: Kapopoulos, 1975) [In Greek].

Healey, Denis, *The Time of My Life* (London: Michael Joseph, 1989).

Hill, Christopher and Lord Christopher, 'The Foreign Policy of the Heath Government' in Stuart Ball and Anthony Seldon (eds), *The Heath Government, 1970–1974: A Reappraisal* (London: Longman 1996).

Holland, R., *The Pursuit of Greatness: Britain and The World Role, 1900–1970* (London: Fontana Press, 1991).

Holland, Robert and Diana Markides, *The British and the Hellenes: Struggles for Mastery in the Eastern Mediterranean, 1850–1960* (Oxford: Oxford University Press, 2006).

Hollowell, Jonathan, *From Commonwealth to European Integration* in Jonathan Hollowell (ed.) *Britain Since 1945* (Oxford: Blackwell Publishers, 2003).

Hollowell, Jonathan, *Twentieth-Century Anglo-American Relations*, (London: Palgrave Macmillan, 2001).

Holden, D., *Greece Without Columns* (London: Faber & Faber, 1972).

Hristopoulos, George and Ioannis Bastias (eds), *History of the Greek Nation*, Vol. 16 (Athens: Ekdotiki Athinon, 2000) [In Greek].

Iraklides, Alexis, *Irreconcilable Neighbours: Greece-Turkey, The Aegean Dispute* (Athens: Sideris, 2007) [In Greek].

James, Alan, *Keeping the Peace in the Cyprus Crisis of 1963–1964* (London: Palgrave, 2002).

Kanellopoulos, Panayiotis, *My Life: The Truth About the Crucial Moments of the Nation's History from 1915 to 1980* (Athens: D. Gialleles, 1985) [In Greek].

Karavia, Maria, *The London Diary: Notes from the Dictatorship Era* (Athens: Agra, 2007) [In Greek].

Kazamias, Alexander, 'Antiquity as Cold War Propaganda: The Political Uses of the Classical Past in Post-Civil War Greece', in Dimitiris Tziovas (ed.), *Re-imagining the Past: Antiquity and Modern Greek Culture* (Oxford: Oxford University Press, 2014).

Keeley, Robert, *The Colonels' Coup and the American Embassy: A Diplomat's View of*

265

BIBLIOGRAPHY

the Breakdown of Democracy in ColdWar Greece (University Park: Pennsylvania University Press, 2011).

Kennedy, Paul, *The Realities Behind Diplomacy: Background and Influences on British External Policy, 1865–1980* (London: Allen & Unwin, 1981).

Kofas, John, *Intervention and Underdevelopment: Greece during the Cold War* (University Park: The Pennsylvania State University Press, 1989).

Koliopoulos, John, *Greece and the British Connection, 1935–1941* (Oxford: Clarendon Press, 1977).

Kolliopoulos, John and Thanos Veremis, *Greece: The Modern Sequel, From 1831 to the Present* (London: Hurst and Company, 2002).

Konstantopoulos, S., *Open Letter to the Members of the House of Representatives and the Senate of the United States of America* (Athens: F. Tsironis Printing Enterprise, 1971).

Konstas, Dimitres and Charalampos Tsardanides (eds), *The Greek Case at the Council of Europe* (Athens: Sakkoula, 1988–89) [In Greek].

Kornetis, Kostis, *Children of the Dictatorship: Student Resistance, Cultural Politics and the Long 1960s in Greece* (New York: Berghahn, 2013).

Kyle, Keith, 'British Policy on Cyprus, 1974–2004' in Hubert Faustman and Nicos Peristianis (eds) *Britain in Cyprus: Colonialism and Post-colonialism, 1878–2006* (Cyprus: Bibliopolis, 2006).

Lee, David, *Wings in the Sun: A History of the Royal Air Force in the Mediterranean, 1945–1986* (London: Her Majesty's Stationery Office, 1989).

Maclean, Donald, *British Foreign Policy Since Suez, 1956–1968* (London: Hodder & Stoughton, 1970).

Mangold, Peter, *Success and Failure in British Foreign Policy: Evaluating the Record, 1900–2000* (London: Palgrave Macmillan, 2001).

Maragkou, Konstantina, 'Anglo-American Attitudes Towards Konstantinos Karamanlis During the Greek Colonels' Regime' in Konstantinos Svolopoulos, Konstantina E. Botsiou, Evanthis Hatzivassiliou (eds), *Konstantinos Karamanlis in the Twentieth Century* (Athens: Ekdoseis Rodakio, 2009).

Maragkou, Konstantina, Anglo-Greek relations during the 'brief decade of the 1960s' in Manolis Vassilakis (ed.), *From the Unrelenting Struggle to Dictatorship*, (Athens: Ekdoseis Papazisi, 2009) [in Greek].

Markezinis, Spyridon, *Contemporary Political History of Greece*, Vol. 3, 1952–1975, (Athens: Papyros, 1994) [In Greek].

McDonald, Robert 'The Colonels' Dictatorship' in Marion Sarafis and Martin Eve (eds), *Background to Contemporary Greece* (London: Merlin Press, 1990).

Meletopoulos, Meletis, *The Dictatorship of the Colonels: Society, Ideology, Economy* (Athens: Papazisis, 2000) [In Greek].

Mercouri, Melina, *I Was Born Greek* (Athens: D. K. Zarvanos, 1983) [In Greek].

Meynaud, Jean, *The Political Forces in Greece* (Athens: Savvalas, 2002) [In Greek].

BIBLIOGRAPHY

Miller, Edward, *The United States and the Making of Modern Greece: History and Power, 1950–74* (Chapel Hill: The University of North Carolina Press, 2009).

Morgan, Kenneth, *Britain Since 1945: The People's Peace* (Oxford: Oxford University Press, 2001).

Murtagh, Peter, *The Rape of Greece: The King, the Colonels and the Resistance* (London: Simon & Schuster, 1994).

Nafpliotis, Alexandros, 'The 1971 Re-establishment of Diplomatic Relations Between Greece and Albania: Cooperation and Strategic Partnership Within Cold War Bipolarity' in Othon Anastasakis, Dimitar Bechev, Nicholas Vrousalis (eds), *Greece in the Balkans: Memory, Conflict and Exchange* (Cambridge: Cambridge Scholars Publishing, 2009).

Nafpliotis, Alexandros, *Britain and the Greek Colonels: Accommodating the Junta in the Cold War* (London: I. B. Tauris, 2012).

Nicolet, Claude, *United States Policy Towards Cyprus, 1954–1974: Removing the Greek-Turkish Bone of Contention* (Zurich: Vivliopolis, 2001).

Glen O'Hara and Helen Parr (eds), *The Wilson Governments, 1964–1970 Reconsidered* (Abingdon: Routledge, 2014).

Ovendale, Ritchie, *British Defence Policy Since 1945* (Manchester: Manchester University Press, 1994).

Pagoulatos, George (ed.), *UK/Greece: A New Look at Relations*, (ELIAMEP, 2001).

Papadopoulos, George, *Our Credo: Speeches of the President of the Government Georgiou Papadopoulou*, 7 Volumes, (Athens: Government Printing Office, 1968–1972) [In Greek].

Papagos, Leonidas, *Notes, 1967–1977* (Athens: Foundation of Goulandri-Horn, 1999) [In Greek].

Papahelas, Alexis, *The Rape of Greek Democracy: The American Factor, 1947–67* (Athens: Estia, 2000, 14th edition) [In Greek].

Papandreou, Andreas, *Democracy at Gunpoint: The Greek Front* (London: Andre Deutsch, 1971).

Papastratis, Prokopis, *British Policy Towards Greece in the Second World War, 1941–1944* (Cambridge: Cambridge University Press, 1984).

Pattakos, Stylianos, *21 April 1967: Why, Who, How?* (Athens: Viovivl, 1993) [In Greek].

Pesmatzoglou, Vassilis, 'The Greek Dictatorship (1967–1974) and the EEC' in Y. Athanasatou and Alkis Rigos et al. (eds), *The Dictatorship 1967–1974: Political Practice-Ideology-Resistance* (Athens: Kastaniotis, 1999) [In Greek].

Pickering, Jeffrey, *Britain's Withdrawal From East of Suez: The Politics of Retrenchment* (New York: St. Martin's Press, 1998).

Polmar, Norman, *Soviet Naval Power: Challenge for the 1970s* (London: Macdonald & Company, 1974).

BIBLIOGRAPHY

Polyviou, Polyvios, *The Diplomacy of the Invasion* (Athens: Ekdoseis Kastanioti, 2010) [In Greek].

Ponting, Clive, *Breach of Promise: Labour in Power, 1964–1970* (London: Hamish Hamilton, 1989).

Porter, Bernard, *Britain, Europe and the World, 1850–1986: Delusions of Grandeur* (London: Allen & Unwin, 1987, 2nd edition).

Rallis, Georgios, *Political Confidences* (Athens: Proskinio, 1989) [In Greek].

Reynolds, David, *Britannia Overruled: British Policy and World Power in the Twentieth Century* (London: Longman, 1991).

Rizas, Sotiris, *The Rise of the Left in Southern Europe: Anglo-American Responses*, (London: Pickering and Chatto, 2012).

Rizas, Sotiris, *Greek Politics after the Civil War: Parliamentarism and Dictatorship* (Athens: Kastaniotis, 2008) [In Greek].

Rizas, Sotiris, *Greek-Turkish Relations and the Aegean, 1973–76* (Athens: Sideris, 2006) [In Greek].

Rizas, Sotiris, *The United States, The Dictatorship of the Colonels and the Cyprus Issue, 1967–1974* (Athens: Pattakis, 2002) [In Greek].

Rousseas, S., *The Death of a Democracy* (New York: Grove Press, 1967).

Sandbrook, Dominic, *White Heat: A History of Britain in the Swinging Sixties* (London: Abacus, 2007).

Stephens, Robert, *Cyprus: A Place of Arms: Power Politics and Ethnic Conflict in the Eastern Mediterranean* (London: Pall Mall Press, 1966).

Stewart, Michael, *Life and Labour: An Autobiography* (London: Sidgwick & Jackson, 1980).

Svolopoulos, Konstantinos, *Greek Foreign Policy, 1945–1981*, Vol. 2 (Athens: Estia, 2007) [In Greek].

Treholt, Arne, 'Europe and the Greek Dictatorship' in R. Clogg and G. Yannopoulos (eds.), *Greece Under Military Rule* (1972), p. 213.

Tsoucalas, Constantine, *The Greek Tragedy* (London: Penguin, 1969).

Ullman, Richard, 'America, Britain and the Soviet Threat in Historical and Present Perspective' in W. M. Roger Louis and Hedley Bull (eds), *The 'Special Relationship': Anglo-American Relations Since 1945* (Oxford: Clarendon Press, 1986).

Valinakis, Yiannis, *Introduction to the History of Greek Foreign Policy, 1949–1974*, (Thessaloniki: Parateretes, 1988) [in Greek].

Valinakis, Yiannis, 'The US Bases in Greece: The Political Context', in Thanos Veremis, *US Bases in the Mediterranean* (Athens: Hellenic Foundation for European and Foreign Policy, 1989), p. 33.

Vasilakis, Manolis (ed.), *From the unrelenting struggle to dictatorship*, (Athens, Ekdoseis Papazisi, 2009) [In Greek].

Vatikiotis, P. J., *Greece: A Political Essay* (Beverly Hills: Sage Publications, 1974).

BIBLIOGRAPHY

Velios, Alexandros, *Karamanlis: The Correspondence of Self-Exile, 1963–1974* (Athens: Roes, 1995) [In Greek].

Veremis, Thanos, *US Bases in the Mediterranean* (Athens: Hellenic Foundation for European and Foreign Policy, 1989).

Veremis, Thanos, *The Military in Greek Politics: From Independence to Democracy* (London: Hurst & Co, 1997).

Vlachos, Eleni, *House Arrest* (London: Andre Deutsch Ltd, 1979).

Vournas, Tassos, *History of Contemporary Greece: Junta, Cyprus Dossier (1967–1974)* (Athens: Pattakis, 2003) [In Greek].

Wallden, Sotiris, *Unseemly Partners: The Greek Dictatorship, the Communist Regimes and the Balkans (1967–1974)* (Athens: Polis, 2009) [In Greek].

Wilson, Harold, *The Labour Government, 1964–1970: A Personal Record* (London: Weidenfeld and Nicholson, 1971).

Winkler, David, *Cold War at Sea: High-Seas Confrontation Between the United States and the Soviet Union* (Annapolis, MD: Naval Institute Press, 2000).

Woodhouse, C. M., *The Rise and Fall of the Greek Colonels* (London: Granada Publishing Ltd, 1972).

Wringley, Chris, *Now You See It, Now You Don't: Harold Wilson and Labour's Foreign Policy 1964–1970*, in R. Coopey, S. Fielding, N. Tiratsoo (eds.), *The Wilson Governments: 1964–1970*, (London: Pinter Publishers, 1993).

Xanthopoulos-Palamas, Christos, *Diplomatic Triptych* (Athens: Ekdoseis ton Philon, 1979, 2nd edition) [in Greek].

Young, John Wilson, *Britain and the World in the Twentieth Century* (London: Arnold, 1997).

Young, John W., *The Labour Governments, 1964–1970: Vol. 2 International Policy* (Manchester: Manchester University Press, 2003).

Young, John, *Britain and European Unity*, 2nd edition (London: Palgrave Macmillan, 2000).

Young, John, Effie Pedalieu and Michael Kandiah (eds), *Britain in Global Politics: From Churchill to Blair*, Volume 2 (Basingstoke: Palgrave Macmillan, 2013).

Young, Hugo, *This Blessed Plot: Britain and Europe from Churchill to Blair* (London: Macmillan, 1999).

Young, Kenneth, *The Greek Passion* (London: J. M. Dent &sons, 1969).

II. Articles

Alexander, Philip, 'A Tale of Two Smiths: The Transformation of Commonwealth Policy, 1964–1970' in *Contemporary British History*, Vol. 20, No. 3 (2006), pp. 303–21.

Anthem, Thomas, 'The Greek Colonels and the USA' in *Contemporary Review*, Vol. 216, No. 1251 (April 1970), pp. 178–183.

Aujourd'hui la Grèce, Dossier in *Les Temps Modernes*, Vol. 25 (July–Sept. 1969).

BIBLIOGRAPHY

Conispoliatis, Helen, 'Facing the Colonels: How the British Government Dealt with the Military Coup in Greece in April 1967', *History*, Vol. 92 Issue 308 (2007) pp. 515–535.

Coufoudakis, Van, 'The European Economic Community and the "Freezing" of the Greek Association, 1967–1974' in *The Journal of Common Market Studies*, Vol. XVI, No. 2 (December 1977).

Craig, Phyllis, 'The United States and the Greek Dictatorship: A Summary of Support' in *Journal of the Hellenic Diaspora*, Vol. III, No. 4 (1976), pp. 5–15.

Danopoulos, Constantine, 'Military Professionalism and Regime Legitimacy in Greece, 1967–1974' in *Political Science Quarterly* (Fall 1983), pp. 485–506.

Fouskas, Vassilis, 'Uncomfortable questions: Cyprus, October 1973–August 1974' in *Contemporary European History*, Volume 14, Issue 1 (February 2005), pp. 45–63.

Gallagher, John and Ronald Robinson, 'The Imperialism of Free Trade' in *The Economic History Review*, Second series, Vol. VI, no. 1 (1953), pp. 1–15.

Hatzivassiliou, Evanthis, 'Heirs of the King-makers: The British Embassy in Athens, 1951–61' in *Diplomacy and Statecraft*, Vol. 18, No. 3 (2007), pp. 573–591.

Kazamias, George, 'Britain in the Cyprus Crisis of 1974', GreeSE Paper No. 42, Hellenic Observatory Papers on Greece and Southeast Europe, December 2010.

Klarevas, Louis, 'Were the Eagle and the Phoenix Birds of a Feather? The United States and the Greek Coup of 1967' in *Diplomatic History*, Vol. 30, No. 3 (2006), pp. 471–508.

Kovertaris, G. A., 'Professional Self-Images and Political Perspectives in the Greek Military' in *American Sociological Review*, Vol. 36 (December 1971), pp. 1043–1057.

Leuprecht, Peter, 'Max van der Stoel: A Tireless Defender of Greek Democracy' in *Security and Human Rights*, No. 3 (2011), pp. 183–185.

Maragkou, Konstantina, 'British Reactions to "The Rape of Greek Democracy"' in *The Journal of Contemporary History*, Vol. 45, No. 1 (2010), pp. 162–180.

Maragkou, Konstantina, 'Favoritism in NATO's Southern Flank: The Case of the Greek Colonels, 1967–1974' in *ColdWar History*, Vol. 9, Issue 3 (2009), pp. 347–366.

Maragkou, Konstantina, 'The Foreign Factor and the Greek Colonels' Rise to Power on 21 April 1967' in *The Journal of Southeast European and Black Sea Studies*, Vol. 6, Issue 4 (December 2006), pp. 427–443.

Pedaliu, Effie, 'Human Rights and Foreign Policy: Wilson and the Greek Dictators, 1967–1970' in *Diplomacy and Statecraft*, Vol. 18, No. 1 (2007), pp. 185–214.

BIBLIOGRAPHY

Pedaliu, Effie, "'A Discordant Note": NATO and the Greek Junta, 1967–74' in *Diplomacy and Statecraft*, Vol. 22 (2011), pp. 101–120.

Reynolds, David, 'A "Special Relationship"? America, Britain and the International Order since the Second World War' in *International Affairs*, Vol. 62, No. 1 (1985–1986), pp. 1–20.

Sakkas, John, 'The Greek Dictatorship, the USA and the Arabs, 1967–1974' in *The Journal of Southern Europe and the Balkans*, Vol. 6 No. 3 (2003), pp. 245–257.

Sulzberger, C. L., 'Greece under the Colonels' in *Foreign Affairs*, Vol. 48, No 2 (January 1970), pp. 300–311.

Tsoucalas, Constantine, 'Class Struggle and Dictatorship in Greece' in *New Left Review*, No. 56 (July–August 1969).

Young, John, 'The Diary of Michael Stewart as British Foreign Secretary, April–May 1968' in *Contemporary British History*, Vol. 19, No. 4 (2005), pp. 481–510.

Young, John, 'Britain and "LBJ's War", 1964–68, in *Cold War History*, Vol. 2, No. 3 (2002), pp. 63–92.

Wall, Michael, 'Greece', Special Issue in *The Economist* (July 31/August 1971).

Xydis, Stephen, 'Coups and Counter-coups in Greece, 1967–1973', in *Political Science Quarterly*, Vol. 89, No. 3 (Fall 1974), pp. 507–538.

III. Newspapers & Periodical Publications

Daily Telegraph, London (1967–74)
Der Spiegel, Hamburg (1967–74)
Eleftheros Kosmos
Financial Times, London (1967–74)
Greek Report, London, ed. by Panayotis Lambrias, (monthly, 1969)
Guardian, Manchester (1967–74)
Hellenic Review, London, ed. by Helen Vlachos, (monthly, 1968)
I Acropolis, Athens (1967)
I Apogeumatini, Athens (1967)
I Kathimerini, Athens (1967, 2002)
I Vradyni, Athens (1967)
Le Monde (1967–74)
The Economist, London (1967–74)
The Greek Observer, London, ed. by George Yannopoulos, (monthly, 1969–70).
The New Statesman, London (1967–74)
The New York Times, New York (1967–74)
The Observer, London (1967–74)
The Sunday Telegraph, London (1967–74)

BIBLIOGRAPHY

The Sunday Times, London (1967–1974)
The Times, London (1967–74)
The Washington Post, Washington (1967–74)
Time (Magazine)
To Vima, Athens (1967)

D) Unpublished Dissertations

Conispoliatis, Helen, 'Facing the Colonels: British and American Diplomacy Towards the Colonels' Junta in Greece, 1967–1970' (Unpublished Ph.D. thesis, University of Leicester, 2003).

Kyriakides, Panayiotis, 'Cyprus After the Suez Campaign: The Perceived Strategic Value and Significance of the Island and Its Military Bases to Britain, 1956–1960' (Unpublished Ph.D. thesis, University of Cambridge, 1993).

E) Interviews

Baxter, Brigadier Harry (Military Attaché, British Embassy in Athens, 1969–71), London, 9 May 2001.

Bendall, David (Counsellor in Washington, 1965–69 & Assistant Under-Secretary of State for Western Europe, 1969–71), Stowmarket, 2 July 2002.

Bridges, Baron Thomas (Head of Chancery, British Embassy in Athens, 1966–68), London, 28 November 2000.

Burley, Anne (Amnesty International Researcher), London, 24 February 2015.

Clogg, Richard (Senior Research Fellow at St. Antony's College, University of Oxford), Oxford, 22 November 2000.

Constantine II of Greece, (ex-King of the Hellenes), London, 29 January 2002.

Davidson, Alan (Head of Central Department, FCO, 1966–68, UK Delegation to NATO, 1969–71), London, 7 February 2001.

Dawbarn, Sir Simon (Commercial Attaché, British Embassy in Athens, 1968–71), London, 29 January 2003.

Dodson, Sir Derek (Counsellor, British Embassy in Athens, 1966–69), London, 4 December 2000.

Fraser, John (Labour MP for Norwood, 1966–97), London, 9 May 2001.

Giles, Frank (Foreign Editor of *The Sunday Times*, 1961–77 and Deputy Editor of *The Sunday Times*, 1967–81), London, 16 January 2003.

Goodenough, Sir Antony (British Embassy in Athens, 1967–71), London, 29 January 2003.

Gorham, Robin (Central European Department, FCO, 1967–69), London, 9 March 2001).

BIBLIOGRAPHY

Grant, Stefanie (Amnesty International Researcher), London, 12 February 2015.

Hitch, Brian (First Secretary at the British Embassy in Athens), Oxford, 15 January 2002.

Kypreos, Konstantinos (Minister of Industry), Athens, 3 November 2001.

Llewellyn-Smith, Sir Michael John (British Ambassador to Greece, 1996–99), 25 September 2003.

Lowenstein, James (US Senate Foreign Relations Committee, 1965–74), Washington, 7 April 2003.

McDonald, Robert (BBC Correspondent in Athens), Athens, 25 November 2003.

Makarezos, Nikolaos (coup arbitrator and Minister for Coordination), Athens, 30 October 2001.

Modiano, Mario (*The Times* Correspondent in Athens), Athens, 13 January 2001.

Packard, Martin (Malta-based British naval intelligence officer, former peace-keeper with the British Army in Cyprus, member of the British resistance to the Colonels), London, 2 July 2015.

Palliser, Sir Michael (Private Secretary to the Prime Minister, 1966–69), London, 3 December 2001.

Palmer, Andrew (FCO, Central Department and later European Department, 1968–72), Amersham, 9 July 2002.

Parsons, Sir Richard (FCO, 1967–69), London, 8 July 2002.

Patras, Loukas (Minister for Social Services), Athens, 1 March 2002.

Pattakos, Stylianos (coup arbitrator & Minister of the Interior and later Deputy Prime-Minister), Athens, 27 October 2001.

Powell-Jones, Sir John (Counsellor and Consul-General at the British Embassy in Athens, 1970–73), London, 16 July 2003.

Prendergast, Sir Kieran (FCO, 1967–69), New York, 21 April 2003.

Rodgers, Lord William (Foreign Office, Parliamentary Under-Secretary of State, 1967–68), London, 26 November 2002.

Spraos, John (Professor at UCL, Chairman of the Committee against Dictatorship in Greece), London, 22 June 2015.

Talbot, Phillips (American Ambassador in Athens, 1965–69), New York, 10 April 2003.

Theodoropoulos, Vyron (Ambassador of Greece to Cyprus), Athens, 21 March 2005.

Tomkys, Sir Roger (Head of Chancery, British Embassy in Athens, 1972–75), Cambridge, 17 November 2000.

Whitaker, Ben (Labour MP for Hampstead, 1966–70), London, 8 March 2001.

Williams, Roger (member of the British resistance to the Colonels), London, 30 September 2015.

INDEX

INDEX

INDEX

INDEX